"A CHARMING AND SENSITIVELY DRAWN MEMOIR OF A YOUNG, UN-WORLDLY AUTHOR-TO-BE GROWING UP IN WARSAW."
—*New York Times Book Review*

"A fine piece of work...the life, law, and lore of the poor Jewish people of War-saw...the man is a master of the art of storytelling."
—*The Critic*

"IN ISAAC BASHEVIS SINGER'S LAND-SCAPES, THE HUMAN SITUATION COMES STUNNINGLY ALIVE."
—*Chicago Tribune*

"These penetrating, philosophical studies of human nature faithfully show the richness of life, the volatile emotions, the depth of religious feeling in old-time Jewish Warsaw."
—*Publishers Weekly*

ISAAC BASHEVIS SINGER

In My Father's Court

FAWCETT CREST • NEW YORK

This book is dedicated to the sacred memory of Cecil
Hemley, who helped me whole-heartedly as a friend, a
publisher, an editor, a translator. His wife Elaine
Gottlieb translated a part of this work, and it was all
done with Cecil's advice. His love for literature was as
great as his taste.

IN MY FATHER'S COURT

THIS BOOK CONTAINS THE COMPLETE TEXT OF THE
ORIGINAL HARDCOVER EDITION.

Published by Fawcett Crest Books, a unit of CBS Publications, the
Consumer Publishing Division of CBS Inc., by arrangement with
Farrar, Straus & Giroux, Inc.

Selection of the Commentary Book Club
Selection of the Literary Guild
Selection of the Jewish Publication Society

Printed in the United States of America

10 9 8 7 6 5 4 3 2 1

Contents

Author's Note

In My Father's Court, or *Beth Din,* as this book is called in the Yiddish original, is in a certain sense a literary experiment. It is an attempt to combine two styles—that of memoirs and that of belles-lettres—and its approach to description and its manner of conveying situations differ from those used in my other writings. The pieces here were first published as a series under my journalistic pseudonym, Isaac Warshawsky, in the *Jewish Daily Forward.* The idea had been with me a long time: when still very young, I had actually thought of writing my recollections of the Beth Din. It was only after the newspaper publication of the series that I decided to release them in book form under my own name, because they portrayed a life and environment that no longer exist and are unique.

This book tells the story of a family and of a rabbinical court that were so close together it was hard to tell where one ended and the other began. The rabbinical court, the Beth Din, is an ancient institution among the Jews. It started when Jethro counseled Moses to "provide out of all the people able men, such as fear God, men of truth, hating covetousness ... and let them judge the people at all seasons." There is a direct line between the Beth Din of today and the Talmudic annotators, Geonim, Princes, Amoraim, Tannaim, Men of the Great Synagogue, and Sanhedrin. The Beth Din was a kind of blend of a court of law, synagogue, house of study, and, if you will, psychoanalyst's office where people of troubled spirit could come to unburden themselves.

That such a mixture was not only feasible but necessary was proved by the continued existence of the Beth Din over many generations.

It is my firmest conviction that the court of the future will be based on the Beth Din, provided the world goes morally forward instead of backward. Though the Beth Din is rapidly disappearing, I believe it will be reinstated and evolve into a universal institution. The concept behind it is that there can be no justice without godliness, and that the best judgment is one accepted by all the litigants with good will and trust in divine power. The opposite of the Beth Din are all institutions that employ force, whether of the right or the left.

The Beth Din could exist only among a people with a deep faith and humility, and it reached its apex among the Jews when they were completely bereft of wordly power and influence. The weapon of the judge was the handkerchief the litigants touched to signify their acceptance of the judgment. I have not attempted to idealize the Beth Din or to endow it with conditions and moods that were not a part of my direct experience. The Beth Din not only differed in every generation, but every Rabbi who participated in it colored it with his character and personality. Only that which is individual can be just and true.

At times I think that the Beth Din is an infinitesimal example of the celestial council of justice, God's judgment, which the Jews regard as absolute mercy.

The pieces in this book were translated by Channah Kleinerman-Goldstein, Elaine Gottlieb, and my nephew Joseph Singer. I am grateful for the editorial help of Robert Giroux and Henry Robbins. I am also grateful to the editors of the following magazines, in which parts of the book previously appeared: *American Judaism, Commentary, The Critic, Harper's Magazine, Jewish Heritage,* and *The Saturday Evening Post.*

                                                            I.B.S.

The Sacrifice

THERE ARE in this world some very strange individuals whose thoughts are even stranger than they are.

In our house in Warsaw—No. 10 Krochmalna Street—and sharing our hallway, there lived an elderly couple. They were simple people. He was an artisan, or perhaps a peddler, and their children were all married. Yet the neighbors said that, despite their advanced years, these two were still in love. Every Sabbath afternoon, after the *cholent,* they would go for a walk arm in arm. In the grocery, at the butcher's—wherever she shopped—she spoke only of *him:* "*He* likes beans...*he* likes a good piece of beef...*he* likes veal..." There are women like that who never stop talking about their husbands. He, in turn, also would say at every opportunity, "My wife."

My mother, daughter of generations of Rabbis, frowned upon the couple. To her such behavior was a sign of commonness. But, after all, love—especially between an elderly couple—cannot be dismissed so easily.

Suddenly there was a rumor that shocked everyone: the old people were going to be divorced!

Krochmalna Street was in an uproar. What did this mean? How could it be? Young women wrung their hands: "Mamma, I'm going to be ill! I feel faint!" Older women proclaimed: "It is the end of the world." The angry ones cursed all men: "Well now, aren't men worse than beasts?" Soon the street was

9

aroused by an even more outrageous report: they
were getting the divorce so that the old sinner could
marry a young girl. You may well imagine the curses
that were heaped upon the old man—a burning in his
belly, a pain in his black heart, a fire in his bowels, a
broken arm and leg, a plague, the judgment of heaven
upon him! The womenfolk spared no curse and
prophesied that he would not live to see his wedding
day, the old billy goat—instead of a wedding canopy
he would find a black coffin.

In our home, in the meantime, the truth, the real
truth, came to light.

The old woman herself came to my mother and
spoke to her in such a manner that my mother's pale
face flushed with embarrassment. Although she tried
to chase me away so that I would not be able to hear, I
did listen, for I was afire with curiosity. The woman
swore to my mother that she loved her husband more
than anything in the world.

"Dear lady," she argued, "I would gladly give my
life to save a fingernail of his. I am, woe is me, an old
woman—a broken shard—but he, he is still a man. He
needs a wife. Why should he be burdened with me? As
long as the children were still at home, one had to be
careful. People would gossip. But now what they say
matters no more to me than the cat's meow. I no
longer need a husband, but he—may he be well—is
like a young man. He can still have children. And
now he has found a girl who wants him. She is past
thirty; the time has come for her, too, to hear the
wedding music play. Besides, she is an orphan and
works for others as a maid; she will be good to him.
With her he will enjoy life. As for me, I am provided
for. He will give me enough to live on, and I do a little
peddling on the side. What do I need at my age? I only
want to see *him* happy. And he promised me that—
after a hundred and twenty years, when the time
comes—I will lie next to him in the cemetery. In the
other world I will again be his wife. I will be his
footstool in Paradise. It has all been settled."

The woman had come, quite simply, to ask my father to arrange the divorce and then perform the wedding.

My mother tried to dissuade her. Like the other women, my mother saw in this affair an affront to all womankind. If all old men were to start divorcing their wives and marrying young girls, the world would be in a fine state. Mother said that the whole idea was clearly the work of the Evil One, and that such love is an impure thing. She even quoted one of the books on ethics. But this simple woman, too, could cite Scripture. She reminded my mother of how Rachel and Leah had given their maidservants, Bilhah and Zilpah, to Jacob as concubines.

Though I was a mere boy, I was not at all indifferent to this affair. I wanted it to come off. First of all, I loved to be present at a divorce. Second, at weddings I always got a piece of sponge cake and a sip of brandy or wine. And third, when Father earned some money, I would be given a few groschen to buy sweets. And then, after all, I was a *man*....

When my mother saw that she could do nothing with the woman, she sent her in to my father, who immediately began to discuss the law. He warned her that after the divorce her former husband would be as a total stranger to her. She would not be allowed to remain under the same roof with him. She would not be permitted to speak with him. Was she aware of this, or had she imagined that she could continue to be with him? The woman replied that she knew the laws, but that she was thinking of *him*, not of herself. For him she was ready to make any sacrifice, even give her life. Father said he would give her an answer. Let her come back the next day.

After the woman left, Mother went into the study and began to argue with my father that she did not want him to earn money by such means. The old man, she said, was a woman-chaser, a goat, a vulgar person, a lecher. She said that if he were to grant this divorce and perform the marriage, the entire community would be aroused against him. Father left to go to his Hasidic study house, to talk the matter over with sensible men. There, too, a heated argument took place, but the final conclusion was that since both parties were in agreement, no one had the right to interfere. One scholar even quoted the verse: "In the morning sow thy seed, and in the evening withhold not thy hand...." According to the Gemara, this means that even an elderly man is still obligated to "be fruitful and multiply."

The next morning, when the old woman returned, this time with her husband, my father began to cross-examine her. I was sent out of the study. Father spoke gruffly, sometimes slowly and sometimes faster, sometimes gently and sometimes in anger. I stood behind the door, but could hear little. I was afraid that any minute now Father would burst out with: "Scoundrels, remember that He has not yet abandoned His world to the rule of chaos!" and chase them out, as was his custom with those who defied the law. But an hour passed and the two were still inside. The old man spoke slowly, in a broken voice. The woman pleaded. Her voice became softer and ever softer. I sensed that she was convincing my father. She whispered intimate secrets to him, such as a man seldom hears from the lips of a woman, such as are only rarely discussed in the heavy tomes of the Responsa. When husband and wife left the study, they looked happy. The old man wiped the sweat off his face with his kerchief. The woman's eyes glowed as on the night after Yom Kippur, when one feels assured that the prayers for a happy year have been answered....

During the weeks that passed between that day and the wedding, Krochmalna Street gaped and wondered. The community was divided into two parties. The affair was discussed everywhere: in the grocery and at the butcher's, at the fish tubs in

Yanash's bazaar and in the fruit shops behind the markets; in the synagogues of the unlearned and in the Hasidic study houses where disciples gathered to tell of the miracles wrought by *their* Wonder Rabbi and to disparage the claims of all rivals.

Most excited, however, were the women. The old wife herself seemed to have lost all shame. She went around praising her husband's bride to the skies, brought presents for the "couple," busied herself with the wedding preparations as though she were the girl's mother. The other women scorned or pitied her. "Heaven help us—it just goes to show how an old woman can lose her mind!" All clung to the same idea: the old woman was crazy, and the husband, the old sinner, wanted to get rid of her. All mocked her, all were outraged, all were puzzled. All asked the same question: "How can such things be?" And the only answer was: "Well, you see..."

Had there been any young hooligans in the neighborhood, they might have molested the old couple or the bride, but our neighbors were quiet people. The husband himself was a good-natured man with a white beard and the mild eyes of the very old. He continued to come to the synagogue regularly. He wound the leather straps of his phylacteries around his arm with a trembling hand. The youngsters made fun of him, but he never showed anger. He touched the ritual fringes of his prayer shawl to his eyes. He kissed the phylactery that is worn on the forehead, and then that which is placed on the arm. A Jew remains a Jew, even when extraordinary events befall him. The truth was that it was not he who had talked his wife into this. On the contrary, it had all been her idea, he confided to my father. She had simply overwhelmed him. The girl was a poor orphan. The old woman herself went about happy, hopeful, smiling. Her eyes shone with a weird joy.

At the same time that husband and wife were preparing for the divorce and the subsequent wedding, they also purchased a cemetery plot. They

invited friends there, to the place of eternal rest, and
served cake and brandy. All was mixed up together:
life, death, lust, boundless loyalty, and love. The old
woman announced that when *his* wife would give
birth she, the ex-wife, would care for the child because
the young woman would have to help earn a living.
Women who heard such talk spat out: "God help us!
Heaven preserve us! May all evil dreams come upon
them!" Others openly declared that these were the
doings of the devil, of Satan himself. And yet there
was something else. Although all were wholehearted-
ly against the marriage, they were eager for it to take
place as quickly as possible. The entire street had
been infected by a fever. Here life was presenting a
drama more exciting than those one read about in the
papers or saw in a theater.

The divorce took place in our home. Two old people
who had loved each other with a great love were now
divorced. The scribe wrote out the document with his
goose quill and wiped the ink on his skullcap. Every
once in a while he would mumble something. His
green eyes threw out sparks. Who knows? Perhaps he
was thinking of his own "better half"?... The
witnesses signed. The old man sat there, bewildered,
his eyes veiled by his brushlike white brows. His
beard lay flat against his chest. It was clear that he,
the chief protagonist, was as perplexed as everyone
else. This idea had not been born in *his* head. From
time to time he took a snuff of tobacco to relieve his
dejection. Occasionally he would glance at his wife,
who sat on the bench. Usually the participants in a
divorce wear modest, even shabby, clothes, but the
old woman had adorned herself with her holiday
bonnet and a Turkish shawl. She replied to his gaze
with a radiant look. Her eyes were simply sparkling
with fire. "*Mazel tov!* See, I do everything for you, for
you! I sacrifice myself for you, I sacrifice myself.
Accept this offering graciously, my lord and master.

...If only I could, I would bare my throat to the Reaper's scythe for you...."

My mother paced impatiently up and down the kitchen. Her matron's wig was awry. An angry flame burned in her eyes. I entered the kitchen and asked for something to eat, but she exclaimed in vexation: "Get out! Get out! Don't grab things from the pot!"

Even though I was only a small boy and her own son, I was at that moment for her a member of the despicable male sex.

I stood by while the old woman held out her wrinkled hands and the old man placed the writ of divorcement in them. My father then gave the customary instructions: that the woman may not remarry immediately but must wait for three months.

The old one with her toothless gums began to laugh. What an idea! She, thinking of remarrying?

I do not remember how much later it was, but I know that eventually the wedding also took place in my father's study. Under the canopy stood an old man and a stout young woman. Four men held the rods of the canopy. Father gave the groom and bride a sip of wine. Everyone said, *"Mazel tov!"* and drank brandy with sponge cake. Then, in another room, a meal was served. The cooking and all the preparations had been done by the first wife. People said that the old woman had had underclothes, slips, and skirts sewn for the bride, for the girl had no proper clothes to wear. So many guests came for the meal that all our rooms were filled and people were standing out in the hallway.

For some time longer Krochmalna Street continued to bubble and boil. People would run after the old man and his new wife and stare at them as though they were performing magicians or Chinese with pigtails, such as occasionally came to our street to sell paper flowers. But after a while they found other things to talk about. After all, what is so unusual

about an old woman losing her senses? Or an old man
marrying a cook? People began to say that the first
wife already regretted what she had done. The new
wife did not give birth. The old man fell ill.

I regret, dear reader, that I cannot report a
dramatic climax. Like everyone else, I too eventually
lost interest. I only remember that the old man died
not long after the wedding, and both women cried at
the funeral. Then the old wife also breathed her last
in some garret room. Even the fire of the Evil
Inclination does not burn forever.

Whether husband and wife finally were reunited in
Eden, and whether she became his footstool there, I
cannot say. When you yourself arrive there—after a
hundred and twenty years—ask for the mansion
wherein dwell the former inhabitants of Krochmalna
Street.

Why the Geese Shrieked

IN OUR HOME there was always talk about spirits of
the dead that possess the bodies of the living, souls
reincarnated as animals, houses inhabited by
hobgoblins, cellars haunted by demons. My father
spoke of these things, first of all because he was
interested in them, and second because in a big city
children so easily go astray. They go everywhere, see
everything, read profane books. It is necessary to
remind them from time to time that there are still

mysterious forces at work in the world.

One day he told us a story that is found in one of
the holy books. If I am not mistaken, the author of
that book is Rabbi Eliyahu Graidiker, or one of the
other Graidiker sages. The story was about a girl
possessed by four demons. It was said that they could
actually be seen crawling around in her intestines,
blowing up her belly, wandering from one part of her
body to another, slithering into her legs. The Rabbi of
Graidik had exorcised the evil spirits with the
blowing of the ram's horn, with incantations, and the
incense of magic herbs.

When someone questioned these things, my father
became very excited. He argued: "Was then the great
Rabbi of Graidik, God forbid, a liar? Are all the
rabbis, saints, and sages deceivers, while only
atheists speak the truth? Woe is us! How can one be so
blind?"

Suddenly the door opened, and a woman entered.
She was carrying a basket in which there were two
geese. The woman looked frightened. Her matron's
wig was tilted to one side. She smiled nervously.

Father never looked at strange women, because it
is forbidden by Jewish law, but Mother and we
children saw immediately that something had
greatly upset our unexpected visitor.

"What is it?" Father asked, at the same time
turning his back so as not to look upon her.

"Rabbi, I have a very unusual problem."

"What is it? A woman's problem?"

Had the woman said yes, I would have been sent
out of the room immediately. But she answered: "No,
it's about these geese."

"What is the matter with them?"

"Dear Rabbi, the geese were slaughtered properly.
Then I cut off their heads. I took out the intestines,
the livers, all the other organs, but the geese keep
shrieking in such a sorrowful voice...."

Upon hearing these words, my father turned pale.

A dreadful fear befell me, too. But my mother came from a family of rationalists and was by nature a skeptic.

"Slaughtered geese don't skriek," she said.

"You will hear for yourself," replied the woman.

She took one of the geese and placed it on the table. Then she took out the second goose. The geese were headless, disemboweled—in short, ordinary dead geese. A smile appeared on my mother's lips.

"And *these* geese shriek?"

"You will soon hear."

The woman took one goose and hurled it against the other. At once a shriek was heard. It is not easy to describe that sound. It was like the cackling of a goose, but in such a high, eerie pitch, with such groaning and quaking, that my limbs grew cold. I could actually feel the hairs of my earlocks pricking me. I wanted to run from the room. But where would I run? My throat constricted with fear. Then I, too, screamed and clung to my mother's skirt, like a child of three.

Father forgot that one must avert one's eyes from a woman. He ran to the table. He was no less frightened than I. His red beard trembled. In his blue eyes could be seen a mixture of fear and vindication. For my father this was a sign that not only to the Rabbi of Graidik, but to him, too, omens were sent from heaven. But perhaps this was a sign from the Evil One, from Satan himself?

"What do you say now?" asked the woman.

My mother was no longer smiling. In her eyes there was something like sadness, and also anger.

"I cannot understand what is going on here," she said, with a certain resentment.

"Do you want to hear it again?"

Again the woman threw one goose against the other. And again the dead geese gave forth an uncanny shriek—the shriek of dumb creatures slain by the slaughterer's knife, who yet retain a living force, who still have a reckoning to make with the living, an injustice to avenge. A chill crept over me. I felt as though someone had struck me with all his might.

My father's voice became hoarse. It was broken as though by sobs. "Well, can anyone still doubt that there *is* a Creator?" he asked.

"Rabbi, what shall I do and where shall I go?" The woman began to croon in a mournful singsong. "What has befallen me? Woe is me! What shall I do with them? Perhaps I should run to one of the Wonder Rabbis? Perhaps they were not slaughtered properly? I am afraid to take them home. I wanted to prepare them for the Sabbath meal, and now, such a calamity! Holy Rabbi, what shall I do? Must I throw them out? Someone said that they must be wrapped in shrouds and buried in a grave. I am a poor woman. Two geese! They cost me a fortune!"

Father did not know what to answer. He glanced at his bookcase. If there was an answer anywhere, it must be there. Suddenly he looked angrily at my mother.

"And what do you say now, eh?"

Mother's face was growing sullen, smaller, sharper. In her eyes could be seen indignation and also something like shame.

"I want to hear it again."

Her words were half pleading, half commanding.

The woman hurled the geese against each other for the third time, and for the third time the shrieks were heard. It occurred to me that such must have been the voice of the sacrificial heifer.

"Woe, woe, and still they blaspheme.... It is written that the wicked do not repent even at the very gates of hell." Father had again begun to speak. "They behold the truth with their own eyes, and they continue to deny their Maker. They are dragged into the bottomless pit and they maintain that all is nature, or accident...."

He looked at Mother as if to say: You take after *them*.

For a long time there was silence. Then the woman asked, "Well, did I just imagine it?"

Suddenly my mother laughed. There was something in her laughter that made us all tremble. I knew, by some sixth sense, that Mother was preparing to end the mighty drama that had been enacted before our eyes.

"Did you remove the windpipes?" my mother asked.

"The windpipes? No...."

"Take them out," said my mother, "and the geese will stop shrieking."

My father became angry. "What are you babbling? What has this got to do with windpipes?"

Mother took hold of one of the geese, pushed her slender finger inside the body, and with all her might pulled out the thin tube that led from the neck to the lungs. Then she took the other goose and removed its windpipe also. I stood trembling, aghast at my mother's courage. Her hands had become bloodied. On her face could be seen the wrath of the rationalist whom someone has tried to frighten in broad daylight.

Father's face turned white, calm, a little disappointed. He knew what had happened here: logic, cold logic, was again tearing down faith, mocking it, holding it up to ridicule and scorn.

"Now, if you please, take one goose and hurl it against the other!" commanded my mother.

Everything hung in the balance. If the geese shrieked, Mother would have lost all: her rationalist's daring, her skepticism which she had inherited from her intellectual father. And I? Although I was afraid, I prayed inwardly that the geese *would* shriek, shriek so loud that people in the street would hear and come running.

But alas, the geese were silent, silent as only two dead geese without windpipes can be.

"Bring me a towel!" Mother turned to me.

I ran to get the towel. There were tears in my eyes.

Mother wiped her hands on the towel like a surgeon after a difficult operation.

"That's all it was!" she announced victoriously.

"Rabbi, what do you say?" asked the woman.

Father began to cough, to mumble. He fanned himself with his skullcap.

"I have never before heard of such a thing," he said at last.

"Nor have I," echoed the woman.

"Nor have I," said my mother. "But there is always an explanation. Dead geese don't shriek."

"Can I go home now and cook them?" asked the woman.

"Go home and cook them for the Sabbath." Mother pronounced the decision. "Don't be afraid. They won't make a sound in your pot."

"What do you say, Rabbi?"

"Hmm...they are kosher," murmured Father. "They can be eaten." He was not really convinced, but he could not now pronounce the geese unclean.

Mother went back to the kitchen. I remained with my father. Suddenly he began to speak to me as though I were an adult. "Your mother takes after your grandfather, the Rabbi of Bilgoray. He is a great scholar, but a cold-blooded rationalist. People warned me before our betrothal...."

And then Father threw up his hands, as if to say: It is too late now to call off the wedding.

A Broken Engagement

I OFTEN SERVED as my father's messenger and would
frequently be sent to summon the parties to a Din
Torah, or rabbinic trial. One such errand has
remained particularly vivid in my mind. A young
man dressed in Western fashion came to see my
father and demanded that his fiancée, who lived at
No. 13 Krochmalna Street, be called to a trial. Father
immediately told me to go for her and her father.

In order to get there from our house, No. 10, one
had only to cross the street. However, No. 13 bordered
on the ill-famed Krochmalna Square, where pick-
pockets and hoodlums loitered and dealers in stolen
goods carried on their trade. The houses facing the
Square also harbored a number of brothels. Even
regular commerce was carried on in an underhand
manner: if one wanted to buy a *tchaste*—a kind of
chocolate-covered cracker—one pulled numbers from
a hat or spun a wooden wheel. Yet in these same
houses dwelt decent men, pious women, chaste girls.
There were even a few Hasidic study houses.

It was summer. The Square was crowded. In the
courtyard of No. 13, children were at play. Boys
played at being soldiers, or cops-and-robbers; girls
jumped hopscotch, played jacks. Top-spinning con-
tests, with nuts as prizes, were going on. I found
many temptations to linger and enter into one of the
games. But a messenger is a messenger...I ran up
the stairs. On the first floor the building still looked

quite presentable. As I climbed higher, however, the
paint on the walls was more cracked, the railing
shakier, the stairs dirtier. Doors stood wide open.
From the kitchens issued steam, the sounds of
hammers, the hum of sewing machines, the songs of
seamstresses and apprentices—even of gramophones. The people to whom I was sent lived in a
garret. I opened the door and saw a man with a full,
dark beard, and a girl who was quite decently
dressed, in modern style. The man was sitting at the
table, eating his dinner. The girl was serving him a
broth, or perhaps a bowl of borscht. He looked up at
me angrily.

"What do you want?"

"You are called to come to the Rabbi for a Din
Torah."

"Who called me?"

"Your daughter's betrothed."

The man muttered something. The girl, too, looked
angrily at me.

"Well, what do we do now?" she asked her father.

"When one is called, one goes!" he answered
sullenly.

He finished eating and hurriedly said the grace.
The girl put on a coat and straightened her hair
before a mirror. Then all three of us started out.
Usually under such circumstances those who had
been summoned would begin to argue with me. But
this time father and daughter maintained silence—
an ominous silence. Thus I brought them to the
house. Father asked the man to be seated. The girl
remained standing: there were no seats for women in
my father's study.

Father now began the customary ritual of questions.

"Who is the plaintiff?"

"I am the plaintiff," answered the young man.

"And what is it you want?"

"I want to break off the engagement."

"Why?"

"Because I do not love her," answered the young man.

My father was visibly upset. I blushed. Just as her father was dark, sullen, bearded, heavy, so the girl was fair, smooth, light. She smelled of chocolate and perfume. Her shoes had high, thin heels. I could not understand how anyone could say that he did not love such a princess. But the young man was himself a dandy. What did he care about a pretty girl?

Father pulled at his beard. "And what else?"

"That is all, Rabbi."

"And you, what do you say to this?" My father asked the question in such a way that it was hard to tell whether he was addressing the father or the girl.

"I love him," said the girl, dryly and almost angrily.

In most cases my father came to a quick decision. Usually he arranged some compromise solution. But what sort of compromise was possible here? He looked at me as if to ask: what do you say to this? But I was as puzzled as he. Then he said something that I had never heard him say. In recent years the custom had been established by the "official" state-appointed Rabbis to call aside one or the other of the parties to a dispute for a *sub rosa* conference. Father had frequently declared his disapproval of this practice—a Rabbi sitting in judgment must not speak secretly with either of the litigants. Yet now I heard him say, "Please come with me."

He stood up and beckoned to the older man. Both went into an adjacent alcove. And I—what did I do? Naturally, I went along. If there was a secret, I wanted to hear it too. The door to the study remained ajar. My ears were directed toward my father and the older man, but my eyes toward the elegant young couple.

And now I saw something most extraordinary. The pretty girl walked over to her fiancé, they talked a while, they argued in an undertone, and suddenly I heard a resounding slap. A minute later, another. I cannot recall who slapped whom first, but I do know that they both did, and yet it was all done quietly— not at all in the manner of Krochmalna Street. They slapped each other and moved apart. Father had heard and seen nothing. I had the impression that the girl's father had sensed something of what was happening, but he acted as though he had not noticed anything. Tears rose to my eyes. For the first time I inhaled the poignant aroma of love, of adulthood, and of the mysteries that hover between man and woman.

I heard my father say: "Since he does not want to marry her, what's to be done?"

"Rabbi, we don't want him, either," answered the man grumblingly. "He is a hoodlum, a spendthrift— everything that's rotten. He runs around with other girls. There's no sin he hasn't committed. We wanted to be rid of him a long time ago, but he gave her presents—and the presents we don't want to return. That's the only reason she says she still loves him. Actually she can't bear him—that is the real truth of the matter. But we will not return the gifts."

"What kind of gifts?"

"A ring, a necklace, a brooch."

"Maybe you can make some compromise?"

"No compromise! We'll return nothing! Nothing!"

"Hm, I see. Go back now and send the young man in, please."

Then Father returned to the study and muttered at the fiancé, "Get in there!"

The young man came in quickly.

"You really don't want to marry her?" asked my father.

"No, Rabbi."

"Perhaps one can still endeavor to make peace between you two?"

"No, Rabbi. It is impossible."

"Peace is the foundation upon which the world stands."

"There can be no peace with *her*."

"She is a good Jewish girl."

"Rabbi, we are not yet married and already she has begun to nag me for money. I have an old mother to support, and she won't let me. I had to render her an account of every kopeck I earned. If it is like that now, what will it be like later? During the busy season I earn forty rubles a week. Her father is a miser. They have money put away. They just want to suck the last penny out of everyone else. Whenever I took her to a restaurant, she ordered the most expensive things on the menu—not because she was hungry but just to take advantage of me. If I ever came to the house without bringing her a present, her father got excited. She even told me exactly what to get her as a Purim gift. And it was like that with everything. They were only afraid that somehow I would fool them.... I never knew there are people like that. And what was it all for? I'm not stingy. Everything would have been hers anyway. But when I gave her the necklace, she ran from one jeweler to another to have it appraised. Rabbi, such a life is not for me!"

"So, then, you really want to end it?"

"Yes, Rabbi."

"And the presents?"

"Let her keep them, and herself!"

"I see. Let us go back in there."

Father surveyed the scene in his study. When he had left it to enter the alcove, he had known nothing about these two. Now it had all become clear. He instructed both sides to declare their acceptance of his decision. He received his fee. Father's decree was that since both parties rejected each other, they could not be compelled to abide by their contract. The bride, however, was to retain possession of the gifts.

The girl appeared to smirk. Something began to glow in her eyes. I thought I could see the glitter of gold reflected in them. Only now I noticed that earrings dangled from her lobes, and a ring with a small diamond glittered on one of her fingers.

"Rabbi, I want him to give her an official writ of forgiveness," demanded the father.

If I remember correctly, both parties wrote out the proper documents of forgiveness, as is the custom in the case of a broken engagement. Both signed their names—itself an unusual accomplishment for Krochmalna Street. When it was all over, the young man remained seated. Apparently he did not want to leave together with them. The father turned to the girl, "Come now, hurry!"

Then the girl said something that has remained indelible in my memory. She said, quickly: "Before I meet with another one like you, may I break both my legs!"

And I, although I was very young, understood that she still loved him. The betrothal had been broken only because of that miser her father.

A Gruesome Question

SABBATH NIGHT always had a holiday-like quality in our house, especially in the wintertime. At dusk my father would sit with his congregation at the closing Sabbath meal. The house was unlit. The men sang

"The Sons of the Mansion" and other table chants. They ate stale *chaleh* and a piece of carp or herring. All his life my father strove to be a Hasidic Rabbi and now he preached to his followers. I always stood behind his chair and listened. My father would lash out with great vehemence against worldly pleasures. He would extol the joys of the pious in heaven, seated on golden chairs with crowns on their heads, as the mysteries of the Torah were unraveled. And while my father talked, the first stars came out, and very often the moon, too. My father's talk of the soul and the "Throne of Glory" were always associated in my mind with the glitter of the stars, the face of the moon, and with the shapes of the clouds. The mysteries of the Torah were one with the mysteries of the world, and I somehow never sensed this quite as acutely as on Saturday after sundown, just before the candles were lit. In another room my mother would sit murmuring softly the prayer "God of Abraham." Our home at this time was permeated by the spirit of God, of angels, of secrets, and filled with a special longing and yearning that defy description.

And finally the beloved Sabbath was over and a new week began. The hurricane lamps were lit, the evening prayers said, and the braided valedictory candle lit. After my father said grace over the wine, the men dipped their fingers in it and daubed their eyes as a charm to insure a prosperous week. During the winter months Mother would go into the kitchen to prepare hot grits. Father recited the chapter, "And God shall give you of the fat of the earth," and the story of the poor saint who sold the prophet Elijah into slavery for 800,000 guldens. And then a fire was kindled in our tile stove to heat the living room.

The men sat in their Sabbath clothes, sipped tea with lemon, and discussed Hasidic matters and world affairs. The house was filled with the odor of burning wax, blessed spices, and with an atmosphere of wonder and miracles. My father was a smoker and he would wait quietly but anxiously all through the

Sabbath for the moment when he could light a cigarette or his pipe.

On this particular Sabbath evening, fresh snow had fallen and the ground outside seemed to take on a special look of brightness. Frost palms blossomed on the windowpanes, reminding me of the Land of Israel.

In the midst of this spirit of hopeful anticipation, with its promise of blessings and fulfillment, the door opened and a poor Jew entered. He was not like an ordinary pauper but like an old storybook beggar. His caftan was full of holes and patches, with the quilted cotton and buckram showing through the lining. His cap was peeling. His beard was icy and I think there were icicles hanging down from it. The man entered and brought with him the harshness of the everyday world and the coldness of the outdoors.

"A good week, Rabbi."

"A good week to you, and a good year. What have you to say?"

I opened my eyes wide. This ragged individual reminded me of the stories of the thirty-six saints who dedicated themselves to a life of poverty as water carriers, wood choppers, and solicitors of alms.

"Rabbi, I want to ask a question."

"Well, ask it."

"Rabbi, may a man sleep with his dead wife?"

A strange silence ensued. I felt a chill go through my body. The men turned pale. My father's face froze.

"I do not understand what you are talking about," my father finally stammered.

"Rabbi, I am not insane," the man said. "My wife died on Friday. I live in a cellar where there are rats. The funeral will take place on Sunday. I cannot leave the corpse on the floor because the rats would, God forbid, gnaw it to bits. I have only one bed. She must lie in that bed. And I, Rabbi, cannot sleep on the floor either. The rats would get me, too. I have already sat up one night, but my strength is gone. So I want to know, Rabbi, may I lie in bed with this corpse?"

As the man uttered these last words, I saw my
father's face as I had never seen it before. It was
flooded with tears. There was one gush and everything was wet—eyes, cheeks, red beard. There was a
stirring among the men, followed by an outcry. There
was a scraping of boots and the drumming of fingers
on the table. My father took out his large handkerchief to wipe his eyes and blow his nose. In a broken
voice, he said: "Men, did you hear? Woe, woe."

"God spare us, God spare us," said one of his
followers.

"Unheard of, unheard of," answered another.

"Well, why are you silent? Let us do something."

The men did not have money in their satin
Sabbath gabardines. But they all lived nearby and
ran home to get money. My father, who kept his
money in a tin box, took out several notes right away.
My mother heard the commotion and came running
in from the kitchen to see what had happened. She
turned pale, reddened, and paled again. Always in
crises like these my mother's wig would become
disheveled as though it were alive; several strands
(made of silk, not human hair) fell on her forehead
and cheeks; a hairpin sprang out; her bun loosened.
My mother went back into the kitchen to get food for
the poor man, and returned with tea, a biscuit, and
some leftover prune stew. The poor man went over to
the waterbarrel to wash his hands. A young man
returned to the house with the news that he had
obtained a makeshift cot for the man. Women
neighbors came into our house, wrung their hands,
and milled around among the menfolk.

"We must go and see," somebody said.

My father was not allowed to enter a room where
there was a corpse, because he was descended from
the priestly caste. But this was not forbidden other
Jews. While the poor man was eating and reviving
himself, contributions poured in from all sides.
Someone brought a padded jacket, a shirt, a pair of

socks, a fur cap. They showered the poor fellow with a
complete wardrobe. After he had finished eating and
said the appropriate blessing, he was taken home by
a host of people, one carrying the cot and others
carrying the food. I was not permitted to go along
because I, too, was descended from the priestly line.
Besides, I had a dread of these things from my
earliest childhood. But my curiosity apparently was
stronger than my fears. The man lived on Krochmalna Street, and as we went into the courtyard, most of
the men remained outside. Others started to make
their way down the dark and dingy stairs. I took a
quick look through the cellar window and saw an
eerie sight. This was not an ordinary cellar apartment, but a cave, a hole in the earth. The walls were
as black as the inside of a chimney. Two dim lights
flickered in the darkness, and on the bed there lay a
human form covered by a shawl. I could not see
clearly because the windowpanes were obscured by
frost and ice, with a clear spot only in the center
where the ice had been melted by the warm breath of
the curious onlookers. This man lived in the ground.
There, in the gloom, in the cold and filth, he pursued
his wretched existence with his wife, waging war on
the hordes of crawling creatures who attacked his
flesh and his scraps of bread. And now these vicious
beasts threatened to mutilate this martyred body.

I was torn between two conflicting emotions. My
fear dictated that I turn my eyes the other way, but
my curiosity demanded just another glance. I knew
that I would pay for each look with nightmares and
torment, but each time anew I leaned forward to see
this living grave. The flames which glimmered below
only served to intensify the darkness. It appeared to
me that I could see all kinds of evil spirits and sprites
romping around this unspeakable place. They
assumed all sorts of fearful shapes. Can a person
survive in such an abyss? Can a man confined to
such a sordid place keep his sanity? I suddenly felt a

tightness in my head and an icy shudder ran down
my spine. Could it be that he who dwells here is
himself a ghost?

Men and women busied themselves in the cellar
and someone moved the candles. They seemed to be
lifting something. I was ready to turn and run, but
now I was in no condition to go home alone. I was
afraid because the steps to our flat were sometimes
unlit and at other times illuminated only by a smoky
kerosene lamp without a chimney and without a cap.
A man agreed to go back with me. I was shaking all
over and my teeth were chattering. Something within
me cried and asked, "How can God permit this?"

When I was led into the house, my mother began to
wring her hands. "Woe is me! Just look at this child!"

They warmed me up and blew on me. My mother
recited an incantation. I was given tea and preserves
and all of the goodies which were in the house. My
father paced back and forth in his study. He chewed
his beard and rubbed his forehead. He was by nature
a believer, but this incident had awakened doubts in
him.

"Dear Father in Heaven ... Woe!" he cried out. "It
is high time for our salvation ... time ... high time."

Our Sabbath night was ruined and the week that
followed was a meager one because my father had
given part of my mother's weekly allowance to the
poor man. Later I heard talk that it was odd indeed
for a Jew to have only one bed in his house. This was
known among peasants, but it was unheard of even
among the most impoverished Jews. But who knows,
perhaps he had a second bed that had been broken?
Perhaps he had to use it for kindling wood? The
squalor that one sometimes finds in large cities is
rarely found in small towns. For a long, long time
afterwards there was talk in our house of this grim
episode and for a long period thereafter I was
afflicted with nightmares. I often saw this man later,
as he went about trading and mingling with the

people. But I was always afraid of him. I always remembered his visit that Sabbath evening, and his gruesome question.

The Washwoman

OUR HOME HAD LITTLE CONTACT with Gentiles. The only Gentile in the house was the janitor. Fridays he would come for a tip, his "Friday money." He remained standing at the door, took off his hat, and my mother gave him six groschen.

Besides the janitor there were also the Gentile washwomen who came to the house to fetch our laundry. My story is about one of these.

She was a small woman, old and wrinkled. When she started washing for us she was already past seventy. Most Jewish women of her age were sickly, weak, broken in body. All the old women in our street had bent backs and leaned on sticks when they walked. But this washwoman, small and thin as she was, possessed a strength that came from generations of peasant forebears. Mother would count out to her a bundle of laundry that had accumulated over several weeks. She would lift the unwieldy pack, load it on her narrow shoulders, and carry it the long way home. She also lived on Krochmalna Street, but at the other end, near Wola. It must have been a walk of an hour and a half.

She would bring the laundry back about two weeks

later. My mother had never been so pleased with any other washwoman. Every piece of linen sparkled like polished silver. Every piece was ironed. Yet she charged no more than the others. She was a real find. Mother always had her money ready, because it was too far for the old woman to come a second time.

Laundering was not easy in those days. The old woman had no faucet where she lived but had to bring in the water from a pump. For the linens to come out so clean, they had to be scrubbed thoroughly in a washtub, rinsed with washing soda, soaked, boiled in an enormous pot, starched, ironed. Every piece was handled ten times or more. And the drying! It could not be done outside because thieves would steal the laundry. The wrung-out wash had to be carried up to the attic and hung on clotheslines. In the winter it would become as brittle as glass and almost break when touched. Then there was always a to-do with other housewives and washwomen who wanted the attic for their own use. Only God knew all she had to endure each time she did a wash!

The old woman could have begged at the church door or entered a home for the indigent aged. But there was in her a certain pride and a love of labor with which the Gentiles have been blessed. The old woman did not want to become a burden, and thus she bore her burden.

My mother spoke a little Polish, and the old woman would talk with her about many things. She was especially fond of me and used to say that I looked like Jesus. She repeated this every time she came, and Mother would frown and whisper to herself, her lips barely moving, "May her words be scattered in the wilderness."

The woman had a son who was rich. I no longer remember what sort of business he had. He was ashamed of his mother, the washwoman, and never came to see her. Nor did he ever give her a groschen. The old woman told this without rancor. One day the

son was married. It seemed that he had made a good
match. The wedding took place in a church. The son
had not invited the old mother to his wedding, but she
went to the church and waited at the steps to see her
son lead the "young lady" to the altar. I do not want
to seem a chauvinist, but I believe that no Jewish son
would have acted in this manner. But I have no doubt
that, had he done this, the mother would have
shrieked and wailed and sent the sexton to call him to
account. In short, Jews are Jews and Gentiles are
Gentiles.

The story of the faithless son left a deep impression
upon my mother. She talked about it for weeks and
months. It was an affront not only to the old woman
but to the entire institution of motherhood. Mother
would argue. "Nu, does it pay to make sacrifices for
children? The mother uses up her last strength, and
he does not even know the meaning of loyalty."

And she would drop dark hints to the effect that
she was not certain of her own children: Who knows
what they would someday do? This, however, did not
prevent her from dedicating her life to us. If there was
any delicacy in the house, she would put it aside for
the children and invent all sorts of excuses and
reasons why she herself did not want to taste it. She
knew charms that went back to ancient times, and
she used expressions she had inherited from generations of devoted mothers and grandmothers. If one of
the children complained of a pain, she would say,
"May I be your ransom and may you outlive my
bones!" Or she would say, "May I be the atonement
for the least of your fingernails." When we ate she
used to say, "Health and marrow in your bones!" The
day before the new moon she gave us a kind of candy
that was said to prevent parasitic worms. If one of us
had something in his eye, Mother would lick the eye
clean with her tongue. She also fed us rock candy
against coughs, and from time to time she would take
us to be blessed against the evil eye. This did not

prevent her from studying *The Duties of the Heart, The Book of the Covenant,* and other serious philosophic works.

But to return to the washwoman: that winter was a harsh one. The streets were in the grip of a bitter cold. No matter how much we heated our stove, the windows were covered with frostwork and decorated with icicles. The newspapers reported that people were dying of the cold. Coal became dear. The winter had become so severe that parents stopped sending children to the heder, and even the Polish schools were closed.

On one such day the washwoman, now nearly eighty years old, came to our house. A good deal of laundry had accumulated during the past weeks. Mother gave her a pot of tea to warm herself, as well as some bread. The old woman sat on a kitchen chair trembling and shaking, and warmed her hands against the teapot. Her fingers were gnarled from work, and perhaps from arthritis too. Her fingernails were strangely white. These hands spoke of the stubbornness of mankind, of the will to work not only as one's strength permits but beyond the limits of one's power. Mother counted and wrote down the list: men's undershirts, women's vests, long-legged drawers, bloomers, petticoats, shifts, featherbed covers, pillowcases, sheets, and the men's fringed garments. Yes, the Gentile woman washed these holy garments as well.

The bundle was big, bigger than usual. When the woman placed it on her shoulders, it covered her completely. At first she swayed, as though she were about to fall under the load. But an inner obstinacy seemed to call out: No, you may not fall. A donkey may permit himself to fall under his burden, but not a human being, the crown of creation.

It was fearful to watch the old woman staggering out with the enormous pack, out into the frost, where the snow was dry as salt and the air was filled with dusty white whirlwinds, like goblins dancing in the cold. Would the old woman ever reach Wola?

She disappeared, and Mother sighed and prayed for her.

Usually the woman brought back the wash after two or, at the most, three weeks. But three weeks passed, then four and five, and nothing was heard of the old woman. We remained without linens. The cold had become even more intense. The telephone wires were now as thick as hawsers. The branches of the trees looked like glass. So much snow had fallen that the streets had become uneven, and on many streets sleds were able to glide down as on the slopes of a hill. Kindhearted people lit fires in the streets for vagrants to warm themselves and roast potatoes over, if they had any to roast.

For us the washwoman's absence was a catastrophe. We needed the laundry. We did not even know the woman's house address. It seemed certain that she had collapsed, died. Mother declared that she had had a premonition, as the old woman left our house the last time, that we would never see our things again. She found some torn old shirts and washed them, mended them. We mourned, both for the laundry and for the old, toilworn woman who had grown close to us through the years she had served us so faithfully.

More than two months passed. The frost had subsided, and then a new frost had come, a new wave of cold. One evening, while Mother was sitting near the kerosene lamp mending a shirt, the door opened and a small puff of steam, followed by a gigantic bundle, entered. Under the bundle tottered the old woman, her face as white as a linen sheet. A few wisps of white hair straggled out from beneath her shawl. Mother uttered a half-choked cry. It was as though a corpse had entered the room. I ran toward the old woman and helped her unload her pack. She was even thinner now, more bent. Her face had become more gaunt, and her head shook from side to side as though she were saying no. She could not utter a clear word, but mumbled something with her sunken mouth and pale lips.

After the old woman had recovered somewhat, she told us that she had been ill, very ill. Just what her illness was, I cannot remember. She had been so sick that someone had called a doctor, and the doctor had sent for a priest. Someone had informed the son, and he had contributed money for a coffin and for the funeral. But the Almighty had not yet wanted to take this pain-racked soul to Himself. She began to feel better, she became well, and as soon as she was able to stand on her feet once more she resumed her washing. Not just ours, but the wash of several other families too.

"I could not rest easy in my bed because of the wash," the old woman explained. "The wash would not let me die."

"With the help of God you will live to be a hundred and twenty," said my mother, as a benediction.

"God forbid! What good would such a long life be? The work becomes harder and harder—my strength is leaving me—I do not want to be a burden on anyone!"

The old woman muttered and crossed herself, and raised her eyes toward heaven. Fortunately there was some money in the house and Mother counted out what she owed. I had a strange feeling: the coins in the old woman's washed-out hands seemed to become as weary and clean and pious as she herself was. She blew on the coins and tied them in a kerchief. Then she left, promising to return in a few weeks for a new load of wash.

But she never came back. The wash she had returned was her last effort on this earth. She had been driven by an indomitable will to return the property to its rightful owners, to fulfill the task she had undertaken.

And now at last the body, which had long been no more than a broken shard supported only by the force of honesty and duty, had fallen. The soul passed into

those spheres where all holy souls meet, regardless of
the roles they played on this earth, in whatever
tongue, of whatever creed. I cannot imagine Eden
without this washwoman. I cannot even conceive of a
world where there is no recompense for such effort.

A Major Din Torah

THE DISPUTES that were brought to my father for
arbitration were usually petty ones. The sums
involved would be about twenty, or at the most fifty,
rubles. I had heard that there were Rabbis to whom
"big" cases, involving thousands of rubles, were
brought, and each side would be represented by its
own arbitrator. But this happened only to the rich
Rabbis who lived in the north of Warsaw, not in our
part of town.

But one winter a major lawsuit was brought to our
house. To this day I do not know why these wealthy
people chose my father to be their judge, for he was
known as a naïve, unworldly man. My mother sat in
the kitchen and worried. She feared that he would not
understand these complicated matters. Early that
morning, Father had taken down the *Hoshen
Mishpat* and immersed himself in it: if he was not an
expert on questions of business and commerce, he
would at least be sure of the law. Soon the litigants
came and brought their arbitrators—themselves
Rabbis. One of the litigants was tall, with a sparse,
black beard and angry, coal-black eyes. He wore a

long fur coat, shiny galoshes, and a fur hat. His lips
held a cigar in an amber cigar holder. An aura of
importance, learning, and shrewdness emanated
from him. When he removed his overshoes, I saw gilt
letters on the red lining and was told that these were
monograms. He had brought an arbitrator—a Rabbi
with a milky-white beard and young, laughing eyes.
The Rabbi had a round potbelly, and a silver chain
dangled across his silk vest.

The second litigant was a small, gray manikin,
dressed in a fox pelt, a thick cigar between his lips; he
had brought a spokesman who had a broad, yellow
beard, a nose like the beak of a bird, and round,
birdlike eyes to match. When he removed his hat he
remained for a few moments bareheaded. Then he
put on a silken skullcap of the style worn by Litvaks.

In our house, the study of Torah was the only
subject of importance, but these men brought with
them an element of worldliness. I gaped and
wondered. The Rabbis—the arbitrators—exchanged
jokes. They smiled well-practiced smiles. My mother
served tea with lemon and cookies left from the
Sabbath, and the Rabbi with the laughing eyes
addressed her jestingly.

"Rebbetzin, perhaps you can do something about
bringing the summer?" He did not avert his eyes, like
my father, but looked straight at her.

My mother reddened like a schoolgirl and seemed
for a moment at a loss. Then she regained her
composure and answered, "If we have winter, it is
probably because the winter is needed." Soon the
actual hearing began; the case involved thousands of
rubles. With all my might I tried to understand what
was being discussed, but I soon lost the thread. It was
about buying, selling, ordering wagonloads of
merchandise. They talked of credit, net value, gross
income, account books, ledgers, interest, notes. The
negotiating Rabbis were well versed in the terminology of business affairs, but my father was constantly
asking for explanations. As his son, I suffered pangs

of shame and embarrassment on his behalf. From
time to time the discussion of the case would be
interrupted by women from the neighborhood who
came to ask whether their freshly slaughtered
chickens were kosher.

The Din Torah lasted not one but several days.
During this time I learned that not all Rabbis
resembled my father. These two took out fountain
pens and scribbled on sheets of paper—lines, circles,
squares. Every few hours I was sent out to buy
refreshments: apples, cakes, even sausages and cold
cuts. My father never touched meat bought in a
sausage shop, even one that was strictly kosher. But
the other Rabbis ate the smoked meats and discussed
them like connoisseurs. At other times the argument
would be halted while one of the Rabbis told a story.
Then the other would not want to lag behind, and he
too would tell an anecdote. Then they got to talking
about foreign countries and different resorts, and I
learned that these Rabbis had been in Germany, in
Vienna, and in other distant places. My father, to be
sure, presided at the head of the table, but he seemed
to shrivel in the presence of these worldly divines and
their smooth conversation.

After a while I began to understand the issues and
realized, to my amazement, that the arbitrators were
not really concerned about who was right and who
wrong, what was true and what false, but each was
looking for twists and turns to justify his party and to
contradict the arguments of his opponent.

I resented these clever Rabbis, yet at the same time
I envied their children. From the way they spoke, I
realized that in their homes there were rugs, sofas,
lovely things of all kinds. Occasionally one of the
Rabbis would even mention his wife, and this was the
greatest wonder of all. Never had I heard my father
refer to my mother when he was speaking with other
men.

The longer the Din Torah lasted, the more
complicated it became. The table was covered with a

thick layer of papers, calculations. They called in a
bookkeeper, who brought a stack of account books.
The moods of the tall man with the black beard were
constantly changing. One minute he spoke calmly,
deliberately, as though each word cost a gold piece,
then suddenly he would begin to shout, banging his
fist on the table and threatening to file suit in a
governmental court. The gray little man answered
sharply, angrily, maintaining that he was not afraid
of any court. For his part, the lawsuit could be
brought before the highest tribunal. And the two
spokesmen, although they were literally waging war
against each other, still chatted amiably, lit matches
for each other's cigarettes, and continued to repeat to
each other the sayings of Rabbis, scholars, and
famous lawyers. My father had almost stopped
speaking, or asking for explanations. From time to
time he would glance longingly at his bookcase. For
the sake of the business quarrels of these rich men he
had had to give up time he would otherwise have
devoted to the Torah, and he yearned for his books
and commentaries. Once again the world, with its
calculations and falsehoods, had intruded into our
life.

I was constantly sent on errands. One minute
someone sent me for cigarettes—and the next for
cigars. For some reason a Polish newspaper was
needed and I was sent for it. But most frequently I
was sent for different things to eat. I had not known
that anyone could eat so much—so many kinds of
sweets and delicacies—and on ordinary weekdays, to
boot. The Rabbi with the laughing eyes wanted a tin
of sardines. Apparently the two Rabbis ate so much
because it was all paid for by the litigants. They said
so openly, albeit as a jest and with a wink of the eye.

On the last day all was shouting and tumult. Every
few minutes one or the other of the litigants would try
to run out, and his Rabbi would hold him back.

Perhaps they were only acting? I had learned that
they often said one thing and meant another. When
they were angry, they spoke softly. When they were
satisfied, they pretended to be enraged. When one of
the Rabbis was away, the other would enumerate all
his sins and weaknesses. Once the Rabbi with the
laughing eyes arrived half an hour earlier than the
others and proceeded to revile his opponent, the
Rabbi with the yellow beard and birdlike eyes. He
said, "That one is no more a Rabbi than I am the king
of England."

My father was stunned. "How is that possible? I
know that he makes decisions on ritual questions."

"His decisions, ha...."

"But if that is so, he could—may such things not
come to pass—cause other Jews to eat forbidden
foods."

"Well, he may know how to look up a reference in
the Be'er Heitev.... He was in America already."

"What did he do in America?"

"He sewed pants."

Father wiped the sweat from his brow. "Are you
serious?"

"Yes."

"Nu, he probably needed the money. It is written
that it is better to flay carcasses than to take
alms...Work is no disgrace."

"True, but not every shoemaker is a Rabbi Yochan-
an...."

My father had told my mother that he would be
almost happy if this Din Torah were taken to another
Rabbi for judgment. He had already diverted too
much of his time from his studies. He could not devote
more energy to all these tangles and "fractions" (a
term my father used for any arithmetical process
more complex than addition, subtraction, and
multiplication). He foresaw that in any case the
litigants might not abide by his decree. He was also
afraid that the suit would eventually be brought into
the civil courts, and he might be called as a witness.

The very idea of standing before a magistrate, taking
an oath on a Bible, sitting among policemen, cast
terror upon him. He groaned in his sleep at night. In
the morning he would rise even earlier than usual, to
be able to recite his prayers in peace and to review at
least one page of the Gemara. He would pace up and
down in his study and pray aloud, in a trembling
voice:

"O my God, the soul Thou gavest me is pure. Thou
didst create it, Thou didst form it, Thou didst breathe
it into me. Thou preservest it within me, and Thou
wilt take it from me, but wilt restore it unto me
hereafter...."

He was not simply reciting a prayer, but seemed
almost to be pleading his case before the Master of
the Universe. I thought that he kissed his phylacteries and the fringes of his prayer shawl with a fervor
more intense than ever.

Yes, the final day was a stormy one. This time, not
only the litigants, but even the negotiators shouted.
The erstwhile amity between the two spokesmen had
evaporated, and they were now quarreling and
abusing one another. They argued and shouted and
gave vent to their pent-up emotions until their
strength was exhausted. At that moment Father took
out his kerchief and ordered the litigants to grasp it, a
token of their submission to his decision. I stood by,
trembling. I was certain that my father had understood nothing of all these entangled arguments and
that he would pronounce a decree as ill-fitted as a
blow for a Sabbath greeting. But now it became clear
that in the course of these past days my father had,
after all, grasped the significance of the issues at
stake. He pronounced his old and tried formula of
compromise: an equal division....

For some time after he had given his decision,
there was silence. No one had the strength to speak.
The man with the sparse beard stared at my father
with savage eyes. The little man made a grimace as
though he had accidentally swallowed something

sour. The Rabbi with the yellow eyes smiled cynical-
ly, displaying a mouthful of yellow teeth. I noticed
that one tooth was gold-covered, and this convinced
me that he had indeed been in America.

When all had had time to recover, they began to
tear my father's decree apart. Insulting innuendoes
were made. Father stated his argument simply. "I
asked you whether you wanted an absolute decision,
or were willing to accept a compromise."

"Even a compromise must be reasonable!"

"That is my decision. I have no Cossacks at my
command to enforce it."

The arbitrators withdrew to confer with their
clients. They muttered, argued, complained. I remember that the loudest protests came from the side that
had actually benefited the most from the decision.
After a while they seemed to have decided that the
compromise was not, after all, so bad and that
perhaps there really was no better way. The litigants,
who were business partners, shook hands. The
Rabbis demanded that I go down to bring refreshments, so that all could recuperate from the fighting
and quarreling. Again the two were the best of
friends, and one even said that he would recommend
the other to handle a case he knew of. At last
everyone had left. In the study there remained only
cigar smoke, a table full of papers, fruit skins, the
remains of various delicacies. Father had received a
generous fee—twenty rubles, I believe—but I could
tell that he felt an unpleasant aftertaste. He asked
Mother to clear the table as quickly as possible. He
opened the doors so that the odors of wealth and
worldliness might escape. The litigants were, after
all, men of business—but the overly clever Rabbis
had caused him deep pain.

As soon as my mother had cleared the table,
Father sat down to resume his studies. He reached for
his books eagerly. There, in the holy books, one did
not nibble on sardines, one did not make innuendoes,
or flatter, or speak words of double meaning, or tell

slippery jokes. There holiness, truth, dedication reigned.

In the Hasidic prayer house where my father prayed, the men had heard of the sensational Din Torah. Businessmen discussed it with my father. They said that he was becoming known in Warsaw, was gaining a reputation, but my father waved this talk aside with his hand.

"No, it is not good...."

At that time, too, my father began to talk to me about the Lamed-Vov—the thirty-six hidden saints—the simple Jews, the tailors, shoemakers, and water carriers upon whom depends the continued existence of the world. Father spoke of their poverty, their humility, their appearance of ignorance so that none would recognize their true greatness. He spoke of these concealed saints with a special love, and he said, "One contrite heart is of greater worth before the Almighty than thirty silk gabardines."

The Family Tree

FATHER'S FAMILY was more distinguished than Mother's, but he seldom spoke of them. My father's father was Reb Samuel, an assistant Rabbi in Tomaszow; his father had been Reb Isaiah Konsker, a Hasid and scholar without ecclesiastical office; Reb Isaiah's father had been Reb Moshe, known as the Sage of Warsaw, and author of *The Sacred Letter*. Reb Moshe's father had been Reb Tobias, the

Sztektcin Rabbi, and his father had been Reb Moshe, the Neufeld Rabbi. This Reb Moshe had been a disciple of the celebrated Baal Shem. Reb Moshe's father had been Reb Zvi Hirsch, the Zhorker Rabbi.

My paternal grandmother Temerl's roots went even further back.

My father's father, Reb Samuel, had refused for many years to become a Rabbi, and instead had given himself to the study of the Cabala. He fasted often and perspired so profusely when he prayed each morning that his wife had to give him a fresh shirt daily—in those days, an unheard-of luxury. Grandmother Temerl's mother had been a jeweler, supporting her husband, and my grandmother did the same. At that time it was a woman's accepted lot to bear children, cook, run the household, and earn a living— while the man studied Torah. Rather than complain, our grandmothers praised God for providing them with husbands who were scholars. In his later years, when Grandmother was no longer able to earn a living, Grandfather consented to become a Rabbi.

For years, Reb Samuel kept to himself, having made an oath of silence. Grandmother Temerl, on the other hand, mingled with people and was liked by them. She was the daughter of Hinde Esther, to whom the famous Rabbi Shalom Belzer had offered a chair when she came to visit him. Grandmother's most fervent wish was that her children study Torah.

Her eldest son, Isaiah, married, and settled in Rohatyn, Galicia, was wealthy and a devoted Belz Hasid. Two of her daughters had married in Hungary, and one son had died. My father, the youngest son, received all his mother's love and attention. She was pleased with him because he was scholarly and devoted to Jewish ways while other young men were beginning to grow worldly, dressing fashionably, and reading the Hebrew newspapers and magazines that sometimes reached Tomaszow. But none of this affected my father, who continued to wear the traditional long hose and half shoes, a kerchief around his neck, and long sidelocks. His childhood ambition had been to become a saint. At fifteen he had begun writing a commentary, and other boys were wary of him and his dreamy ways, resenting his lack of interest in their games of goat or wolf (or cards on Hanukkah), his superiority and aloofness.

Grandmother had wanted Father—who already grew a red beard at sixteen—to marry young, but old-fashioned young men did not attract wealthy prospective fathers-in-law, and to make things more difficult, Grandmother insisted that the bride came from a family of Rabbis, not merchants. Finally, when my father did become betrothed, his bride-to-be died, and he was called up for conscription. There was nothing worse for a young man of my father's kind than to serve the Tsar, but Grandmother would not permit Father to maim himself and his only recourse was to pray to God.

In those days it was customary to have a drawing at which the recruits with the highest numbers were excused from service. Father drew a high number, thus saving himself even the preliminary embarrassment of stripping before a doctor. For years he referred to the mercy God had thus shown him.

It was only after his release from service that Father's family realized what an old bachelor he was—twenty-one! In his long hose, half shoes, sash about his loins, skullcap beneath his velvet hat, full beard, and long sidelocks, he looked like an elderly Hasid. With only one desire—to live as a Jew—he was entirely immersed in piety and had very little to say to anyone. The only item missing from his habit was the prayer shawl worn by married men. Other young men, in their polished boots and gold-rimmed glasses, would joke about Pinhos-Mendel's longing to be a Wonder Rabbi, but this was the truth. Father wanted to purify his soul to such a degree that he would be capable of performing miracles. He would read, besides the Gemara and the Scriptures, Hasidic books and an occasional book of the Cabala.

Although his conduct pleased his mother, it was out of fashion with others. Daughters of rabbinical families read modern books, dressed modishly, visited spas, walked about unchaperoned, spoke "German," and even occasionally wore modern hats.

It was necessary for young Rabbis to know something of practical matters, commerce, and world affairs, and Father was not the kind of son-in-law who would fall into this pattern.

Then a match was proposed with the daughter of the Bilgoray Rabbi, who was well known in the region, having formerly been Rabbi of Maciejew, which is near Kowel, and prior to that, of Purick in the Szedlce province. He was the kind of Rabbi who lived in the past. Once, when a troupe of actors appeared in Bilgoray, he put on his coat, went to the barn where they were performing, and drove them out, along with the audience. Even though Bilgoray was near enlightened Zamoscz and Shebreshin, where the "heretic" Jacob Reifman lived, Grandfather kept Bilgoray to itself, assisted by the town elders and the Hasidim. To the few sophisticates in Bilgoray, Grandfather was a fanatic, a purveyor of darkness, but despite this, he was respected and feared. Tall, broad, and powerful, retaining all his teeth and hair through old age, he was also known as a mathematician and an expert in Hebrew grammar. His command was like that of the ancient leaders, and while he lived, Bilgoray remained pious.

The projected proposal caused Father some anxiety, because, despite the piety of the Bilgoray Rabbi, he was known to be so rooted in the traditional that even Hasidism seemed impure, with its gesticulations, chants, visits to rabbinic courts, and mystic aspirations. He ruled his town despotically; his own household trembled before him. In addition, his two sons were known for their sharp wit. Father was afraid he would not fit in there.

But it wasn't easy to turn down the opportunity.

Mother was sixteen at the time, and known for her wisdom and erudition. Two matches had been proposed to her—one with my father and one with the son of a wealthy Lublin family. Grandfather asked whom she preferred.

"Which is the better scholar?" she asked.

"The one in Tomaszow."

That settled it for her. But her family was disgraced during the signing of the Articles, because of the appearance of Father's family. Grandmother Temerl wore a satin dress that would have been stylish a hundred years before, and her bonnet was a mass of knots, corals, and stripes that no one had seen anywhere. Even her manner of speaking was archaic, and Father looked more like a father-in-law than a bridegroom. His father, Reb Samuel, kept silent. My father said nothing to the other betrothed young men, who tried to talk to him about stores, houses, watches, travel, and politics. He knew of nothing but service to God, spoke no Polish or Russian, could not even write his address in the Gentile script. Outside of the Torah and prayer, the world was to him full of evil spirits, demons and goblins.

Mother, when she met her prospective husband, was embarrassed by this man with his full red beard. But when she heard him discuss religious questions with her father, she respected and even admired him. She told me that it also pleased her to have a bridegroom five years her senior. Grandmother Temerl presented Mother with a gold chain so heavy it was barely wearable. It might have been two hundred years old. For months afterwards, Mother was showing it to her girl friends. It had the kind of clasp goldsmiths no longer made.

My maternal grandmother, Hannah, was a bitter, skeptical woman who, without detracting from her piety, could wound profoundly. Grandmother Temerl, on the other hand, was all sweetness and biblical quotations. Where Hannah was melancholy,

Temerl was joyous, and where Hannah criticized everything, Temerl exclaimed constantly about the wonders of God. Grandmother Hannah had a premature curiosity about how Father would support his family when his eight board years were over, but Grandmother Temerl insisted lightheartedly that God would provide, as He always had. Hadn't He given manna to the Jews in the desert?

Hannah answered dryly, "That was long ago."

"God doesn't change," Temerl said.

"We're not worth miracles any more," Hannah countered.

"Why not?" Temerl replied. "We can be just as good and pious as our ancestors."

This was more or less the way they talked. Later, convinced that her son's future was in the right hands, Temerl went home happily. Reb Samuel continued to say nothing, the Bilgoray grandfather returned to his books, and Hannah's sense of loneliness increased. She was convinced that her youngest daughter would end up a pauper.

After the Wedding

MY GRANDFATHER, even though he ruled Bilgoray, was not too close to his adherents. Nothing but the Talmud and the eternal questions interested him. Having no time for pettiness or small talk, he gave his legal decisions or religious interpretations of law, and said no more. Gossip and town feuds did not

concern him, even though there were always oppos-
ing parties trying to destroy each other in the affairs
of ritual slaughterers, elders, flour for Passover,
Community jobs. As the Talmud says one must close
one's ears to gossip, so he did, and in a fit of rage
called out warnings, even to prominent citizens, that
they must desist.

The citizens, although accepting the warning
never to try to involve Grandfather in intrigue, would
develop a feeling of hostility toward him.

On the other hand, the simpler Jews, artisans,
peddlers, and sievemakers—the so-called "rabble"—
revered Grandfather and would allow no one to harm
him. He advised them even when they came to him
with their private problems. They joined him at the
third Sabbath meal and sang hymns with him.

There were two kinds of Hasidim in town, the
Turisk and Sandzer, and since Grandfather had,
when young, visited the court of the Turisk Rabbi, it
was that group to which he belonged. Nevertheless,
he was at odds with the old Rabbi's sons, Reb Jacob
Leibele and Reb Mottele Kuzmer, who visited
Bilgoray every year, competing for followers. They
stayed with Grandfather and were always stirring up
trouble. Grandfather kept in his yard a Succoth booth
with wings that could be lifted and lowered by ropes.
When either of the Rabbis came to visit, he would
move into the booth with his books, pens, inkwell,
paper, and a samovar, and sit there, drinking
steaming tea as he studied Torah and wrote commentaries that were more likely to be burned than
printed. Both Rabbis were afraid of Grandfather,
perhaps because he told everyone the truth, thus
demonstrating the saying, "The scholar's words are
like burning coals..."

Joseph and Itche, Grandfather's sons, were witty
but did not have their father's strength of character.
He preferred his daughters, the favorite being the
youngest, Bathsheba, my mother. Like her father,
she was wise, devout, passionately interested in

books, and had even taught herself Hebrew. A blue-eyed, fair-skinned redhead, she was thin and frail, lacked appetite, and was always aching somewhere. Her nose was thin, her chin pointed, and her shoes, as cobblers had assured her, were the smallest in town. She liked to primp, and before leaving the house would polish her shoes a hundred times with a brush or an old stocking.

By the standards of the time, Bilgoray was a fair-sized town. It lay near the Austrian border, and many soldiers were stationed there. Cossack officers danced with Russian women or played cards in the military club. Cossack soldiers rode whip in hand through the streets, wearing a single earring and round caps. The Polish Gentiles lived on side streets, and the three nationalities remained separate, speaking in their own tongues and celebrating their own holidays.

Mother and Father's wedding, which occurred after Pentecost, was a noisy one. Mother often told us how tumultuous it had been. All the girls had sewed dresses for this occasion, and had learned the latest dances. But my father, because his mother wanted him to dress in his best clothes, had to wear a fur coat, even though it was summer, thus providing great entertainment for the town dandies.

It did not take long for Father to realize that he could not fit into the household of his severe, patrician father-in-law, with whom it was almost impossible to speak. His brothers-in-law jeered at my father's piety, the way he concentrated on being a Jew. More than once, he could not find his way home from the study house, and since he never looked at a woman he could not recognize my mother and might easily have mistaken Grandmother or a sister-in-law for his wife. Even at that time, such unworldliness was rare. To become an official Rabbi, one had to take an examination in Russian and speak to the governor, but, though my uncles had done this, my father refused. During the eight-years boarding

period, he went home frequently and sometimes
visited Wonder Rabbis. He wanted to become the
disciple of a saint, but couldn't find one that met his
requirements.

When the eight years were over, Father looked for
a small rabbinate where he would not need a Russian
examination. My mother's brothers, as well as her
mother, urged her to divorce this dreamer, but my
mother already had children, my sister Hinde Esther,
and my brother Israel Joshua. Grandfather said
nothing, becoming more secretive and silent with
age.

Because there were always so many fights among
the Hasidim concerning positions—for which one
needed influence—no one believed Father would find
a rabbinate. He did, nevertheless, in a tiny village,
Leoncin, by the river Vistula, not far from Nowy
Dwor, Zakroczym, and only a few miles from
Warsaw. My parents lived there for ten years and my
younger brother Moishe and I were born there,
although we were listed officially as having been
born in Radzymin. Leoncin, I needn't describe, since
my older brother has already done so in *Of a World
That Is No More*. But there are a few things I would
like to mention about Radzymin.

My father left Leoncin and became assistant to the
Radzymin Rabbi as a result of the following events.
Radzymin had become the vortex of a new rabbinical
dynasty founded by Reb Yekele, a miracle worker,
formerly connected with the Hasidic courts of
Przyscha and Kotzk. To the women who visited him,
he would present charmed coins and pieces of amber
that cured illness. Young men would seek his prayers
to free them from induction. It was said that his
incantations revived those who were dying. It was
rumored that his rebukes helped even more than his
blessings. When a woman came to him crying about
her sick baby, he would shout, "Oh, go to the devil,
you and your bastard..." And the child would
recover immediately.

Reb Yekele loved coins, copper, silver, and gold,

which he kept in earthen jars. It was said that even
corpses came to him for purification so that they
might enter Paradise. He would complain that the
transmigrant souls would soon collapse his attic with
their weight. Once when he fell from his bed at night
and the beadle ran in, the Rabbi cried out, "He's as
much a fool dead as alive. Why does he come to me in
his shrouds when he knows what a coward I am?"
And he ordered a candle left burning in his room all
night.

His son, Reb Shlomele, died young, and his
grandson, Reb Aaron Menachem Mendel, became
Rabbi, inheriting a large estate from his grandfather,
a following, a house of worship, and buildings in
Warsaw. There was no great heritage attached to the
Radzymin dynasty, but Reb Aaron Menachem
Mendel married the Bialer Rabbi's daughter, whose
lineage was distinguished. Nevertheless, the Radzymin Rabbi lacked the prestige of other great
Rabbis; few noble Jews and Rabbis visited his court;
and his following was made up of small storekeepers,
artisans, and coachmen. Also, he was not an unusual
scholar, and the commentaries he had written needed
revision. He opened a yeshivah but had no one to
direct it and study with the boys.

The position went to my father.

We put our possessions in a wagon and rode to
Radzymin, and even though I was only three at the
time, I remember the journey. All the Jews in town
came to bid us goodbye, and the women kissed
Mother. Then we rode through fields, forests, and
past windmills. It was a summer evening, and the
sky seemed ablaze with blowing coals, fiery brooms,
and beasts. There was a buzzing, a humming, and the
croaking of frogs. The wagon had halted, and I saw a
train, first a large locomotive with three lamps like
suns, then freight cars trailing behind in a slow,
preoccupied way. They seemed to come from nowhere
and to go to beyond the end of the world, where the
darkness loomed.

I began to cry. Mother said, "Why are you crying,

silly? It's just a train." I know exactly what I saw
at that time—a train with oil cars, but there was a
sense of mystery about it then that still remains
with me...

To Warsaw

A HUGE MAN with an enormous belly and great
yellow beard, the Rabbi would clap his hands, stamp
his feet, and carry on as he prayed. On the Sabbath,
the Rabbi ate at the study house, closing his eyes as
he recited the Torah. Then one of the beadles would
remove his boots and walk over the tablecloth in
stocking feet, pouring wine for everyone.

The Rabbi had a numerous following, and his
court included a house of prayer, a ritual bath, a large
house for the young Rebbetzin, the Bialer Rabbi's
daughter, and a small house for the Rabbi's mother.

The young and old Rebbetzins did not get along,
because the younger one acted too much the lady and
was childless as well. The old Rebbetzin often
advised her son to divorce this woman, who despite
her beauty, intellect, and eloquence could not produce
an heir to the Radzymin dynasty. But it was the
opinion of doctors and specialists that this was the
Rabbi's fault, and Hasidim from other courts knew
about it, and laughed. In Radzymin, enlightened
young men made bawdy jokes, at which the girls
blushed. It was said that the Rabbi would not bathe
with the other men, but had his own private ritual
bath.

I remember visiting both Rebbetzins with my mother. Red-faced and wrinkled as a market woman, the old one had a little white beard, angry eyes, and used snuff, which made me sneeze when she pinched my cheek and gave me a crumbling cookie. Wearing a dilapidated cloak, she held a decaying religious book, a woman's Pentateuch.

The younger Rebbetzin was quite the opposite. Ascending a red staircase, we were admitted by a maid in a white apron who led us into a parlor with rugs on gleaming floors, draperies on the windows, and gold tapestries on the walls. In glass bookcases there were leather- and silk-bound books, and objects of silver, ivory, and mother-of-pearl were displayed everywhere. The Rebbetzin's wig was made of silk; she was still young and pretty, brown-eyed and fair, dressed in satin and laces, and wearing precious gems on her long fingers. She received my mother with the graciousness of one aristocrat greeting another, and gave me cake and wine in a silver beaker. She smelled of good things, and the colorful fan she fluttered had an ivory handle.

Their initial polite remarks gave way to whispered secrets and sighs. The Rebbetzin brushed away a tear with a lace handkerchief. She kept plying me with sweets and offering playthings. When I became enthralled with a bead on her cloak, she took a scissors and lavishly removed a whole string of beads for me to play with.

Father too visited the young Rebbetzin, and her unhappy face would break into a smile when she saw him. "Welcome, Leoncin Rabbi," she would say, kissing me. They discussed Torah and Hasidism and even worldly things. She had visited all the foreign spas, knew all the rabbinical courts, and wrote Hebrew in a fancy script. Although both my parents liked her, my mother evinced some jealousy, and once, when my father said that she might soon be divorced, my mother remarked, "Now you can marry her."

Father's sympathy for the young Rebbetzin didn't

help him with the Rabbi, who began to persecute him.
He would send his beadle for Father, who when he
arrived would be prevented by another beadle from
entering. Once, in the middle of the night, Father was
summoned to be told that the Rabbi didn't like the
way he was directing the yeshivah and rewriting the
Rabbi's manuscript.

The old Rebbetzin, who had more influence with
her son than his wife did, also opposed my father.
When Father had taken the job, the Rabbi had
promised him a good living bu⁺ had not mentioned
terms. He used to dole out a few rubles now and then;
there was no salary, and we were in great need. In
Leoncin my sister and older brother had been pious,
but the Rabbi's behavior had changed their attitude.
My brother would imitate the Rabbi, shouting as he
prayed, rolling his eyes as he dealt out food to the
Hasidim. Father warned Mother that if she didn't
stop abusing the Rabbi before the children they
would proceed from doubting the Rabbi to doubting
God. But Mother herself was the daughter of an
opponent of Hasidism and had inherited some of her
father's causticness. Even though Father resented
the Rabbi, he felt that he had to defend him at home.

Despite our distress at home, the insecurity of
Father's position, things went well for me. The young
Rebbetzin was always giving me presents. I played in
the courtyard and in an orchard nearby, among
gooseberries, currants, and cherries. Standing there,
I would gaze at the horizon. Was that the end of the
world? What happened there and what was beyond
it? What were day and night? Why did birds fly and
worms crawl? I tormented my mother with questions.
My Father always answered, "That's how the Lord
made it."

"Where is He?"

"In heaven."

"Show me."

"Don't be silly. No one can see God."

He had created everything but could not be seen.

One had to thank Him before eating a cookie, wear ritual fringes and sidelocks for Him. I pointed to a cloud and asked, "Is that him?"

Father became furious: "Idiot, that's a cloud. It absorbs water and pours out rain..."

I found friends: Leah, Esther, and Benjamin. We ran about, chattering, digging holes, playing with shards; Benjamin and I were fathers, the girls mothers. In a pile of dirt in the Rabbi's courtyard, one could always find broken dishes, papers, boxes, and boards. For days I played with a dried palm branch I had found there. One Sabbath morning, in a fit of rage, I cut Leah's face, and the blood ran. Mother called me an Esau for this. But after the Sabbath meal I felt that I must see Leah, even though it seemed like a dangerous thing to do. I went to her courtyard, from which one could see meadows, a pasture, and cattle, and stood there waiting until her father appeared, shouting, "You bully, you outlaw!"

And he hit me. I sobbed mournfully, as bullies always do.

After a while I was enrolled in a heder run by Reb Fishl, an old man, whose pupil the Radzymin Rabbi had once been. He taught me my alep-beth, and I spent the rest of the time playing with the other boys on stacked logs in the courtyard. From here, too, one could see green fields and forests, and a road leading to the Vistula.

One day the Rabbi's court and many other houses caught fire. I remember it as if it were yesterday. Mother, emptying her slop pail, saw two heavy columns of smoke. "Woe is me," she cried.

Packing our possessions in sheets, we carried them into the garden. My sister, who was seventeen at the time, took my younger brother and myself by the hand, moaning in a singsong voice, "Where shall I take the children?" There were many places to go, the town wasn't surrounded by flames, but my sister enjoyed drama.

My brother Joshua fetched water from a well and

helped extinguish the fire. I felt deliriously happy. People were running about, carrying parcels; someone led horses, a trumpet was blowing; Jews carried sacred books and scrolls of the Law. It was like a holiday. I had heard people speak of the Messiah, of God, Gehenna, and Paradise, and it seemed to me that I was experiencing it all at one time. The sun shone and flames leaped at the sky. People ate outside. Gentiles and Jews mixed together. An elderly man approached me, asking, "Who am I?"

"I'm afraid of you," I said.

"Why?"

"Because you're a frog."

"Why a frog?"

"Just because."

I found myself in a strange house where people asked me all kind of questions and laughed at my answers. I tried to hide behind the stove, and crawled under the bed. I was half crazed with excitement.

Suddenly one day there was talk at home about going to Warsaw. I remember the day exactly.

Wearing a new pair of shoes, I went out to play with my friends, but Esther, Leah, and Benjamin were sitting under a torn parasol, which they had stuck in the ground, and would not admit me.

"Let him in," Leah finally said. "He has new shoes."

Later I sat next to my parents, my sister, and my younger brother in the little train that traveled from Radzymin to Warsaw. My older brother Joshua was riding in the wagon that carried our furniture.

Through the train windows I saw trees, buildings, and people moving backwards. A horse-drawn wagon had wheels that seemed to move in reverse. Cows were grazing and horses nuzzled each other in meadows. It all seemed mysterious. Things that I did not understand were happening. My brother Moishe fell asleep in Mother's lap; he was a beautiful child with blue eyes and silken blond hair.

Leaving the train, we climbed into a droshky and rode over the bridge from Praga to Warsaw proper. A broad river with the sky in it stretched beneath us. Ships floated by. Over the bridge, which had intricate ironwork columns, trolleys and omnibuses raced. We came upon tall buildings, crooked roofs, ironwork balconies. It looked as if there was always a fire raging in Warsaw, because people kept running and shouting. It seemed like an endless holiday. I saw a tremendous pillar, and on it a figure with a sword in his hand. It was the monument of King Zygmunt. Beneath him, four stone mermaids drank from large beakers. It was impossible to ask questions any longer, because I was confounded by everything. After passing the better neighborhoods, we arrived at Krochmalna Street. It was evening, and people thronged the streets. Stopping before one of the houses, the driver said, "This is it."

The Oath

WHENEVER he conducted a Din Torah, Father repeated the same speech: that he was opposed to the taking of oaths. Not only did he object to oaths, he objected even to pledges, words of honor, or hand-shaking as guarantees for the fulfillment of a promise. One can never fully trust one's own memory, Father argued; therefore, one must not swear even to what one believes to be the truth. It is written that when God proclaimed, "Thou shalt not take the name of the Lord...," heaven and earth trembled.

I would often picture this scene in my imagination:

Mount Sinai enveloped in flames; Moses standing there, holding the Tablets of the Law. Suddenly an awesome voice is heard—the voice of God. The earth begins to totter and quake, and with it all the mountains, the seas, the cities, and the oceans. The heavens tremble, together with the sun, the moon, the stars...

But the woman with the large black matron's wig, with the masculine face and the Turkish shawl draped around her shoulders, absolutely craved to take an oath. I no longer remember what that Din Torah was about. I remember only that it involved the one woman and several men. They accused her of something. Perhaps it was in connection with a legacy, or about moneys that had been concealed. It did involve, if I recall correctly, a rather large sum. The men spoke harsh words; they pointed their fingers accusingly at the woman. They called her a swindler, a thief, and all sorts of insulting epithets. But the woman did not take it without protest. She had an answer for every argument. For every insult, she hurled back an insult or a curse. Hair sprouted on her upper lip—a woman's mustache. On her chin there was a wen from which grew a small, pointy beard. Her voice was rough like a man's, full of vigor. Yet, although she was an aggressive woman, apparently she could not swallow the accusations. After each one she would shriek: "Rabbi, light the black candles and open the Ark! I want to swear by the Purity [the Torah scroll]!"

Father was shaken. "Hasten not to swear oaths!"

"Rabbi, it is permissible to swear to the truth. I am ready to swear before black candles and a purification bier!"

The woman must have come from the provinces, for the women of Warsaw were not familiar with such oaths and expressions. She clenched her hand into a fist and hit Father's table so that the tea glasses trembled. Every few minutes she ran to the door, as though she were ready to escape and leave the others

The Oath

sitting there. But soon she would return with new protestations of her innocence and new arguments against her accusers. Suddenly she blew her nose so violently and with such a trumpeting sound that one might have thought someone had blown a shophar. I stood behind my father's chair, frightened. I was afraid that this Tartar of a woman would go completely wild—break the table, the chairs, Father's lectern; tear the books; beat the men mercilessly. Mother, a frail person, opened the door every few minutes and looked in. An uncanny force emanated from this woman.

The argument grew more and more heated. One man, with a reddish nose and a small gray beard, found his courage anew and began to accuse the woman once more of being a liar, an embezzler, and such like names. Suddenly the woman jumped up. I thought she would pounce upon the little gray man and kill him on the spot. But she did something quite different. She flung open the door of the Holy Ark, impetuously took hold of the Torah scroll inside, and called out in a heart-rending voice: "I swear by the sacred scroll that I am telling the truth!"

Then she enumerated all the assertions to which she was swearing.

Father jumped up as though to tear the scroll out of her hands, but it was too late. Her adversaries stood motionless, petrified. The woman's voice became hoarse, was broken by sobs. She kissed the coverlet of the scroll and began to cry with such a broken, wailing voice that one was reminded of an excommunication, of a funeral.

For a long time there was a heavy silence in the study. Father stood, his face pale, and shook his head as if in negation. The men stared at each other, confused, perplexed. There was, obviously, no more to be said, nothing further to be argued. The woman left first. Then the men left. Father stood for a while in a corner and wiped the tears from his eyes. All these years he had avoided taking even a pledge—

and now a woman had sworn by the Torah, in our house, before our scroll. Father feared a harsh retribution. Mother paced the kitchen, deeply upset. Father walked over to the Ark, opened the door slowly, moved the scroll, straightened the scroll holders. It was almost as though he wanted to ask the scroll's forgiveness for what had happened.

Usually after a Din Torah, Father would talk over the arguments with the family, but this time all remained silent. It was almost as though the adults had made a pact not to mention the incident by so much as a word. For days an ominous silence hung over our house. Father lingered over his prayers in the Hasidic study house. He no longer chatted with me. Once, however, he said he had only one request to make of the Almighty: that he might no longer have to earn his living as a rabbi. I frequently heard him sigh his familiar sigh and whisper the plea: "Ah, woe is us, dear Father ..." And sometimes he would add: "How much longer? How much longer?"

I knew what he meant: how much longer will this bitter exile last? How much longer will the Evil One hold sway? ...

Slowly we began to forget the incident. Father again became approachable, began to tell stories and to repeat Hasidic lore. The Din Torah had taken place during the summer. Then came the Three Weeks of Mourning for the destruction of the temple, followed by the Nine Days, and the Ninth of Ab. Then on the Fifteenth of Ab, Father again began to study in the evenings. The month of Elul came, and in the Hasidic synagogue in our courtyard the shophar was sounded every day to frighten away Satan, the accuser. Everything was taking place just as in every other year. Father would rise early. By seven he had already performed the morning ablution and was preparing to study his daily portion of the Talmud. He made his preparations quietly, so as not to wake Mother and the children.

But one morning, at the break of day, we heard a

tempestuous knocking on the outer door. Father was alarmed. Mother sat up in bed. I jumped out of my bed. No one had ever knocked on our door so early in the morning. People do not come to ask ritual questions before the day has fully dawned, nor to settle disputes. Knocking with such force and anger for us could mean only the police. On the Sabbath a small congregation gathered in our house for prayers, and for this we had no license. Father always lived in the fear that he might, God forbid, be imprisoned. According to Russian law he was not even licensed to perform weddings or to grant divorces. True, by way of a certain "fixer" he regularly sent small sums to the local precinct chief and captain. But who knows what the Russian police would suddenly decide to do? Father was afraid to open the door. He did not speak a word of Russian or Polish. Mother put on her robe and went to the door. I crept into my pants and boots, and followed her. I was thrilled at the prospect of seeing a uniformed policeman right in our house. Mother began to speak Polish even before she opened the door.

"Kto tam?"

"Open the door!" a voice was heard in Yiddish.

I ran to tell Father the good news that the stranger was a Jew and not a policeman. He quickly praised the Lord of the Universe.

I rushed back into the kitchen, where, to my astonishment, I recognized the woman who had sworn the oath before the Torah scroll. A little later Mother brought her into the study. Father entered from the bedroom.

"Hmm, what is it?" he asked irritably.

"Rabbi, I am the woman who swore the oath..." she began.

"Hmm, nu? Nu?"

"Rabbi, what I have to tell you is confidential."

"Leave the room," Father said to the family.

Mother went out and took me with her. I had a tremendous desire to eavesdrop, but the woman had cast a gloomy look upon me, indicating that she was wise to my tricks. Her face had become gaunter, pointier, ashen. From the study I could hear a mumbling, sighs, a silence, then again a muttering. Something was happening in there on that cool Elul morning, but I could not discover what it was. Mother went back to bed. I also undressed again. But although I was tired and my eyelids were heavy, I could not fall asleep. I was waiting for Father to return, but an hour passed and they were still whispering secrets in the study. I was just beginning to doze off when the door opened and Father entered. His face was white.

"What happened?" asked my mother.

"Oh, woe, woe!" answered my father. "Woe is us—this is the end of the world, the end of all ends!"

"What is it?"

"It were better not to ask. It is time for the Messiah to come! Everything is in such a state... 'for the waters are come in unto my soul...'"

"Tell me what happened!"

"Alas, the woman swore falsely. She has been able to find no rest.... She confessed of her own free will.... Think of it: she swore falsely before a Torah scroll!"

Mother remained seated on her bed, silent. Father began to sway, but there was in his swaying something different from other days. His body rocked back and forth like a tree tossed by a storm wind. His earlocks quivered with every motion. Outside, the sun was rising and cast a reddish net over his face, and his beard glowed like a flame.

"What did you say to her, Father?"

Father looked angrily toward my bed. "What, you are not asleep? Go back to sleep!"

"Father, I heard everything!"

"What did you hear? The evil inclination is strong, very strong! For a little money, one sells one's soul! She took an oath, an oath before the Torah!... But she has repented. Despite everything, she is a true

Jewess. Repentance helps in every need!" Father exclaimed suddenly. "Even Nebuzradan, when he repented, was granted forgiveness. There is no sin that cannot be wiped out by penitence!"

"Will she have to fast?"

"First of all, she has to return the money, for it is written: 'That he shall restore which he took violently away...' Soon it will be Yom Kippur. If one repents with all one's heart, the Almighty—blessed be His name—forgives. He is a merciful and forgiving God!"

I heard later that nightmares had tortured the woman. At night she could not sleep. Her dead father and mother appeared to her in her dreams, dressed in shrouds. My father imposed a penitence upon her, to fast Mondays and Thursdays, to give money to charity, to abstain from meat for some time, except on the Sabbath and holidays. In addition she must have returned the money, for I recall seeing, one more time in our house, the men who had accused her.

Years later Father still told this story. If ever, during a Din Torah, anyone mentioned an oath, he would tell the story of this woman. To me it always seemed that the Torah scroll, too, remembered, and that whenever Father retold the incident, there, on the other side of the velvet curtain that covered the Ark, the scroll was listening...

The Purim Gift

OUR HOME was always half unfurnished. Father's
study was empty except for books. In the bedroom
there were two bedsteads, and that was all. Mother
kept no foods stocked in the pantry. She bought
exactly what she needed for one day, and no more,
often because there was no money to pay for more. In
our neighbors' homes I had seen carpets, pictures on
the walls, copper bowls, lamps, and figurines. But in
our house, a rabbi's house, such luxuries were
frowned upon. Pictures and statuary were out of the
question; my parents regarded them as idolatrous. I
remember that in the heder I had once bartered my
Pentateuch for another boy's, because the frontis-
piece of his was decorated with pictures of Moses
holding the Tablets and Aaron wearing the priestly
robe and breastplate—as well as two angels. Mother
saw it and frowned. She showed it to my father.
Father declared that it was forbidden to have such
pictures in a sacred book. He cited the Command-
ment: "Thou shalt not make unto thee any graven
image, or any likeness..."

Into this stronghold of Jewish puritanism, where
the body was looked upon as a mere appendage to the
soul, the feast of Purim introduced a taste of luxury.

All the neighbors sent *shalach-monos*—Purim
gifts. From early afternoon the messengers kept
coming. They brought wine, mead, oranges, cakes,

and cookies. One generous man sent a tin of sardines; another, smoked salmon; a third, sweet-and-sour fish. They brought apples carefully wrapped in tissue paper, dates, figs—anything you could think of. The table was heaped with delicacies. Then came the masked mummers, with helmets on their heads and cardboard shields and swords, all covered with gold or silver paper. For me it was a glorious day. But my parents were not pleased with this extravagance. Once a wealthy man sent us some English ale. Father looked at the bottle, which bore a colorful label, and sighed. The label showed a red-faced man with a blond mustache, wearing a hat with a feather. His intoxicated eyes were full of a pagan joy. Father said, in an undertone, "How much thought and energy they expend on these worldly vanities."

Later in the day Father would treat the Hasidim with the wine. We did not eat the Warsaw cakes, for we were never certain just how conscientious Warsaw Jews were about the dietary regulations. One could not know whether the pastries had been baked with chicken fat and must therefore not be eaten together with any milk foods.

The mummers, too, were disposed of quickly, for the wearing of masks and the singing of songs smacked of the theater, and the theater was *tref*—unclean. In our home, the "world" itself was *tref*. Many years were to pass before I began to understand how much sense there was in this attitude.

But Krochmalna Street did not wish to take note of such thoughts. For Krochmalna Street, Purim was a grand carnival. The street was filled with maskers and bearers of gifts. It smelled of cinnamon, saffron and chocolate, of freshly baked cakes and all sorts of sweets and spices whose names I did not know. The sweetshops sold cookies in the shapes of King Ahasuerus, Haman the Wicked, the chamberlain Harbona, Queen Vashti, and Vaizatha, the tenth son of Haman. It was good to bite off Haman's leg, or to swallow the head of Queen Esther. And the noise-

makers kept up a merry clamor, in defiance of all the
Hamans of all the ages.

Among betrothed couples, and boys and girls who
were "going with each other," the sending of Purim
gifts was obligatory. This was part of the customary
exchange of engagement presents. Because of one
such Purim gift, an argument arose that almost led to
a Din Torah in our house.

A young man sent his betrothed a silver box, but
when she opened it—in the presence of her sister and
her girl friends, who were impatiently awaiting the
arrival of the gift—she found it contained a dead
mouse! She uttered an unearthly shriek and fainted.
The other girls screeched and screamed. After the
bride-to-be had been revived with compresses of cold
water and vinegar, and her friends had collected
their wits, they began to plot revenge. The bride-to-be
knew the reason for her boyfriend's outrageous deed.
Several days before, they had quarreled. After much
talk and discussion, the young women decided to
repay the malicious youth in kind. Instead of a dead
mouse, however, they sent him a fancy cake—filled
with refuse. The baker was party to the conspiracy.
The girls of Krochmalna Street looked upon this
conflict as a war between the sexes, and Krochmalna
Street had something to laugh about that Purim. The
strange part of it was that the young man, although
he had committed a revolting act, had not expected
an equally odious retaliation, and was no less
stunned than his fiancée had been. People quickly
added imaginary incidents. The girls of Krochmalna
Street always believed in laughing. One often heard
bursts of uncontrolled laughter that might have come
from an insane asylum. This time they chortled and
chuckled from one end of the street to the other. The
young man, too, had been surrounded by friends at
the festive Purim meal. He, too, had been aided and
abetted in his prank.

Yes, that Purim was a merry one. But the next
morning everyone had sobered up and the warring

clans came to us for a Din Torah. The room was jammed full with people. The bride-to-be had brought her family and her girl friends, and the groom was accompanied by his relatives and cronies. All of them were shouting as they climbed up the stairs, and they kept on shouting for half an hour or more, and my father had yet to learn who was the accuser, who the defendant and what the tumult was about. But while they were yelling, screaming, hurling insults and curses, Father quietly pored over one of his books. He knew that sooner or later they would grow calm. Jews, after all, are not bandits. In the meanwhile, before more time had been wasted, he wanted to know what Rabbi Samuel Eliezer Edels meant by the comment in his book, *The Maharsha:* "And one might also say..."

I was present in the room and soon knew all about the affair. I listened attentively to every insult, every curse. There was quarreling and bickering, but every once in a while someone ventured a mild word or the suggestion that it was senseless to break off a match for such foolishness. Others, however, raked up the sins of the past. One minute their words were wild and coarse, but the next minute they had changed their tune and were full of friendship and courtesy. From early childhood on, I have noted that for most people there is only one small step between vulgarity and "refinement," between blows and kisses, between spitting at one's neighbor's face and showering him with kindness.

After they had finished shouting, and everyone had grown hoarse, someone at last related the entire story to my father. Father was shocked.

"Shame! How can anyone do such things? It is a violation of the law: 'Ye shall not make your souls abominable...'"

Father immediately cited a number of biblical verses and laws. First, it was impious; second, it was loathsome; third, such acts lead to anger, gossip, slander, discord, and what not. It was also danger-

ous, for the victim, overcome by nausea, might have
become seriously ill. And the defilement of edibles,
the food which God had created to still man's hunger
and over which benedictions were to be recited, was
in itself a sacrilege. Father recalled the sage who used
to say that he merited long life if only because he had
never left bread crumbs lying on the ground. He
reminded them that, in order for a cake to be baked,
someone had to till the soil and sow the grain, and
then rain and dew had to fall from heaven. It was no
small thing that out of a rotting seed in the earth a
stalk of wheat burst forth. All the wise men of the
world together could not create such a stalk. And
here, instead of thanking and praising the Almighty
for His bounty, men had taken this gift and used it to
provoke their neighbors—had defiled what He had
created.

Where formerly there had been an uproar, silence
now reigned. The women wiped their eyes with their
aprons. The men bowed their heads. The girls
bashfully lowered their eyelids. After Father's words
there was no more talk of a Din Torah. A sense of
shame and solemnity seemed to have overcome
everyone. Out of my father's mouth spoke the Torah,
and all understood that every word was just. I was
often to witness how my father, with his simple
words, routed pettiness, vain ambition, foolish
resentment, and conceit.

After Father's admonition the bride- and groom-to-
be made peace. The mothers, who just a few minutes
before had hurled insults at each other, now em-
braced. Talk of setting a date for the wedding was
heard. My father received no fee, for there had been
no actual Din Torah. His words of mild reproach had
damaged his own livelihood. But no matter, for the
weeks between Purim and Passover were a time of
relative prosperity for us. Together with the Purim
delicacies, the neighbors had sent a half ruble or a
ruble each. And soon the pre-Passover sale of
leavened bread would begin.

When the study had emptied, Father called me over and cautioned me to take heed of what may happen to those who do not study the Torah but concern themselves only with the vanities of this world.

The next Sabbath, after the *cholent*, the Sabbath stew, I went out on the balcony. The air was mild. The snow had long since melted. The pavements were dry. In the gutter flowed little streamlets whose ripples reflected the blue of the sky and the gold of the sun. The young couples of Krochmalna Street were starting out on their Sabbath walks. Suddenly the two who had sent each other the ugly gifts passed by. They walked arm in arm, chatting animatedly, smiling. A boy and his girl had quarreled—what of it?

I stood on the balcony in my satin gabardine and my velvet hat, and gazed about me. How vast was this world, and how rich in all kinds of people and strange happenings! And how high was the sky above the rooftops! And how deep the earth beneath the flagstones! And why did men and women love each other? And where was God, who was constantly spoken of in our house? I was amazed, delighted, entranced. I felt that I must solve this riddle, I alone, with my own understanding.

The Suicide

ALL SORTS of topics were discussed in our home. The
older children read the daily papers, including the
serialized novels. I heard them talking about veiled
ladies, horrible secrets, and fatal passions. Even
Father sometimes spoke of irresponsible men who
fall in love with immoral women and who, if they
cannot satisfy their lusts, take a revolver and shoot
themselves. But most of all I was fascinated by the
story of a man who had heard of a harlot in a far-
distant land who demanded four hundred gulden as
her hire. He came to her and she prepared a golden
couch for him. Then he sat down beside her naked,
and she too was naked. But suddenly the fringes of
his prayer shawl lifted themselves and smote against
his face. In the end both the man and the woman
repented. He married her and the couch of sin became
a sanctified marriage bed.

This story, which the men used to recite immediately after the Psalms, puzzled me greatly. Why
should a man desire a harlot? And why should they
sit beside each other naked? And why did he later
marry her? I knew that it was useless to ask these
questions. My parents always had the same answer
for me: Such things are not for children. When you
grow up, you will understand.... But time dragged
on, and I was still only a boy. The years crept by so
slowly.

In the meantime a tragedy struck Krochmalna

Street. Usually on the morning of the Sabbath the
street was quiet. The shops were all closed with iron
bars and padlocks. The young fellows who used to
loiter around the square had nothing to do, because
they could neither smoke nor gamble, and nothing
was for sale—no lemonade, no halvah, no licorice, no
chocolate-covered cookies or fritters. The thieves'
hangouts were also closed. At that time no one yet
dared to desecrate the Sabbath openly. Among the
thieves and their fences there were even some who
attended the synagogue. On the Sabbath before the
cholent, Krochmalna Street was peaceful.

But that day there was an uproar in the street. A
crowd collected. I went out on the balcony. Was it a
fire? If so, where were the firemen? Where were the
patrols? Where were the fire wagons with their
stomping horses, the water hoses, the ladders, all
that noisy machinery? And why were there no brass
helmets to be seen? No, it was neither a fire nor a
fistfight. The crowd was made up not only of
youngsters, but also of older men and women. I called
down to one of the boys to ask what had happened,
and he answered that a young man who worked at
shoemaking had poisoned himself.

"Why did he poison himself?"

"Because he was in love!"

The small group of worshippers who assembled in
our house talked of nothing but the shoemaker,
before, after, and even during the service. He had
been in love with a girl. He warned his parents that if
he could not marry her, he would do something
terrible: if they would not set up his wedding canopy,
they would have to dig his grave.... But the parents
remained stubborn—her parents as well as his. The
life of the young people was embittered. On Friday
night he had gone for a last walk with her in the
Saxony Gardens. In the morning, when his mother
went to wake him, she found him dead. Next to his
bed stood a vial of poison. On the table they found a
note which he had written on Friday night....

Krochmalna Street seethed. Women wept, wrung their hands, wiped their eyes with their aprons. Men talked, whispered. Boys scampered about everywhere, trying to listen.

As on every Sabbath, I went to the baker to fetch the *cholent*. The bakery seemed to have been swept by a holocaust. Girls were talking, crying, cursing the fanatics who barred the path of young lovers. One woman stood in the middle of the room, holding a large *cholent* pot, and moaned, "Woe is us, such a slender sapling! He was as handsome as a count! The street brightened when he stepped out of the door!"

Yes, love was powerful—not only in far-off days and distant lands where harlots prepared golden couches, but right here, on Krochmalna Street.

Whenever there was excitement in the street, I knew that sooner or later the parties involved would come to our house. We were still sitting at the dinner table. Mother was serving the *cholent*. Father was chanting the Sabbath table hymns. Suddenly the door opened and the mother of the suicide entered. She did not walk in. She collapsed into the room, her face red, her eyes swollen, a shawl over her head—a reminder of the weekday world, an embodiment of anguish. Father broke off his singing. Mother put down the *cholent*. Our Sabbath rest, too, had now been destroyed.

"Rabbi, holy Rabbi! ..."

Father uttered the usual phrases of consolation. One may not weep on the Sabbath. Alas, the poor boy had committed a grievous folly, but by now he had surely found divine forgiveness. God is merciful. ...But the woman would not be comforted. Her fingers clawed at her cheeks as though she were trying to tear herself apart.

"Such a devoted son! Such a good soul! ... Rabbi, what shall I do—where can I turn? He has brought dishonor upon me. My face is blackened before the world. It were better that he had died in childhood and not lived to this day! ... My husband is sick. In our house today is Tishah b'ab—the day of destruction!"

Father's eyes became damp, and he swayed from side to side. Mother ran into the kitchen to weep unseen. After much further talk, it became apparent that the woman had come to ask my father to use his influence so that her son might be given a decent burial—not behind the cemetery fence, in the ground reserved for suicides.

"He did not know what he was doing! The girl had driven him mad. May she become mad.... May she run through the streets like a wild woman.... May her body be tossed by chills and fevers.... May she be struck with epilepsy! Dear Father in heaven, let her taste of my woe, of the bitterness of my heart.... May she follow the coffins of her children to the grave. ... The whore, the slut, the hussy!"

Father covered his ears.

"Do not curse! Today is the Sabbath. Even during the week it is forbidden to curse!"

"If this thing could happen, there is no God!" screamed the woman in an inhuman voice.

"*No man is judged in his hour of grief*," murmured my father, perhaps to me, perhaps to no one. He explained the verse immediately: "When someone blasphemes in a time of great affliction, his words may not be weighed too closely."

Father promised the woman to try to see to it that the boy was buried decently within the cemetery proper. But what influence did he carry in the councils of the Warsaw community? Who would heed an insignificant Rabbi from Krochmalna Street? It is different with the Lord of the Universe. Anyone may come to plead before Him. To Him every man may pour out his heart....

Father hardly tasted the *cholent*, the noodle pudding, the meat, the candied carrots. He closed his eyes, swayed back and forth, back and forth. Here, in the house, amidst the holy books, the peace of the Sabbath reigned again, but the street outside was full

of shouting, turmoil, theft, robbery, war, injustice. A
year or two before we had come to live in Warsaw,
there had been a revolution. People still spoke about
"bloody Wednesday" and the bomb Baruch Schul-
man had thrown at a policeman. Jewish boys were
still in jails or working in prison camps deep inside
Russia. Father himself never stepped out on the
balcony, except on very hot summer evenings, when
the heat indoors was unbearable. The balcony was
already a part of the street, of the crowd, of the
Gentile world and its savagery. He even frowned at
my going out on the balcony. He would always cite
the verse: "The king's daughter is all glorious
within...." For the children of a king, he would say, it
is more seemly to remain within the palace—and all
Jews are the children of a great King....

Usually, on the Sabbath after the meal, Father
would take one of his books and lie down. But this
time he remained in the study with me.

At first he spoke words of ethical advice and moral
instruction, but after a while he began to discuss the
Cabala.

"It is not a simple matter, not simple at all," he
said. "The world is filled with mysteries, everything
happens according to its decree, everything contains
the secret of secrets...."

"Father, do you know the Cabala?"

"You speak like a child. Can a man empty the
ocean? Every word, every letter of the Torah contains
thousands upon thousands of mysteries. Even the
zaddikim, the righteous sages, did not understand a
thousandth part of it. Even Moses, our great teacher,
did not know it all.... Everyone merits understanding according to his soul, as befits his spiritual
elevation. As long as the soul is imprisoned within
the body, it cannot fully grasp the worlds above.
...But everything is just, everything is just. Man
was created in the image of God. His soul emanates
from the Throne of Glory. A second after its mortal

release, the soul of a water carrier may understand more than the greatest living zaddik...."

"Father, what is love?"

"What is love? One must love the Almighty. 'And thou shalt love the Lord thy God with all thy heart and with all thy soul....' See, I love you because you are my child. But who created you? The Creator of the Universe. If I love you, obviously I must love the Creator, for without Him neither you nor I would exist. The meaning of this is that all love belongs to the Creator, and to Him only. A wise man understands this and traces all love back to its source."

"Father, is that Cabala?"

"What does it matter whether it is or not? It is the truth."

"Father, what will happen to the shoemaker in the next world?"

Father waved the question aside with his hand.

"He made a terrible mistake. But the Lord of the Universe is a merciful and compassionate God. The soul will be purified and will return to its source. For we are all His children, and how can a father harm his child? If the child soils itself, the father washes and cleanses it. The child cries because it has no understanding, but the father means everything for the best. He knows that uncleanness can cause vermin and disease..."

Father spoke to me for a long time. He told me that there is a particle of the divine in everything. Even the mud in the gutter contains divine sparks, for without them nothing could continue to exist. Finally he began to yawn and blink his eyes. He gave me the *Rod of Chastisement* and said, "Read the translation. It is a holy book."

Father went to the bedroom. No sooner had he lain down than I ran down into the courtyard. Boys were running about. Girls were whispering secrets, playing with nuts, singing, dancing. A crazy man was screaming and a street urchin hurled a stone at him.

Suddenly a window opened and a woman poured a pail of water over the head of the young rowdies who would not let her sleep.

A hunchbacked boy came out of a cellar and asked me, "Do you want to play the button game?"

"No, you're not allowed to touch them on the Sabbath."

"Well, will you play hurl-the-stick?"

"It's forbidden on the Sabbath."

"Pious dolt!" was his answer.

"Hunchbacked thief, I'd rather have sweets!" shouted a boy behind his back.

"Hey you, will you play cops-and-robbers?" one of the other boys called across to me.

We chose sides and I became a "robber." I ran to hide in a cellar, but there fear overcame me. I remembered the shoemaker who had poisoned himself, and my father's words about the secrets of the Torah: we are all the children of God. In each one of us dwells a soul that came from the Throne of Glory. There are Divine sparks even in the mud.... I remained standing on the steps leading down into the cellar, and closed my eyes. I actually *felt* that there was a holy soul inside me, a particle of the Godhead. In the darkness I beheld a fiery flower, glittering like gold, luminous as the sun. It opened up like a chalice and bright colors leaped forth: yellow, green, blue, purple—colors and forms such as one sees only in a dream.

Someone tugged at my hand. I shuddered. It was a "cop" who had caught me, the "robber." Suddenly the game bored me, and I walked off alone towards Gnoyna Street....

To the Land of Israel

SOME PEOPLE seem to have their destinies written on
their faces. Such a man was Moshe Blecher of No. 10
Krochmalna Street. He was a simple tinsmith, and a
poor man, but there was something about him which
intrigued me. First of all he looked like a Jew from the
Holy Land, like a Yemenite or someone from the land
of old King Ahasuerus. His face was dark, sun-
burned, wrinkled, and had a yellowish hue as though
a tropical sun had shone on it since days of old.
Second, there was a dreaminess about his eyes which
one never saw in these parts. It seemed as though his
eyes were able to see secret things of the past and
possibly the future. Moshe Blecher was something of
a biblical scholar and in his discussions with my
father he would dwell on one subject, the advent of
the Messiah. He was familiar with all the verses and
all the commentaries dealing with the Messiah. He
had a special affinity for the obscure passages of
Daniel. He was always absorbed in these prophesies
and whenever there was reference made to them his
dreamy eyes would take on an even more faraway
look.

Often I would spy Moshe Blecher on a roof. The
roofs in Warsaw are crooked and perilous. But Moshe
Blecher walked across them with the sureness of a
somnambulist. I was overcome with fear each time I
would watch him at work high above the gutter

paved with cobblestones. Standing at such a height,
Moshe Blecher appeared to be a man of extraordinary strength, accustomed to miracles, a man not
subject to the ordinary laws. He would stop suddenly,
lift his head skyward as though he expected a
momentary visitation from an angel or seraph
announcing the coming of salvation.

Sometimes he would pose very difficult questions
to my father. He found contradictions in the Talmud.
He wanted to know how long it would take between
the martyrdom of the first Messiah, Son of Joseph,
and the appearance of the second Messiah, Son of
David. He talked about the ram's horn announcing
the Messiah, about the ass on whose back the
Messiah would ride, and about the legend of his
pausing at the gates of Rome unwinding and
rewinding the bandages of his wounds. Moshe
Blecher was very indignant about the prediction of
the sage Hillel that the Messiah would not liberate
the Jews because he was already "consumed" during
the time of King Hezekiah. How could a saintly man
say such a thing? And what is the meaning of the
thought expressed in the Mishnah that all that
separates the present from the Messianic Age is the
acquisition of a Jewish kingdom? Can that be all?
How long, for example, will it be from the coming of
the Messiah until the resurrection of the dead? And
when will the fiery temple be brought down from
above? When? When?

Moshe Blecher lived in a cellar apartment, but it
was neat and clean. A kerosene lamp was always lit.
The beds were made. There were no rags lying around
as in other cellar apartments. Next to the wall there
was a cabinet lined with books. I used to visit him
because he read Yiddish newspapers and I would
borrow them from him. He would sit at his table, his
eyeglasses resting on his nose, thumbing through his
newspapers in search only of news of Palestine and
of the countries where the War of Armageddon will
take place, where God would hurl down stones from

heaven. He was interested in the places where Paradise was thought to be, and the river Sambation, where the Ten Tribes are supposed to have been lost. Moshe Blecher knew all about the lost tribes, and he more than once let it slip that if he could see to it that his family was taken care of, he would set out to find the vanished brethren.

And then suddenly the news spread that Moshe Blecher was going to the land of Israel with his entire family. I do not recall all the members of his family. I do remember that he had a grown boy, or perhaps two. Moshe Blecher's decision to go to Palestine was not capricious, but the result of a deep-seated urge. Everybody wondered why he had waited so long.

The details are blurred and I recall only isolated incidents because I was only a child at the time. People kept going to see the tinsmith in his cellar apartment. He was given written messages to be placed near the Wailing Wall, at Rachel's grave, or perhaps at the Cave of Machpelah. Elderly people asked him to send them bags containing holy soil. Moshe Blecher walked around full of exhilaration, with a look of longing and expectation in his eyes, and a blissfulness that is not of this world. The Holy Land seemed to be engraved on his face, which somehow resembled a map.

One early evening a wagon rode up to our house. It was so huge that it looked more like an omnibus. I cannot to this day figure out why Moshe Blecher hired such a wagon. Perhaps he took his furniture with him? Krochmalna Street was suddenly crowded with Jews. They came to say farewell. They kissed him, wept, and expressed the wish that the Messiah would come and bring an end to the Diaspora. Moshe Blecher's voyage seemed to suggest the coming of the Redeemer, as though he were his forerunner or minion. If Moshe Blecher is leaving for Palestine with his entire family, this must be a sign that the End of Days is close.

Months passed. Then I heard the sad tidings. My

father received a letter which said that Moshe Blecher could not find work in the Holy Land. He was suffering privation and want. For months he and his family subsisted only on rice and water. Our household was greatly distressed by this news because everyone loved Moshe Blecher and hoped that he would settle in the Holy Land and send for all the Jews of Krochmalna Street. Moshe Blecher seemed somehow to be related to everyone.

It was the day before Yom Kippur. Services were held in our house and at the afternoon prayers plates were put out into which coins were thrown to support various charitable causes, the care of the sick, poor brides, and yeshivahs. My father put out a plate on which he placed a piece of paper inscribed thus: "For Reb Moshe Blecher." Underneath the inscribed paper lay the letter which Moshe Blecher had written to my father.

The men and women who came to services at our house were not accustomed to throwing money around. Four groschen, six groschen, or ten groschen were considered adequate contributions. But this particular plate had a magical quality about it. Into it went forty-groschen pieces, half rubles, and rubles. Somebody put in a three-ruble note. The news that Moshe Blecher and his family were living on rice and water saddened everybody. It was as though this was an omen that salvation was a long way off.

After Yom Kippur my father sent the money to Moshe Blecher. For that amount he could buy a considerable supply of rice and water. (In those days in the Holy Land water had to be purchased.) But it appeared that he just could not make his way; or perhaps the romantic Moshe Blecher could not adjust to the thought that he was finally in the Land of the Holy. Perhaps the dream was sweeter to him than the reality. Perhaps he could not make peace with the fact that the Turks ruled in God's land. Or maybe he took objection to the nonbelieving colonists who shaved their beards and did not live by the Torah.

The word spread that Moshe Blecher was returning home.

And return he did. He looked even more sun-burned, swarthier, and had more gray hairs in his beard. He had a quaint gleam in his eyes. His was the look you might expect to see on the face of someone who has died, gone through purgatory, and then to Paradise, but for some reason was ordered back to earth.

He came to visit us. My father questioned him for hours. He answered all of the questions put to him. He had traveled everywhere. Yet we could not find out exactly what drove him home. It was as though he were hiding something.

I saw Moshe Blecher on the roofs again. He stopped more and more frequently. He was looking somewhere, searching for something in the heights. He came to my father again to talk about verses in the Bible. He had brought back a sack of chalk-white sand from Palestine and many pebbles, fragments taken from old ruins and from headstones on holy graves. Every time someone died, Moshe Blecher contributed some earth from the Holy Land for the grave. The mourners wanted to pay him, but he did not want to traffic in sacred objects.

It is possible that I have erred somewhat in my story. But if memory serves, it happened this way. Moshe Blecher's children married; he was left with his wife. He needed to work less, and he stayed home more often, pouring over sacred tomes. It seems that before he went to Palestine Moshe Blecher opposed the Zionists, who attempted to translate his dreams into a practical reality. Moshe Blecher wanted the Messiah and only the Messiah. But with the passage of time he grew more sympathetic to the Zionist ideal. After all, if the Messiah does not want to come, must Jews wait indefinitely? Perhaps God wants the Jews to force the coming of the Messiah? Perhaps Jews must settle in the Holy Land first and then the Messiah will bring salvation. I remember that he began to argue with my father. My father looked upon Zionists as nonbelievers, villains, blasphemers who would bring contamination to the Holy Land. But Moshe Blecher would answer: "Perhaps it is destined to be so. Perhaps they are the vanguard of the Messiah, Son of Joseph? Perhaps they will repent and become pious Jews. Who can tell what the heavens have ordained?"

"A man must be a Jew before he can go to the Holy Land," my father said.

"And what are they? Gentiles? They are making sacrifices for Jews. They drain swamps and contract malaria. They are true martyrs. Is this to be minimized?"

"'Except the Lord build the House, they labor in vain that build it.'"

"The first temple was also built by men, not angels. King Hiram sent slaves and cedar trees to King Solomon."

The arguments grew more heated. My father began to suspect that Moshe Blecher had been taken in by the Zionists. To be sure, he was still a pious Jew, but he had become very confused. He even approved of Dr. Herzl. After a while the arguments came to an end. Moshe Blecher seemed to wander about in a state of bewilderment. He would carry on discussions not only with adults but with the children. Boys in the study house would question him: "Is it true that the stars in the Holy Land are as large as plums?"

"True, children, true."

"Is it true that Lot's wife is still standing near the Dead Sea with oxen licking the salt on her body?"

"Somewhere I heard this."

"Can you hear Rachel weeping for her children?"

"I did not hear it, but a saintly man might."

"Reb Moshe, do they eat bread in the Holy Land?"

"If they have it, they eat it."

It began to appear that Moshe Blecher was growing senile. However his behavior must have been the result of his deep nostalgia, because one day

Moshe Blecher returned to the Holy Land.

This time, no large wagon came for him. There was no kissing in the street and no messages sent with him. Moshe Blecher and his wife just disappeared. After a little while he was missed and inquiries were made about him. It was learned that he no longer could suppress his yearning for the land of his ancestors, the land of the fig trees and dates and almonds, where the goats eat St. John's bread and modern men build colonies, plant eucalyptus trees, and speak the holy tongue on weekdays.

Years passed and no word was received of Moshe Blecher. I thought about him for a long time. Is he living on rice and water again? Can he earn his bread? Has he perhaps gone in search of the Red Jews on the other side of the river Sambation? You could expect anything from a man like Moshe Blecher.

The Dispensation

FROM TIME TO TIME someone would come to my father to obtain his signature for a "dispensation by a hundred Rabbis." Long ago Rabbi Gershom promulgated the prohibition against polygamy, but there are exceptions. What was a man to do if his wife was insane? An insane woman cannot be given a divorce. And what should a man do if his wife ran off to America and was never heard from again? Things like that did happen. The husband in that case would

obtain a certificate from a Rabbi who was familiar
with the circumstances, and a hundred other Rabbis
had to sign the dispensation to permit him to marry a
second wife.

Men of means did not make the rounds themselves
but sent agents, and there were some who made their
living in that way—traveling from town to town to
obtain rabbinical signatures for deserted husbands.

This time, however, the husband himself came. He
was a youngish man with a blond beard, metal-
rimmed spectacles, a small hat, and a tie knotted
under his collar. His gabardine was shortened, not
reaching quite to his ankles, and had a slit in the
back. He looked pious but prosperous, and wore
polished low boots. He took out a sheet of paper on
which there already were about fifty or sixty rabbinic
signatures and seals in various shapes—circular,
square, triangular, stamped in blue ink, black ink,
red ink, green ink. And how different the signatures
were! Some Rabbis had signed their names in small,
neat letters, others took up an entire row with their
unwieldy script; some had signed only their own
names, others had added those of their fathers and
even their grandfathers. The signature of one Rabbi
was an illegible scribble-scrabble—such wild, unruly
letters, each one dragging behind it hooks and tails,
blots and smudges. The letters of another were round,
pot-bellied, exuding an air of indescribable self-
complacency. Father studied the signatures for a
long time. He knew some of the Rabbis personally;
others, he had heard of. Then he began to read the
document itself. From time to time he would shake
his head. "Really? Heaven have mercy—she is mad!
And a shrew besides ... a pity! And she won't accept a
divorce? She made your life miserable? Certainly, I'll
give you my signature."

Father signed his name. The young man took a
scrap of blotting paper out of his pocket and carefully
dried the fresh ink.

"Rabbi, you cannot imagine what I suffered because of this accursed woman!" he said.

"It is all described in the paper."

"Rabbi, that's not even a thousandth part of it!"

"Nu, I can imagine."

"Have you ever heard of a woman who—on the night of the Seder—breaks all the dishes and pours the dumpling soup over the bedding?"

"Indeed? She is obviously insane, poor soul," answered my father.

"She is mad," said the young man, after a moment of thought. "But she is even more malicious than mad. I always knew that there were evil people, but such a viper is really beyong the limits of the natural! It started when we were first betrothed. Her father invited me, as is the custom, and we had the opportunity to look each other over. These are, after all, modern times. Young people nowadays want to become acquainted, to talk about things. Her mother insisted on it. It did not really befit my family, for my father is a scholar—an intimate disciple of the Alexander Rabbi. But we gave in to them. She took me aside into her room and began to talk to me—but in such a voice! She made fun of me. I simply did not know how to answer her. And her parents were waiting outside. Anyway, I thought nothing would come of it. Had I told my dear father about this, he would have torn up the engagement contract straight-away. But I thought to myself: it doesn't really matter. She's just been affected by some of these newfangled ideas. What did I know? The matchmaker smoothed over everything, poured oil on thick: it's nothing, don't worry... They should have cut her hair before the wedding, but she wouldn't let them. My dear mother is the daughter of a Rabbi—she was ashamed to show her face! My mother-in-law made up excuses, said they would cut her hair the morning after the wedding. And while we were eating the golden chicken broth at the wedding meal, she just sat there and laughed at everything. Later on she ..."

He looked at me. "Let him go out!"

"Leave the room," ordered my father.

I walked slowly, with small steps. I went out but left the door slightly ajar. My ears pricked, I remained standing there. But the young man apparently suspected that I was eavesdropping. He talked in an undertone, a mumble. I heard my father exclaim. "The mercy of heaven upon us—how dreadful!"

"Wait, there is more ..."

Again the young man began to whisper. All I could hear was a sort of plaintive humming. Father coughed and blew his nose.

"Nu, nu," he interrupted, "that's enough, enough already."

"It is true, every word."

"Even so, one may not defile the ears ..."

"But you have heard nothing as yet ..."

I opened the door. "Father, may I come in now?"

"Yes, but don't listen. This is not for a child. Take a book and study."

I took a book, and heard the young man say: "I wanted to run away, but I was ashamed. You get married, you incur expenses—my dear father had gone into debt for my sake—and then, it's all over. What can I tell you? I suffered. Who knows?—I thought to myself—perhaps it is only a temporary madness that will pass. But soon she really started on me—showed her true colors, as the saying goes. She actually never slept. All night long she sat up in bed and blasphemed, poured out fire and brimstone. She insulted her own parents. If I were to tell you only a thousandth part of it, you would be shocked and stunned. She nursed grievances against the whole world. Everybody mistreated her. She invented things that never happened—no shred of truth to them—and wept bitter tears. She drenched the bed with her tears. But most of all she complained about me. And why should she have complained about me—here we were just married and I was as innocent as a lamb.... But there was a demon in her. Later she herself confessed to me that she had been in love with another man."

"In love?"

"Yes. He was a shoemaker and was taken into the army. I heard afterwards that he didn't want her. Anyway, how could she even consider an ordinary shoemaker? Her father is a respected man in the community, even if he is a misanthrope and has a vicious temper. The entire family has vicious tempers. When angry, they can tear you limb from limb. They say that my father-in-law once fell into a rage because one Sabbath he was called up to lift the Torah before the congregation, when he had been expecting one of the greater honors. He took the Torah scroll and hurled it to the ground, and then he had to fast for forty days as a penance. I don't believe the story is really true, but with people like that anything is possible. My mother-in-law used to beat her daughters—my wife's sisters—with a wooden club. On Friday nights, if my father-in-law didn't like the fish, he would leave the table in the middle of the meal and go to bed. Don't ask—I got myself into a real mess!"

"At least you'll be rid of it now."

"Be rid of it, you say? It's a miracle I'm not sick. First she wanted me to shave off my beard, and then she wanted to go to America. The shoemaker had gone there, and she probably missed him, I told her, 'Be reasonable—everything must be done with reason.' But can you reason with a madwoman? My dear mother heard of what was happening, and started to demand that I get a divorce, but *she* didn't like that either. 'Why—' she said—'should I divorce you? So you can marry someone else? You stay right where you are. For my part, you can lick the dust.' Those were her very words. It's to be expected—her people come from somewhere in Lithuania, or the devil knows where. My mother-in-law actually comes

from Great Poland, but on the father's side they're
from Meseritz. I said to her, 'Why do you torture me?'
After a sleepless night, I simply wouldn't know what
was going on around me the next day. When I wanted
to perform the morning ablution, I'd pour out the
water in the bowl by mistake. And she cared only
about her floors—they had to sparkle like crystal. It
was dangerous to walk on them, they were so
polished. What sort of town was it, anyway?
Everybody there had a temper. Everyone talked
about everyone else—they tore each other apart. The
young fellows picked a quarrel with me—I have no
idea why or what for. They wanted me to quit the
Alexander Rabbi and go over to the Porissover. But I
am not a Porissover disciple. Anyway, they were just
looking for trouble. At first my father-in-law took my
part, but soon he went over to them too. I was a
stranger in the town, and all of a sudden there was a
burning dispute all around me. I wanted to go home,
but they warned the coachman not to take me. Every
time I came to him he had another excuse—too many
passengers, this, that—stuff and nonsense. My
father-in-law—may he pardon the liberty—is a bully,
in league with all the town's roughnecks. People are
afraid of him because he is a friend of the customs
officials, too. And his wife is a bitter woman—pure
gall. They almost refused to feed me. I even wanted to
walk home, but they hid my clothes.... Perhaps you
don't believe me?"

"Why shouldn't I believe you? There are wicked
people in this world."

"Wicked, you say? Satan himself! And then they
spoke such a peculiar language among themselves
that I wanted to laugh and cry at the same time. One
minute they were about to come to blows—a danger to
life and limb! The next minute they start to laugh and
it's all a grand joke. Then there's another outburst of
fireworks—just like in the theater! In the meantime
the government Rabbi had left the town, and my
father-in-law wanted me to take his place. He's a big

man in the community, and on friendly terms with all the officials. But one has to pass an examination. So they tell me, 'Study Russian!' I didn't really like the idea, but—there are these little pamphlets, Neimanovitch's textbooks. Well—to make a long story short— I saw soon enough that this was not for me, and I told them so. Then all hell broke loose. She began to beat me. Just like that—she beat me mercilessly. She threw pots, dishes—anything she could lay her hands on. She even ripped my prayer shawl. I wanted to run away—but just as she can torment one, she can all of a sudden become soft and gentle. 'Why make a fool of yourself? Can't you take a joke?' And the whole family became soft as melted butter, as the saying goes. Fine, I'm one of them now. My father-in-law even wanted to take me into his business. Hardly a week passed—and the clouds are back. She beats me, she insults me—and her little sisters call me names and attack me like wild animals. I ask her, 'What did I do now?' But one might as well talk to a wolf! To make a long story short—my dear father came and said, 'This dough will never rise!' We summoned them to appear before the Rabbi, but they didn't come. I was told that they had hired hooligans to attack me. They could, God forbid, even kill me...

"How can I tell you everything. I tormented myself this way for four years, and every day was like the tortures of the damned in hell. How I lived through it, I myself don't understand. The heart of the strongest might have burst. Fifty times she agreed to a divorce—but when it came to carrying it out, it all came to nought. The Rabbi himself is afraid of them. They wouldn't hesitate to take the bread out of a man's mouth. And when they gang up on someone, his life becomes bitter as gall. They are not simply scoundrels, but crazy scoundrels..."

My father mopped his brow with his kerchief.

"Thank God that you were able to escape from their snares."

"Now people are trying to make peace between us."

"Peace... after all that? What is the sense of that?"

"There is, after all, some sense to it..."

"But you have been traveling all this time—how do they know where you are?"

"I went home for the holidays."

"Is your home in the same town?"

"It's nearby..."

"But what is the use? 'There is no peace, saith the Lord, unto the wicked....' One cannot make peace with scoundrels."

"Of course not. But people are always meddling. They send messengers. Now she claims it was all her mother's fault..."

My father did not answer. The young man also remained silent. He took off his spectacles and polished them with a soiled handkerchief. Then he wrinkled his forehead and asked, "If... somehow... we should come to an agreement after all... do we need to go through the marriage ceremony again...?"

"What...? What for? The dispensation does not annul your marriage."

"But in the meantime, I want to collect all the necessary signatures..."

And again the young man began to mumble to himself—a mumbling that was half singing and half weeping.

The Secret

THE KITCHEN DOOR opened and a woman wearing a kerchief over her head (a rare sight in Warsaw), with a yellowish face, a wide nose, heavy lips, and yellow eyes entered. There was something ordinary, lower-class about her entire appearance. Her bosom thrust forward like a balcony. A large apron covered her chest and stomach. Her shoes were shapeless. She looked like a servant or a poor stallkeeper in a market. Women of this class usually asked at once whether the Rabbi was in, and Mother would send them into the next room. But this woman remained standing near the door, looking at my mother with questioning, pleading eyes. Mother slowly went toward her.

"Do you want to ask a ritual question?"

"Dearest Rebbetzin, I myself don't know what I want. Purest soul, I must bare my heart to someone. I cannot stifle it all inside me any more. May you be preserved from all evil—I am choking. Horo, right here...."

The woman pointed to her throat. At the same time she began to sob. The weeping seemed to burst forth from her and within a minute her face had become red, wet, washed with tears. I was sitting on a footstool in the corner, reading a storybook. I sensed immediately that I was about to hear an unusual tale. My mother had apparently forgotten my presence, and the other woman had not noticed me. She began to speak.

"Dearest being, I have sinned. My heart is crushed...."

Again she began to sob and blow her nose into her apron. Her eyes became a mixture of weeping and laughing, as always when one weeps with great intensity. Mother asked her to be seated on the trunk that also served as a bench.

"If one sincerely repents one's sin, God accepts the penitence." Mother spoke in the manner of a scholar. She knew the text of the Bible even better than my father. She was also familiar with difficult books such as *The Duties of the Heart* and *The Path of the Righteous*—not in translation, but in the original Hebrew. She knew a veritable ocean of law and could cite hundreds of rabbinic sayings and homiletic parables. Her words carried weight.

"How can I do penitence while the heathen yet lives?"

The woman spoke and sobbed. "Who knows whether he is not himself a Jew-baiter? Who knows whether he does not beat Jews? What help can my remorse be to me? Every time I see a dogcatcher, a drunkard—I fear it may be he. Oh, Rebbetzin, my affliction is great! At night I cannot sleep. The older I get, the worse it becomes. I toss upon my bed and cannot close my eyes. How much better if I had never been born...."

Mother remained silent, and I could tell by her face that she understood. But I could not fathom what was going on. Soon I learned what it was about.

Years ago this woman had abandoned an illegitimate child. Some man had seduced her. She had left the infant in a basket near a church, and when she returned a few hours later he was gone. He had probably been taken to a foundling home—or the black demons knew what had become of him. She was a poor girl, an orphan. She was afraid to make inquiries; she forced herself to forget. Years later she had married and borne other children. Now she was a grandmother. She had worked hard all her life and

had almost succeeded in forgetting her misfortune.
But as she grew older, it tormented her more and
more. She was the mother of a Gentile! Who could
know? Perhaps he was the policeman on the street?
Perhaps he was wicked, another Haman? Perhaps he
had fathered a host of heathen sons and daughters?
Woe to her and woe to her old age! How could a sin like
hers be forgiven? How long did she still have to live
on this earth? How would she defend herself in the
other world? Cursed be the day when she had let
herself be persuaded to do this evil! Her life was an
endless torture. She was ashamed to enter a synagogue. She was impure, defiled. How could such a
one as she dare to utter a holy prayer? She should be
spat upon. Would that God send the Angel of Death to
release her....

Again the woman broke into lamentation and
wailing. My mother was pale; her lips were clenched.
The fact that she did not immediately attempt to
comfort the woman was an indication to me of how
grievous was the sin she had committed.

At last Mother spoke. "What can you do? Only to
pray to the Almighty." And after a while she added,
"Our father, Abraham, also brought forth Gentile
nations."

"Rebbetzin, do you think I should speak to the
Rabbi?"

"How can he help you? Give money to charity. If
you are strong enough, fast. But you cannot do more
than your strength permits."

"Rebbetzin, people say that such children become
firemen and are never permitted to marry, so that
they will always be ready to rush to a fire when they
are called."

"What? In that case, at least he will not be the
father of unbelievers."

"Rebbetzin, he should be about forty years old
now. Someone told me that if I were to light forty
candles and recite a secret incantation, he would
die."

My mother shuddered.

"Who told you that? Life and death are in God's hands. And after all, it is not *his* fault. Wherein is he guilty? There is a Talmudic expression for such as he—*a child taken captive*. He is not to be blamed. Were not many Jewish children baptized by force in the days of Chmielnicki? The Almighty keeps the reckoning. Whoever told you about the candles does not know whereof he speaks. One is not permitted to pray for the death of any human being—unless one knows as a certainty that he is wicked and commits evil...."

"How can I know that? I—may God pity me— know only that my life is dark and bitter. I walk through the streets and stare at the Gentiles. If my heart does not break, it must be stronger than iron. I walk from one street to the next, and every Gentile who passes by seems to be my son. I want to run to him, to question him, but I am afraid. People will think I have gone mad. How it is that I do not indeed go mad, only God knows. Rebbetzin, if someone were to lick at my heart, he would be poisoned!"

"You have probably already atoned for your sin."

"What shall I do? Give me counsel!"

"How did it happen? Where is the father?"

The woman began to tell a tale whose exact details I no longer remember. She had been a servant in the house of a well-to-do family. She met a workingman who promised to marry her. He had seduced her with his false tongue, his glib speeches. When he learned that she was pregnant, he disappeared. Does a man worry about a thing like that? Years later she had married a widower. The woman began to speak softly, ever more softly, almost to whisper. Mother nodded her head. After a while it was decided that they would ask Father's advice, but Mother was to go in first and explain the matter to him. The woman remained in the kitchen. Mother entered Father's study. It was not long before my father was sighing. Krochmalna Street would give him no peace: it constantly broke in upon him with its tumult, its unruliness and coarseness.

Then the woman, too, went into the study. Father had taken a stack of books from the bookcase. He searched, scanned, turned pages, tucked at his beard. In his holy books he had often read about murderers, robbers, thieves, depraved men, seducers—but there, in the books, they were part of the Law. Expressed in the holy tongue, written in the sacred script, even these retained the flavor of Torah. But in ordinary, everyday Yiddish, such things sounded quite different. A woman of Krochmalna Street had abandoned an infant. He had been baptized, become a Gentile. The holy books described the atonement for such a sin, but would the woman be prepared to undertake such a penance? And would it not be beyond the limits of her strength? The generation of today was weak. Father was afraid he might go too far, might cause the woman to become ill. Then he would have committed a sin greater than hers. . . .

I stood in a corner of the study and heard Father question the woman. Was her heart in good condition? Did she suffer from any illness? Did she not, perhaps, have a persistent cough? Finally Father prescribed for her this penance: to abstain from meat on weekdays, to fast on Mondays and Thursdays—if her health permitted; to recite the Psalms, to give money to charity. The woman began again and again to weep and lament, and Father comforted her. Of course one should avoid sin, but there are always ways of rectifying an error. Man must do what lies in his power and for the rest he must rely upon the Creator, for "from Him proceedeth not evil." Even that which appears evil will eventually become good. In reality, there is no evil. Father likened the world to a fruit and its outer husk. The husk cannot be eaten. A foolish child might think the husk is useless, but it was made to protect the fruit. Without it the fruit would rot or be eaten by worms. So, too, the Gentile nations are needed. It is even written that God offered

the Torah first to Esau and Ishmael, and only when
they refused it did He offer it to the Jews. At the end of
days they, too, will recognize the truth, and the
righteous of the Gentile nations will enter Paradise....

Father's words melted the woman's heart like wax,
as the saying goes. Her weeping became even more
intense, yet now there was in it something of joy. She
looked upon Father with shining eyes. In essence he
had told her exactly what my mother had already
said, but somehow his words seemed warmer, more
intimate. The woman left, pronouncing countless
blessings upon all of us—my father, my mother, even
me. She regretted only that all these years she had
stifled her woe within herself. She should have
conquered her shame long ago and come to the
zaddik, to pour out the bitterness of her heart before
him. He had lifted a heavy burden from her breast....

When the woman left, Father began to pace up and
down the study. I returned to the kitchen and my
storybook. There I read about emperors, about
princes and princesses, about wild steeds, caves, and
robbers. The story of the woman seemed to become
part of this fantastic tale....

A few days later a fire broke out in a house across
the street. I ran out on the balcony and saw it all: the
arrival of the advance patrol and of the firemen with
their long wagons and the horses that seemed about
to break out of their traces. Within a minute a ladder
had been erected and firemen in shiny helmets, with
hooks on their belts, placed the ladder with incredible
speed against the window from which the smoke was
belching forth. Others unrolled a hose. The street
glittered with brass and with all sorts of machinery
whose use for putting out a fire was difficult to
discern. Even though policemen kept chasing them
away, hordes of children came running from all the
courtyards, and the street was black with people.
Some boys climbed up lampposts, and the walls of
nearby houses. I stood on the balcony and saw it all.
Suddenly it occurred to me that that woman's son

might be among the firemen. I began to look for him
and recognized him at once. Yes, it was the one with
the long face and the dark mustache. He stood by and
did nothing, just looked up at the sky. From minute to
minute I became ever more sure that it was indeed
he....An extraordinary idea took hold of me.
Perhaps I should go down and tell him the truth?
Perhaps I should throw down a note? But he would
not know Yiddish....I stared at him until it seemed
that he had felt my gaze. He raised his eyes, looked at
me in surprise, and then raised a threatening fist
toward me—the usual gesture of the Gentiles toward
Jewish children.

"You are a Jew! A Jew! A descendant of Abraham,
Isaac, and Jacob!" I whispered to him. "I know your
mother....Repent!"

He disappeared amid the other firemen. He had
run away from my words, as Jonah had run away
from God....I was so engrossed in my fantasy that I
did not actually see how the fire was put out. A
terrifying thought had entered my mind. Perhaps I,
too, had been abandoned as an infant? Perhaps I was
not really the child of my father and mother, but had
been placed in Mother's cradle by some servant girl,
and Mother only thought I was her child....If
children can be abandoned and exchanged, how can
anyone know which child belongs to whom? Many
questions arose in my mind, many puzzles. The
grownups were keeping something from us children.
There was a secret behind it all. Perhaps Mother
knew that I was not really her child, and that was
why she scolded me so often?

A lump formed in my throat, and tears rose to my
eyes. I ran into the kitchen and asked, "Mama, am I
really your son?"

Mother opened her eyes wide. "God have mercy,
have you gone crazy?"

I remained silent and she exclaimed, "We will have
to send you back to the heder. You are growing up like
a wild animal!"

The Will

THE DOOR OPENED, and a man with a beard so long
I've seen its equal only once in my life, entered. The
great beard, black as pitch, and with a rich gloss and
density that made one think of a thickly foliaged tree,
reached to the man's knees, and then branched out
into a separate little "beardkin." The man was short
and stoutish, dressed in an expensive-looking overcoat, goatskin boots, and silk hat. He wore gold-
rimmed spectacles padded with cotton at the bridge
to protect his nose. An aura of complacency and
Hasidic good nature enveloped him.

My father welcomed the stranger into the study
and bade him be seated. Soon my father asked, "And
what good news do you bring us?"

"I wish to draw up my will," said the stranger.

My father sat motionless. I, who was also present,
became frightened. My father began to stammer. It
was rare that anyone came to him with such a
request, and the few who did were very old men. He
turned toward his visitor. "But you look like a man in
the prime of life."

"First of all, I'm not a youngster. Secondly, one
never knows what tomorrow may bring."

And the visitor cited verses from the Bible and the
Talmud to prove that every man should be prepared
at all times for his death. Even as he spoke, he lit a
cigar. Then he took out a snuffbox and offered it to

my father. It was an unusual box, made of ivory decorated with carving, the kind of souvenir one brought back from a summer resort. He removed his overcoat and remained in his brand-new coat and a vest with a gold watch-chain dangling over it. He took out his watch and I saw that it had three lids and a face with Hebrew letters instead of numerals. It was obvious that this was a man of some wealth and of a Hasidic background steeped in traditional Jewish ways.

"What is your profession?" My father asked the direct question without ceremony.

"I own a bookstore on Swietokrzyska Street."

"Books?"

"Not the books of the Enlightenment, God forbid, but books for Gentiles, in Polish, Russian, German, French—all languages. The Yiddish and Hebrew books of the atheists, I don't take into my shop."

"And you know all these languages?"

"I frequently speak with the most famous professors at the universities. If they need a Polish or a Latin book, they come to me and I tell them where to look. I am known throughout Poland. I receive letters from professors in Kracow. I have a worldwide reputation. I am what is known as a bibliographer."

"As long as it is for the Gentiles ..." my father said.

After a while the man began to dictate his will to my father. It was a will to cast terror upon the listener. He prescribed what prayers were to be recited at the moment he drew his last breath; how the body was to be carried; what Psalms were to be said by those keeping watch before the funeral; how he was to be handled at the moment of burial. He was well-versed in the wills of famous Rabbis, and whenever my father objected that something was not according to the Law, he would cite one or another such testament and my father was unable to refute him. He knew everything better. My father covered a large sheet with his fine script and the man read it over slowly and apparently with great satisfaction.

Then he signed: "These are the words of the deceased." He embellished his signature with fine flourishes.

The man paid three rubles for the writing of the will. He confided to my father that although he looked well enough, his lungs were diseased and the doctors had given him but little longer to live. Strangely enough, he had discussed only questions of religious ceremony in the will: prayers, charities, scholarly quotations, the observance of the annual anniversary of his death. He had dictated nothing about his business affairs. For the worldly matters he had perhaps had another will drawn up by a notary public.

After the writing of the will, the stranger seemed to have developed an appetite. He sent me down to fetch half a buttercake and a pint of boiled milk. He washed his hands and pronounced the benediction. When he finished eating, he recited a leisurely grace. Then he smoked a cigar, exhaling rings of smoke, and turned to me.

"Are you studying?"

"Yes."

"What are you learning?"

"Babba Kama."

He questioned me on this beginner's text from the Talmud and pinched my cheek. I was frightened. Although the man's fingers were soft and warm, I felt as though a corpse had touched me. He gave me a coin and said, "Don't get into any mischief now."

Three rubles were a welcome addition to my father's meager income, but there was an uncanny silence in our house when the stranger had left. He had expressed such precise wishes about how his shroud should be sewn, how his body was to be purified. He had already bought a plot and ordered his headstone, in the cemetery on Gesia Street. He had specified to the last detail how the pallbearers were to carry the coffin, and how they should arrange the head, the hands, the feet, the boards. It was too much. At the same time I had the eerie feeling that the man took a perverse kind of pleasure in the morbid details. He had indeed eaten the cake I brought him, with a hearty appetite, and when a crumb fell into the tangle of his beard, he had carefully extricated it and swallowed it down. He had also warned me to be sure that the boiled milk had formed a skin.

Some time later I had occasion to be on Swietokrzyska Street. Perhaps I even went there just to see this man. He stood in his shop, which was filled with books. University and high-school students, boys and girls crowded around the shelves, searching, browsing. The man was arguing with someone in Polish. On his face shone the joy of doing business, the pleasure of a man of means. Behind the counter stood a plump woman wearing a matron's wig, together with a young girl—probably their daughter. I stood at the window and looked in. Not only old books were on display, but other antiques too: a porcelain figurine with a naked belly, a plaster-of-Paris bust, all sorts of candlesticks (but not the Jewish kind), and other bric-a-brac of brass, copper, and bronze. Everything in the shop looked pagan, strange. But the owner was a Jew immersed in Torah and the hereafter.

A long time passed. Suddenly the man appeared once more in our house. A few gray hairs showed in his pitch-black beard, but otherwise he looked as stout and as fresh as the first time. It was winter and he wore a rich fur coat and galoshes lined with a soft material. He carried an umbrella with a silver handle. He explained that he had come to alter his will.

"How is your health?"

"What is the good of asking about my health?" he answered. "I am—may no evil befall you—a very sick man."

"The Almighty will grant you a full recovery."

"Of course, He—blessed be His name—can perform miracles. But if nature takes its course, I cannot keep going much longer. How long can a man live without lungs?"

Father paled and reminded the man of the miracle that had been performed on behalf of the wife of Rabbi Hanina ben Dussa. One Friday, instead of filling the lamp with oil, she had filled it with vinegar. But Rabbi Hanina said: "He who commanded oil to burn can also command vinegar to burn." And the lamp burned on that Sabbath just as on every other Sabbath. The same is true of lungs—if the Creator desires that a man should live, he will live.

The man did not receive my father's comforting words kindly. He coughed, spat into his handkerchief, and cited a verse of the Gemara in answer: "Not every day does a miracle occur."

"One of our sages declared that even the normal course of nature is miraculous."

"Of course, of course. But yet, without lungs one cannot breathe, and when you don't breathe.... After all, the body is only a body...."

The changes in the will were thoroughgoing. He had in the meantime studied countless other wills, and he now introduced all sorts of innovations. He wanted the shards placed over his eyes in a very special manner. The switch, or myrtle twig, that is put in the hands of the deceased was to be different, too. The purification of the body was to be done with the yolk of an egg and with a silver spoon he had bought in some distant town, a spoon that had been used by an old-time burial association.

I could tell by the look on my father's face that the exaggerated interest the man took in these melancholy matters was not to his liking. He raised his eyebrows and silently seemed to say: Too much ... too much.... But the candidate for the next world spent hours upon hours in our house. He worked out a list of instructions with a multitude of details. From time to time he would ask for something to be erased, and

something else substituted for it. All during this time
he smoked, took snuff, sneezed. Again he felt hungry
and again I went down to buy milk and cake. .

From that day the man came every year, and
sometimes twice a year. His beard turned gray
slowly, without haste. His face remained rosy and
fat, and his rolling black eyes shone with the joy of
life and the pleasures of a successful businessman.
He kept changing his will, adding new paragraphs
each time. My father was far from being a humorist,
but even he began to make occasional jests about the
man who so steadfastly maintained that he already
had one foot in the grave. Many apparently healthy
men during these years had passed onto the next
world. But the bookseller of Swietokrzyska Street
was still rewriting his will. My father barely
managed to suppress a smile whenever he appeared
at our door. Even I, who had once been so afraid of
him and his morbid conversation, began to get used
to him. This was a man who played with death as the
children in the street played their games. The three
rubles he paid for rewriting his will became a regular
part of our income.

Gradually his beard grew white as milk. As it had
formerly glistened in its blackness, it now sparkled in
its whiteness. In order to complete the story, I must
rush time on. The war broke out. The Germans
entered Warsaw. But even amid battles, famine, and
uprising, the bookseller did not forget his will. He
now paid marks instead of rubles for amending it.
The will itself had become a thick brochure. My
mother stitched the pages together with heavy
thread.

In 1917 my mother left Warsaw with us children.
But a short time before our departure from the capital
I passed Swietokrzyska Street. The bookseller still
stood busily behind his counter, and students were
still searching through the shelves. This time there
were also German officers in the shop.

Eventually, I suppose, the man died. By then he

must have been quite old, and I doubt whether his will was ever carried out. It would have required an entire squadron of members of the burial association, who would have had to spend days studying and memorizing his instructions. Most probably no one read or seriously thought about his will. But while the man lived, this document had given him a great deal of pleasure.

A Day of Pleasures

WHEN TIMES WERE GOOD, I would get a two-groschen piece from Father or Mother every day. For me this piece—or kopeck—represented all worldly pleasures. Across the street was Esther's sweetshop, where one could buy chocolates, jelly beans, candy squares, ice cream, caramels, and all sorts of cookies. Since I had begun at an early age to write copy exercises, and had a weakness for drawing and coloring with crayons, which cost money, a kopeck proved not nearly so large a coin as Father and Mother made it out to be. There were times when I was forced to borrow money from a heder classmate, a young usurer who demanded interest—for every four groschen, I paid a groschen a week.

Now imagine the indescribable joy that I felt when I once earned a whole ruble—that is, one hundred kopecks!

I no longer remember exactly how I came to earn that ruble. I think it happened like this: Someone had ordered a pair of kidskin boots from a shoemaker, but upon delivery the boots proved to be either too tight or too loose. The man who had ordered them refused to accept them, and the shoemaker summoned him to a Din Torah. Father sent me to another shoemaker to ask him to appraise the value of the boots or perhaps even to buy them, since he also dealt in ready-made footwear. It so happened that the second shoemaker had a customer who wanted the boots and was prepared to pay a good price for them. I do not recall all the details, but I remember that I carried a pair of brand-new boots around, and that one of the litigants rewarded me with a ruble.

I knew that if I stayed home my parents would ruin that ruble. They would buy me something to wear which I would have got in any case, or they would borrow the ruble from me and, though they would never deny the debt, I would never see it again. I therefore took the ruble and decided for once to indulge myself in the pleasures of this world, to enjoy all those good things for which my heart yearned.

I quickly passed through Krochmalna Street. Here everyone knew me too well. Here I could not afford to act the profligate. But on Gnoyna Street I was unknown. I signaled to the driver of a droshky, and he stopped.

"What do you want?"

"To ride."

"Ride where?"

"To the other streets."

"What other streets?"

"To Nalewki Street."

"That costs forty groschen. Have you got the money to pay?"

I showed him the ruble.

"But you'll have to pay me in advance."

I gave the driver the ruble. He tried bending it to see whether it was counterfeit. Then he gave me my change—four forty-groschen pieces. I got into the droshky. The driver cracked his whip and I almost fell off the bench. The houses began to move backward. The seat under me bounced on its springs. Passers-by stared at the little boy riding alone in a droshky, without any bundles. The droshky made its way among trolley cars, other droshkies, carts, delivery vans. I felt that I had suddenly assumed the importance of an adult. God in heaven, if I could only ride like this for a thousand years, by day and by night, without stop, to the ends of the earth....

But the driver turned out to be a dishonest man. When we had gone only halfway, he stopped and said, "Enough. Get down!"

"But this is not Nalewki Street!" I argued.

"Do you want a taste of my whip?" he answered.

Oh, if only I were Samson the Strong, I'd know how to take care of such a bandit, such a boor! I would have pulverized him, chopped him into little pieces, beaten him up! But I am only a small weak boy, and he is cracking his whip.

I got down, shamed and depressed. But how long can you mourn when you have four forty-groschen pieces in your pocket? I saw a sweetshop and went in to select my merchandise. I bought something of every kind. And as I bought, I tasted. The other customers looked at me with disdain; they probably suspected I had stolen the money. One girl exclaimed, "Just look at that little Hasid!"

"Hey, you ninny, may an evil spirit possess your father's son!" one boy called out to me.

I left, laden with sweets. Then I reached Krasinski Park. I was nearly run over while crossing the street. I entered the park and ate some of the delicacies. A boy passed by and I gave him a chocolate bar. Instead of saying thank you, he grabbed it and ran off. I walked over to the lake and fed the swans—with chocolate. Women pointed their fingers at me, laughed, made comments in Polish. Daintily dressed girls, with hoops and balls, came over to me and I chivalrously and prodigally distributed my sweets among them. At that moment I felt like a rich nobleman distributing largess.

After a while I had no more candies, but I still had some money. I decided to take another droshky. When I sat in the second droshky and the driver asked where I wanted to go, I really wanted to say, "To Krochmalna Street." But someone inside of me, an invisible glutton, answered instead, "To Marszal-kowska Street."

"What number?"

I invented a number.

This coachman was honest. He took me to the address and did not ask for the money in advance. On the way another droshky rolled alongside ours; inside sat a lady with an enormous bosom and a big hat decorated with an ostrich feather. My driver chatted with the other driver. Both spoke in Yiddish, which the lady did not like at all. Even less did she like the little passenger with the black velvet hat and the red earlocks. She threw angry looks at me. From time to time both droshkies stopped to let a streetcar or a heavily laden wagon pass by. A policeman who stood near the tracks stared at me, at the lady, seemed for a minute about to come over and arrest me—and then began to laugh. I was terribly afraid. I was afraid of God, of my mother and father, and I was also afraid lest a hole had suddenly appeared in my pocket and my money had fallen through. And what if the driver was a robber who would carry me off to some dark cave? Perhaps he was a magician. And perhaps all this was only a dream. But no, the driver was not a robber, and he did not carry me off to the twelve thieves in the desert. He took me exactly to the address I had given him, a big house with a gateway, and I paid him the forty groschen.

"Whom are you going to see?" he asked me.

"A doctor," I answered without hesitation.

"What's the matter with you?"

"I cough."

"You're an orphan, eh?"

"Yes, an orphan."

"From out of town?"

"Yes."

"From where?"

I gave him the name of some town.

"Do you wear the fringed garment?"

This last question I did not answer. What concern of his were my ritual fringes? I wanted him to drive off, but he remained there with his droshky, and I could delay no longer—I had to enter the gateway. But behind the gate there lurked a gigantic dog. He looked at me with a pair of knowing eyes that seemed to say: you may fool the coachman, but not me. I know you have no business here. And he opened a mouth full of sharp, pointed teeth.

Suddenly the janitor appeared. "And what do you want?"

I tried to stammer something, but he shouted at me, "Get away from here!"

And he began to chase me with a broom. I started to run, and the dog let out a savage howl. The droshky driver was probably a witness to my discomfiture— but alone against a broom, a janitor, and a dog, a small boy cannot be a hero.

Things were not going well with me, but I still had some money left. And with money one can find pleasures anywhere. I saw a fruit store and went in. I ordered the first fruit I saw, and when it came to paying, my money was just barely enough. I parted with my last groschen.

I no longer remember what kind of fruit it was. It must have been a pomegranate or something equally exotic. I could not peel it, and when I ate it, it had a poisonous taste. Nevertheless I devoured it all. But then I was overcome by a horrible thirst. My throat was parched and burning. I had only one desire—to drink. Oh, if only I had money now! I could have emptied a gallon of soda water! But I had nothing and, furthermore, I was far from home.

I started to walk home. I walked and suddenly I felt a nail inside my boot. It pierced my skin at every step. How did the nail happen to be there just then? I stepped into a gateway. Here there were no dogs and no janitors. I took off the boot. Inside, right through the inner sole, a pointy nail was sticking out. I stuffed some paper into the boot and set out again. Oh, how bitter it is to walk when an iron nail pricks you at every step! And how bitter it must be to lie on a bed of nails in Gehenna! This day I had committed many sins. I had said no blessing before eating the sweets, I had not given even one groschen of all my money to the poor. I had only gorged myself.

The way home took about two hours. All manner of frightening thoughts beset me as I walked. Perhaps something terrible had happened at home. Perhaps I had not been lying when I told the coachman I was an orphan, but at the very moment when I said it I was in truth orphaned. Perhaps I had no father, no mother, no home. Perhaps my face had changed, like that of the man in the storybook, and when I came home Father and Mother would not recognize me. Anything was possible!

A boy saw me and stopped me. "Where are you coming from? Your mother has been looking for you everywhere!"

"I was in Praga—I rode on a trolley," I said, telling lies now just for the sake of lying. Because once you have eaten without a blessing and committed other sins, then you can do anything—it no longer matters.

"Whom did you visit in Praga?"

"My aunt."

"Since when do you have an aunt in Praga?"

"She just came to Warsaw."

"Go on, you're fibbing. Your mother is looking for you. Swear you were in Praga."

I swore falsely too. Afterward I came home, tired, sweating—a lost soul. I pounced upon the water faucet and began to drink, to drink. Thus must Esau have devoured the mess of pottage for which he sold his birthright.

Mother wrung her hands.

"Just look at that child!"

The Salesman

THINGS HAPPEN IN LIFE so fantastic that no imagination could have invented them.

One day the door to our kitchen opened and a man entered who looked different from any Jew I had ever seen. He wore a hat in the rabbinic style, but his alpaca jacket reached only to the knees, in the German fashion. He had a white beard, but it was too even to have grown naturally; it had been trimmed by shears. His trousers were striped, his boots glistened. But he also had white earlocks. His face was young and rosy, not at all like the face of an old man, and in his black eyes shone a youthful vitality and a strange pensiveness. His Yiddish was heavily Germanic.

"Is the Reverend Rabbi at home?" he asked.

Neither my mother nor I was used to hearing my father called "the Reverend Rabbi," but after a moment's hesitation my mother realized who was meant and indicated to the visitor that he should go into the next room.

My father welcomed the man with an open-hearted greeting, as he welcomed everyone rich or poor, and asked him to be seated. After a while he asked why he had come, but the visitor did not answer directly. It appeared that he had come simply to chat. In his Germanized speech, he began to demonstrate his familiarity with Jewish learning, and I saw that my father was impressed by his knowledge. He apparent-

ly knew the Mishnah by heart. He cited several
scholarly books, and from memory recited a few
lengthy passages. The conversation became more
and more dense. Although my father was a scholar
and the author of a number of commentaries, he
could barely keep up with him. The man knew
everything by heart. He even remembered the exact
pages on which certain passages were to be found. He
tossed quotations from Maimonides around like
nutshells. He seemed to pull commentaries and laws
out of his sleeves. He led the conversation around to
what the Aramaic translator had said about a certain
Biblical verse, and then recited passages of Onkelos
and Jonathan ben Uzziel.

As a rule, my father refrained from praising a man
to his face, but this time he could not hold back. "How
can a man—may no evil befall you—have such a
memory? You are indeed to be compared to 'a limned
cistern that loses not a drop,'" he exclaimed.

"Permit me to show you some affidavits..."

The stranger took out a packet of letters bearing
the seals of many Rabbis. Famous Rabbis called him
"genius," "Prince of the Torah," "one who uproots
mountains and reduces them to dust..." One Rabbi
attested that he had examined this man and that "his
hands were filled" with the Babylonian Talmud, the
Jerusalem Talmud, Sifri, Sifra, Tosefta, Mehilta.
Father rubbed his forehead and almost smacked his
lips. He said, "It is a privilege to have you in my
house!"

He sent me to tell Mother to bring tea and
refreshments for his guest. A little later he himself
came into the kitchen to tell her about the visitor.
Mother, herself the daughter of a renowned Rabbi,
was equally enthralled. In our house, learning was
looked upon as the greatest wealth. I stood with my
ears cocked, so as not to lose a word. Father asked the
stranger whence he came, and it turned out that he
was originally from Hungary and had visited many
lands. He had even studied with a Sephardic

Hacham in one of the provinces of the Turkish empire. He had been in Palestine and had wandered as far as Damascus and Babylon. He had traversed the world and knew several languages—Russian, Hungarian, German, and Arabic. With great deliberation, he took out an Austrian passport and showed my father the many, many visas issued by all sorts of consulates. This was the first time I heard the words "visas" and "consulates." On the whole, my father attached little value to such secular matters, but when they accompanied learning such as this, he considered it a combination of Torah and worldly glory. He called me over and ordered me to shake hands with this extraordinary man. Apparently he wanted me to have the honor and privilege of touching the visitor's hand. The man pinched my cheek and asked, "What are you studying?"

Then he recited by heart not only the passage of the Gemera that I was studying at the time, but added to it bits of Rashi and the other commentaries.

In the meantime my mother had served tea, cookies, and fruit. She seemed almost embarrassed by this modern-looking scholar. Father told the visitor whose daughter she was, and I was pleased to hear that he knew my grandfather by reputation.

After a while he whispered something to my father, who turned to me and said, "Leave the room now."

Mother had already gone out, and after a slight demurral I slowly made my way to the kitchen. I greatly desired to listen to this man's scholarly Germanic speech, but such was the way of adults: as soon as the conversation became really interesting and every word began to draw me like a magnet, they would suddenly decide to "send the boy away." As I went out, I left the door slightly ajar, but the stranger himself walked over and closed it firmly. Obviously, he had an extraordinary secret to confide.

In the kitchen Mother began to lecture me. "How does one become a scholar like that?" she argued. "By studying, not by being idle. But, instead of studying, you read foolish storybooks, about things that never were and never will be." Then she told me a story she had read in a newspaper. A professor had a wife who never had dinner ready on time and every day he had to sit around waiting. Suddenly it occurred to him that he could utilize this time and he began to write a book. A few years later he published the work he had composed entirely in the time spent waiting for dinner. Now if scholars can show such diligence in secular knowledge—for which there is no divine reward—how much more important is such effort in the study of Torah? One could become a scholar and at the same time attain merit for the hereafter.

Mother's words made a deep impression upon me. Yet I was also filled with curiosity as to what the stranger from those faraway lands was telling my father so secretively. Through the closed door I could hear whispering, mumbling, sighs. From time to time I even thought that I heard a stifled cry. The voice was my father's, and it sounded as though he were angry at someone, barely restraining himself from erupting into a towering rage. But why would Father be angry at this man? What was going on inside? Mother, too, began to look curious, for the voices that came from the study were rising higher and higher. There was no longer any doubt that a dispute—indeed, a quarrel—was taking place. Could they be arguing so heatedly about a passage from the Gemara, or over the interpretation of a law? Somehow that did not seem likely. Mother went over to the door and tried to listen. Then she said, almost resentfully, "Why is your father shouting?"

Suddenly the door was flung open and my father appeared. I had never seen him so flushed, so disheveled and upset. His forehead was covered with beads of sweat. His red beard trembled. His earlocks, which were nearly black, quivered. Confusion, dismay, and fright were apparent in his eyes. He called out to Mother: "Give me some money, quickly!"

"How much do you need?"

"As much as you have."

Mother was upset.

"But I cannot give away my last groschen!"

"I beg of you, don't keep me waiting. I don't want that vile creature in my house another minute! May his name and memory be wiped out..."

"Why is he a vile creature?"

"Give me the money—if not, I'll leave the house at once! His very presence defiles..."

Tears rose to my eyes. With trembling fingers, Mother began to search the drawer of the kitchen table. She had grown pale. I could see our visitor through the door. He stood in the center of the study, plucking at his beard and examining our oil lamp. My father returned to argue with him a while longer. Then the door of the study opened again and the stranger came out. He looked at my mother and said, in his precise neo-German, "Good day."

A minute after he had left, Father stormed into the kitchen and cried out: "Woe is us—such a thing has not been heard of since the days of the creation! The man is a heretic—a spiteful apostate—an insolent heathen—a willful sinner! Such learning—and yet he is the lowest of curs!"

"Why are you shouting so? What did he want of you?"

"He came to sell me eternal life..." Father's voice did not sound like itself.

"What?"

"Yes, you heard right. He wanted to sell me his share in the hereafter for a hundred rubles."

"He must be a lunatic."

"No, he's not a lunatic. He is an atheist! A total unbeliever! An Elisha ben Abuya!"

And my father, still upset and barely able to speak, told how the man had made his offer. Since he had amassed so much knowledge in the Torah and sacred lore, he claimed he had acquired a great portion of eternal life and he had come to sell it to my father.

Father argued that an unbeliever has no share in the hereafter, but the visitor had cited Talmudic passages to prove that through the learning he had acquired he had earned a share in the world to come, and that it is possible to sell one's share of eternal life. He argued that since he needed the money, and since he himself did not believe in life after death, he was willing to do business with his portion of it.

Mother looked at Father with reproach in her eyes.

"And why did you give him our last few rubles?"

"I had to get rid of him. He threatened that he would not leave the house without the money..."

"But how shall I prepare for the Sabbath now?"

Father did not know what to say. He ran to the sink and washed his hands, as though to cleanse away the defilement of that creature. He remained standing, his head bowed, confused, almost as though he had been struck by a fist. So much learning—and such heresy! Such a scholar—and such a reprobate! Esau had given away the rights of the first-born for a mess of pottage, and this scoundrel was prepared to throw away eternal life for a few rubles...

"World's end! World's end!" my father muttered to himself. "How many days are left him on this earth? He is already an old man..." Then he looked scowlingly at me and added, "Let this be a lesson to you!"

Soon we heard that the stranger had visited all the Rabbis, scholars, and men of substance in Warsaw. To each he had offered the same unholy business deal, and everywhere he had received at least a few rubles. This *schnorrer* practiced psychology on his victims: first he inspired admiration, then anger, abhorrence, and fear, and finally he let himself be paid off just for going away. It was even rumored that here and there he snared a rich fool who actually paid the hundred rubles. This, then, was his merchandise; with these wares he made his way through the world.

Reb Chayim Gorshkover

THERE WAS a group of "habitués" who visited our
house regularly—men who came simply to see the
Rabbi, to unburden their hearts, to seek advice, or
just to talk. There were even some among them who
would sit in the kitchen and talk to my mother. One of
these was Reb Chayim Gorshkover.

Reb Chayim was a poor man, and his poverty was
inscribed on his face. He had a red nose and a long
beard, which was a mixture of blond, brown, gray,
and many other colors. From under his bushy brows
gazed eyes such as only a poor Jew can have. Their
color was amber. In them glowed an ancient
goodness and a submissiveness formed by generations of exile and suffering. There was in him a
respect and reverence for every adult and every child,
for every living creature. The saying "He would not
hurt a fly" fitted him literally. Frequently a fly would
alight on his red nose, but he would not chase it away.
Was he, Chayim Gorshkover, to presume to tell a fly
where it was permitted to stand and where not?

In the eyes of Reb Chayim Gorshkover my father
was the right hand of God, and he looked upon my
mother with a mixture of awe and admiration. He
himself did not know how to write, and my mother
wrote letters for him to his children in America.
Mother was a scholar in her own right. Whenever he
came to our house, he tried to serve her in some way.

He was willing to sweep up, to run an errand, but Mother would not permit a man to do such menial tasks for her.

Reb Chayim was, in the fullest meaning of the word, a pauper. His wife worked as a chicken plucker in Yanash's court. They lived in a cellar. His shoulders were bent and round. His voice was that of a rooster. His clothes were ragged and patched. Often the interlining could be seen through the rents. Bunches of hair sprouted from his ears and nostrils. His beard covered his face almost to the eyes.

This man had two passions.

One was to recite Psalms or other holy words. Even as he sat and talked with my mother, his sunken lips would begin to mumble, and we knew that he was hurriedly reciting a verse, or even an entire chapter, from the book of Psalms. He knew almost all the Psalms by heart.

His second passion was to speak of Gorshkov. He had left Gorshkov many years ago, but it had remained the source of all his yearnings. All that was beautiful and good was in Gorshkov. All that was ugly and pagan was in Warsaw. Gorshkov was, for Reb Chayim, the Promised Land—a foretaste of Paradise.

A journey to Gorshkov would have required two full days, for the train went only as far as Rejowiec and after that one had to proceed by horse and carriage. Such a journey was for him an utter impossibility, a dream that could not be fulfilled. He could only yearn for Gorshkov. At the mere mention of Gorshkov, tears would rise in Reb Chayim's eyes and fall upon his beard.

Difficult as it was to believe, Reb Chayim actually owned a building in Gorshkov—a one-room shack, a ruin rather than a house. It was inhabited by a relative who paid no rent. This shack caused Reb Chayim all kinds of trouble. A sanitation commission dispatched by the governor of Lublin found that a wall was about to cave in, and Reb Chayim was fined. Since he could not pay the fine, he went to jail. He spent eight days in prison among thieves and hoodlums. We did not know what had happened to him. When he was released and came to tell us of his misfortune, my mother tried to persuade him to sell this "property," or even to give it to the relative who lived in it, but Reb Chayim demurred. "As long as the house is mine, I am still a Gorshkover, my name is still remembered there."

It did not take long for Reb Chayim to be fined again. The chimney sweep had long neglected to clean the soot from the flue, and a fire broke out. The shack did not burn down, but Reb Chayim was fined and once more went to prison.

Both my parents came from that part of the country and we children knew why Reb Chayim came and what he was waiting for.

I would say, "Reb Chayim, what's new in Gorshkov?"

There would be a deep sigh, a sigh torn from the soul's innermost depths. The beard would begin to quiver like the tail of a chicken. His mustache would begin to tremble, and from the toothless mouth would come a wheezing and rumbling like an old clock preparing to strike the hour.

"Gorshkov, eh? Gorshkov was a Garden of Eden, and here we are in Gehenna. What do we know here of the Sabbath, of the holidays? Can one be a real Jew in Warsaw? Does life here have a value? Everyone rushes, everyone runs. In Gorshkov we began to prepare for the Sabbath on Wednesday. My mother—may she intercede for us in the other world—herself baked the Sabbath bread. A little dough remained in the bucket and during the week it turned into yeast.

"Who ever heard of coal in Gorshkov? A peasant brought wood from the forest. My father—may he rest in peace—sawed and chopped it himself. Then we would carefully arrange the kindling in the stove and light it with a shaving. At once the stove would begin to get warm. Can you warm yourself properly in Warsaw? Coal is a curse. If you close the vent, the room is filled with smoke. If you leave it open, you might as well be out in the frost. In Gorshkov, when one made a fire there was a pleasant warmth. Mother baked her own cookies. Warsaw bread is too fresh and has no body. You can eat and eat it and remain hungry. But in Gorshkov, every piece of bread had the taste of Paradise. And if you spread chicken fat on it and covered it with crisp strips of chicken skin—it just melted in your mouth!

"And the Sabbath loaves in Gorshkov! What is the taste of store-bought challah? In Gorshkov, caraway seeds were caraway seeds, and poppy seeds were poppy seeds. Mother would dip a feather in the yolk of an egg and spread it over the braided loaves. And the cookies! And the *cholent!* Here the *cholent* is either half done or burnt. You have to keep it in the baker's oven together with hundreds of other *cholents*. But in Gorshkov my mother kept the *cholent* in her oven and sealed the oven door with dough.

"And the pudding! Does anyone in Warsaw know how to prepare a real pudding? When my mother made a noodle pudding or stuffed a derma, or baked a pie, it took your breath away. And the candied fruits? There was a pear tree in our yard that bore tiny hard pears. Mother would dry these until they became as sweet as sugar. When they were cooked in a casserole with a stick of cinnamon, their fragrance filled the house.

"Nu, and the synagogue? Does anyone really pray in Warsaw? One rushes through the prayers. Before they have completed the Aleinu, they already rush out. Back home, one did not cheat while praying. When our cantor sang 'Welcome, O Bride,' on Friday nights, the very walls sang with him.

"And the Gorshkov wine! Here one buys a bottle from the wine merchant, and it tastes like vinegar. My father made his own raisin wine. First he would cook the wine for more than an hour, then he would squeeze it through a cloth—and when you drank it for the Friday-night kiddush, it raced through every limb of your body."

Mother would smile. She heard this paean every week. She also knew that the raisin wine of Gorshkov was not nearly as fabulous as Reb Chayim imagined. But in the presence of this simple man she would not utter a word in defense of Warsaw or against Gorshkov. She listened to him and nodded her head. I, however, being already somewhat brazen, would ask, "Was there a streetcar in Gorshkov?"

"May God give you good health! What need was there for a streetcar in Gorshkov?"

"And were there any buildings four stories tall?"

"Who needs to climb up so many stairs? In Gorshkov one walks straight into the parlor, even in the houses of the richest men."

But, as if Warsaw were not heathenish enough, it was Reb Chayim's sad fate that all his children had gone to New York. One had gone first and sent for the others, and before Reb Chayim had quite realized what had happened, he was childless. His sons wrote that in comparison with New York, Warsaw was a mere village. In New York, trains ran across the rooftops. The buildings were so tall one had to twist one's neck to see the top. If one wished to go to another part of the city, one rode in an underground train.

Reb Chayim's children wrote long letters full of horrible misspellings. No one except my mother could decipher them. Once even she was stuck on a word that took up an entire line. Everyone in the house tried to read it, but it was illegible. Suddenly, after she had nearly despaired of unscrambling this mystery, Mother suddenly burst into laughter. The word was simply a running-together of the phrase "Hol Hamoed Sukkoth"—the intermediary days of the Feast of Tabernacles! It was truly a model of how many mistakes could be made in one word.

Reb Chayim had an eldest daughter whom we did not know, for she had gone to America before my

parents came to Warsaw. This daughter complained
bitterly about America in every letter. The food was
tasteless. The bread was not real bread, the challah
not real challah, the Sabbath no Sabbath, the
festivals no festivals. Photographs arrived showing
Reb Chayim's sons, daughters, sons-in-law and
daughters-in-law all dressed up, the men even in stiff-
brimmed hats, sometimes top hats and tails. Reb
Chayim hardly recognized his children. As if
Warsaw were not enough of a Sodom, his children
had to wander off to a world where people walked on
their heads, where everything was topsy-turvy!

Year after year the letters from New York became
more and more difficult to understand, for they were
full of English phrases. Over there, apparently, they
had forgotten that in Warsaw people did not speak
English. All the children begged Reb Chayim and his
wife to come to New York. There the old folks would
be able to enjoy life. They wanted to send them
steamship tickets. But Reb Chayim smiled sadly and
shrugged. Did he not have troubles enough in
Warsaw that he should seek new ones in New York?
Was there not enough heathenishness in Warsaw
without his going to New York to seek it?

Reb Chayim had only one dream: to return to
Gorshkov for his last days and to be buried in its
cemetery. If it had not been God's will that he live his
life in Gorshkov, let him at least find his last resting
place there. But the First World War broke out.
Warsaw was under German rule, while Gorshkov
belonged to Austria. In order to reach Gorshkov, one
needed a passport, a visa, a permit to cross the border.

When the Germans entered Warsaw and the great
famine began, I heard Reb Chayim speak longingly
of the paradise Warsaw had been before the war—
when everything was cheap, when his wife brought
home for the Sabbath half a goose, derma, giblets,
challah, cakes. Again his tears flowed. But now we no
longer scoffed. We, too, were hungry. I was half
grown by then, and I would say to him, "Reb Chayim,

do you remember how you used to complain about
Warsaw? You yearned only for Gorshkov."

Reb Chayim raised his yellowish eyes. His moist
glance said silently, "Who dares even think of
Gorshkov now?"

Reb Moishe Ba-Ba-Ba

HE WAS KNOWN as Reb Moishe Ba-ba-ba. Why "Ba-
ba-ba"? Because that was how he talked. "Ba-ba-ba,
the Almighty will help.... Ba-ba-ba, the Messiah will
come and the world finally will be redeemed.... Ba-
ba-ba, it is good to be a Jew. What greater pleasure
can there be than being a Jew? I'll give up all
theaters, all riches, all delicacies for one Minhah
prayer, for one chapter of Psalms, one *Asher Yotzar!*
If a person were to offer me all the gold in the world,
all the palaces and fortresses and soldiers and
Cossacks, on condition that I skip one blessing, I
would laugh in his face. These are vanity, trifles, not
worth an empty eggshell. But when I recite the
blessing: 'By whose word all things exist,' I feel
renewed strength in my very bones. Just think of it:
'Blessed art Thou, O Lord our God, King of the
Universe, by whose word all things exist.' All things,
all! The heavens, the earth, I, you, even—forgive the
comparison—the dog in the street. All were created
by Him, the Creator, and to us He gave the power to
praise Him. Is not this sufficient earthly pleasure? I'd
exchange all fancy balls and all pleasure resorts for

the words of one saint—his sighs and his gestures.
You are only a boy—what does a boy understand?—
but I give you my word, the second night of a festival
at the court of Kuzmir was a pleasure greater than
can be known by any worldling, emperor, general, or
reveler. Every minute savored of Paradise. He who
has never spent a holiday in Kuzmir, has no idea of
true pleasure, ba-ba-ba!"

Reb Moishe must have been very old, for he had
been a frequenter of the court of Rabbi Haskele
Kuzmirer. He looked to be nearly a hundred. His
white beard was turning yellow. The hairs of his
earlocks were falling out, and his brow was wrinkled
like parchment. He wore an old-fashioned gabardine,
a velvet hat with a high crown, half boots, panta-
loons, and white socks. His ritual fringes reached
below his knees. His sons supported him. Reb Moishe
himself had only one occupation: being a devout Jew.
He was always either praying, or studying, or poring
over the Zohar, or reciting the midnight service. He
never had a minute to spare. But he found time to
visit my father and talk of Hasidic lore. Reb Moishe,
having been to the courts of almost all the miracle
Rabbis of Poland, was an expert on the Hasidic
dynasties.

As long as we lived at No. 10 Krochmalna Street,
Reb Moishe had no difficulty in visiting us. There the
entrance gate was wide. But when we moved, years
later, to No. 12, the trouble began. The gate was
narrow and right in the middle sat Mirele, the baker's
daughter, by her side baskets heaped with bread,
Sabbath loaves and rolls. Mirele was a girl of
seventeen, but she had the bosom of a mature
woman. Her chest filled half the entryway. Also,
Mirele had the habit of keeping her money in her
stocking. Whenever she was handed a paper bill, she
lifted her skirt and displayed a leg as round as a
cholent pot. Her stocking was held up by a pink
garter. Mirele had no false modesty. And there was
always a group of women and girls standing around

her, feeling the rolls to see whether they were fresh
and their crusts crisp. Some young fellows were also
usually there, gossiping with Mirele and the servant
girls who came to buy her wares.

To pass through such a gate, filled with women
and the lure of the Tempter, was something Reb
Moishe could not do. He would approach and begin to
pound with his walking stick—a signal for the
women to clear his path. Once Mirele angrily shouted
at Reb Moishe: "You pious old oaf, what are you so
afraid of? What makes you think that I want *you*?"

But Reb Moishe would continue pounding with his
stick until Mirele and the women stepped aside out of
his way. Then Reb Moishe would grab the nearest
boy and pass through the gate holding on to him. For,
according to the Law, two men together may walk
through a group of women, since one can guard the
other.

Not only the gateway, the entire courtyard was
filled with obstacles. Servant girls sang, and Reb
Moishe stopped his ears, for *the voice of woman leads
to lewdness*. The sound of gramophones came
through open windows, and sometimes a troupe of
magicians and acrobats gave a performance in the
courtyard; a half-naked girl, wearing short breeches
and a beaded jacket, walked on her hands. Every step
of the way was fraught with danger. Servants sat on
the stairs, grating horseradish and slicing onions.
All the world's females seemed to be waylaying Reb
Moishe Ba-ba-ba, trying to deflect him from the
narrow path of righteousness and lead him to
Gehenna. But Reb Moishe carried his weapon—his
walking stick. He closed his eyes and pounded the
stone flags with his stick.

"Nu!...nu!...nu!..."

Even passing through our kitchen was not easy.
My mother was indeed a pious woman, a Rebbetzin.
But a female is still a female. Reb Moishe would not
even ask her whether my father was at home: he did

not wish to hear her voice. He went straight into the
study. Only there did he open his eyes and call out:
"Ba-ba-ba! Praised be the Almighty!"

"Welcome, Reb Moishe!...Sit down...."

And they would begin to talk about "good Jews"—
that is, Hasidic miracle Rabbis. Reb Moishe told of
one such Rabbi who prayed that he might have only a
small group of followers. He told of another who
performed so many miracles that they sprawled
under the tables and benches of his court. Of a third
he related that even the dead came to see him, and
that he therefore never extinguished the light in his
chamber. I was fascinated most by the story of the
Rabbi who, six nights a week, slept fully dressed.
Why? Because the Messiah might come at any
moment, and the Rabbi did not want to waste time
dressing. This way he would be able to run to greet
him at once. Then, why didn't he do the same on
Sabbath nights? The Messiah will not come on the
Sabbath, for the holiness of the Sabbath is so great
that even the redemption is, by comparison, a
profane thing....All these stories Reb Moishe told
with extraordinary brevity. At the same time he
would mutter to himself, gesticulate with his hands,
pluck at his beard, and call out from time to time: "Ba-
ba-ba." My father each time was astonished over
again by his tales of the saints.

Mother would enter to serve tea. At once Reb
Moishe turned his head and closed his eyes. The
notion that my mother might arouse the evil
inclination in anyone seemed very farfetched to me. I
saw her as an elderly woman, well in her thirties....

"Reb Moishe, how did Reb Haskele look?" my
father asked.

Reb Moishe good-humoredly pretended to be
annoyed by the question.

"How he looked? Like an angel of God! Who could
look straight at his face? One's eyes were blinded. On
Friday nights he would wear a white gabardine, like

the saints of ancient times. He himself recited the
benediction over the Sabbath lights. That was his
way."

"Not the Rebbetzin?"

"The Rebbetzin too."

"It is the first time I have ever heard of that!" my
father exclaimed.

"What do you youngsters know?" Reb Moishe
showed his irritation with my father. "You are
children...mere schoolchildren. You missed it all. Is
this what you call a generation? Boys, only boys.
...Are there today any true Hasidim? You sit in a
train and ride to the Rabbi. What art is there in that?
In my days we went on foot. If you wanted to reach
Kuzmir for Rosh Hashanah, you left home right after
the Sabbath following Tishah b'ab. You went from
inn to inn, and drank a toast in each. The journey
there was a great event in itself. We walked through
the fields and sang Kuzmirer melodies. Sometimes
we spent a night in the woods. In one tavern they
used to keep a keg of brandy in the main room. There
was a straw stuck in the keg, and whoever came in
took a sip. To the side, there was some cold veal, and
everyone had a bite. Hasidim from every town and
city met together and talked for days. When older
Hasidim talked in those days, the young fellows did
not dare to interrupt. Now every snot-nose has
something to say....There was a time when, if a
young fellow was insolent, they held him down on a
wooden bench and gave him a thrashing. And
afterward he had to treat the entire company to
drinks....Approaching within a few miles of Kuzmir, one could already feel its sanctity in the air. We
began to dance and danced our way into Kuzmir...."

"Was it easy to see the Rabbi in person?"

"Easy? Why should things be easy? Sometimes the
Rabbi made his appearance immediately, and
sometimes he remained secluded in his chamber, and
one had to wait for days. The beds in the lodging
houses were made up for us, but we slept on the hard
benches in the study house, just in case the Rabbi

should come out of his chamber. But when the Rabbi did at last appear, the study house was filled with light, literally full with light...."

While Reb Moishe spoke, the door opened and a girl in a red dress, with red slippers on her bare feet, entered.

"I came to ask the Rabbi...."

"Nu, ask!" said my father.

"We were cooking a meat broth, and on the stove some milk boiled over and spilled into it."

"How much was there? How much were you cooking?"

"Ten pounds of meat and two chickens."

"All in one pot?"

"Yes."

"And how much milk spilled into it?"

"Half a quart."

"Half a quart of milk spilled into the broth? How much milk were you boiling?"

"Six quarts."

My father was constantly amazed by the size of the cooking pots used in Warsaw. We never cooked more than a pound of meat at a time, and if one wanted milk, one boiled a half pint or a pint. But it seemed that the Jews of Warsaw were great eaters. They used, not ordinary pots, but veritable caldrons. Again Father asked the girl for the particulars. He could hardly believe that half a quart of milk could boil over all at once. According to the Law, in order for the broth to remain kosher, there had to be sixty times as much meat as milk. He questioned her over and over. It was no light matter to pronounce food unclean that had been bought with hard-earned money. After much hesitation and thought, my father declared: "It is *tref*. The broth may not be eaten, nor may it be sold even to a non-Jew. It must be poured into the sewer."

The girl laughed. "But we've already eaten the broth and the meat too."

My father shuddered. "When? And why did you come to consult me now?"

"I came about the pot."

"But why did you eat without asking? You have
eaten forbidden food!" Father shouted at her.

"Well, everybody was hungry. Mother was not
home...my older sister was serving...."

While the girl spoke, Reb Moishe hissed like a
snake. Had it not been a girl, but a man, he would
have slapped his face. "First they eat unclean food,
these scoundrels, and afterward they come to ask
questions of the Rabbi....Woe is us, the world has
been abandoned!..." Reb Moishe began to grumble,
to cough, to grimace. "They rebel against their
Creator. They devour all manner of vileness and
defilement. Is it any wonder that the coming of the
Messiah is delayed? Is it surprising that we are
sinking into the iniquities of the Egyptians?..."

The girl left. Reb Moishe shook his head from side
to side. "Nu-nu-nu, ba-ba-ba!"

Father tried to resume the talk about Kuzmir, but
Reb Moishe would no longer discuss Hasidic lore.
That the gateway and the courtyard were filled with
levity—that was an old story. But lawlessness could
enter even here, into the Rabbi's own study. Then
there was no escape! Reb Moishe stamped his foot.

"I am fortunate. I am already an old man," he
declared. "But I pity you young men. I pity you. There
may be—God have mercy—another deluge...."

"Who can tell? Perhaps this is the beginning of the
end?" my father half asked, half answered himself.

"Even wickedness must have a limit."

Suddenly Reb Moishe looked at me.

"Come, you will take me through the gate!"

I went down to the courtyard with Reb Moishe and
we approached the gate together. Mirele was about to
give a customer change and was searching through
the paper money in her stocking. Never again have I
seen such a heavy leg. The higher up, the heavier.
Unbelievably fat and thick....

Reb Moishe began to pound with his stick, and
grabbed my shoulder. Mirele stuck out her tongue.

"Here he is banging away again, the Freemason! Such an old billy goat . . . as though I were likely to sin with him!"

"Nu-nu-nu, you hussy!"

Mirele moved aside. Reb Moishe passed by. He leaned heavily upon me, and I thought of the sacrificial animals in the Temple upon whom the Priest laid his hands. Once outside, Reb Moishe took out his kerchief and his snuffbox in order to refresh his disturbed spirit.

"And you—are you studying, ha?"

"Yes, I'm studying."

"You will grow up to be a Jew?"

"Of course."

"Be a real Jew. Perhaps in your day the Messiah will come."

Traitl

IT WAS a summer evening. Father had returned from the evening prayers. He was sitting at the table and eating his customary summer supper: rice boiled in milk. The windows were open. A light breeze blew in from the balcony, bringing with it a hint of smoke. The bakers were already heating their ovens for tomorrow's baking. Suddenly, someone knocked at the kitchen door. My mother, who was also in the study (in the summertime, the ways of our household were somewhat more relaxed than in the winter), sent

me to open the door. A tall man with a white beard
and wild eyes entered. He wore a heavy overcoat and
a fur hat. I was frightened.

"What do you want?"

"So you're Yitshak, eh? You look just like your
grandmother Temerl. You're named after your great-
grandfather, Rabbi Itche Hersh. Aha! Exactly the
same face! He was a wonderful Jew, A saint. Oh, how
quickly the years pass!"

And without more ado, he entered the study. There
he greeted my father.

"Pinhos-Mendel, don't you recognize me? I'm
Traitl."

Father clapped his hands. "Traitl! I can hardly
believe my eyes! *Shalom aleichem.*"

"Yes, I'm Traitl. I've become an old man, eh? I
didn't even know that you're living in Warsaw now."

I had never heard my father called by his first
name or spoken to in such an informal manner. But
this stranger with the heavy boots, long coat, and
wintry hat in the middle of summer, addressed my
father as though he were a mere youngster. Mother
had disappeared into the kitchen.

"Have you just come from Tomaszow?" Father's
tone, too, was friendly and informal.

"No, I haven't been in Tomaszow for years."

"Then where have you been all this time?"

"Where haven't I been? Through the length and
breadth of Poland. I even got as far north as
Lithuania. I travel around."

"Why are you traveling?"

"What do you mean, why? I have to marry off my
daughters. I had seven children, but two died. Moishe
married a girl from Izhbitz. Chave—she is named
after our grandmother Chave—married into a
Yonever family. The other three—Sarah Mindl, Baile
Broche, and Itele—are still at home. How can I marry
them properly without a dowry? The cursed inform-
ers made me a beggar. They—may their name and
memory be wiped out—accused me of being an

embezzler. Sarah Mindl, poor soul, is almost forty
already. An old maid. But I'm collecting a dowry for
each of them. I won't leave this world until I've led
them all to the wedding canopy."

Father grew thoughtful. He was pondering something, and I could see a deep frown on his forehead.
Somehow, I guessed that he was mentally calculat-
ing Sarah Mindl's age, and that by his reckoning she
was well past forty. He began to tuck at his beard.

"Go and wash. You'll eat dinner here."

"I've eaten already. I eat only once a day, at four
o'clock. For years now."

"I see. But where are you staying?"

"I'll spend the night with you."

"Nu, that will be our pleasure. Perhaps you'll take
a glass of tea? A little rice and milk? That's only a
snack."

"I don't drink tea. I eat no dairy foods. After four
o'clock, I never take another bite. But how is it that
you moved to Warsaw? I, you see, have become a
wandering beggar. Do you think I had any choice?
First they informed against me to the authorities;
then they got the Piosker thieves to rob my store.
They took everything and left me with the empty
shelves. I thought I would take a job as a ritual
slaughterer, but the other slaughterers spread the
rumor that my hands are shaky. They are all my
enemies—they'd like to drown me in a thimbleful of
water. It's because I have some learning, and they are
all ignoramuses. I soon saw that things were in a bad
way, so I swallowed my pride and set forth. A dowry
for a bride is an important matter. The matchmakers
wanted to arrange marriages with ignorant louts, but
I wouldn't hear of it. Surely you remember the verse
in the Talmud: 'One is obligated to sell one's house
rather than marry his daughter to an ignorant
man.'"

"But will you at least go back for the holy days?"

"No. I shall be in Rovno, or in Ludmir, or
somewhere else for the holy days. How can I go home

without money? I won't go back until I have a dowry for each of them."

Mother now brought in refreshments: tea and cookies. But the strange visitor would touch nothing.

"I've made my way throughout the world. I've been as far as Russia, into one of the easternmost provinces. When an opportunity comes my way, I'm off. I had no idea you live in Warsaw, but I met someone from home and he told me. What's his name, eh? I've forgotten it already. My memory is a bit weak. What can you know of my miserable lot? If there's a wagon going my way, I ride. If not, I walk. How is your mother?"

"May she live and be well for many years."

"A saintly woman, but yet she is as nothing compared to your grandmother, Hinde Esther. She wore ritual fringes just like a man. Whenever she came to Belz, the Rabbi—Reb Shalom—himself would offer her a chair. She was wise and pious—a rare woman. She bought and sold jewelry and dealt with the courts of the nobility. And your father, may he rest in peace, tasted no meat for seven years and no one knew of his vow except your mother. He was a Cabalist, a holy man. Now among the Lithuanians things are quite different. They have great men too, but they are different. They have a great scholar whose name is Reb Yoisl. Here we would never use such a name. And at the court of the Rabbi of Lubavitch they do not wash before reciting the grace after meals. Such is their custom. In Trisk, I saw a dibbuk. Ordinarily she was a quiet girl, but suddenly she would begin to howl like a dog, and to speak with a man's voice. Then she sang like a cantor, and her voice was as powerful as the roar of a lion. She knew all the prayers by heart. The Rabbi of Trisk gave her an amulet, but it didn't help. Even the saints of today are not the equals of the saints of the past. But yet, people everywhere help me. The world is large and in every corner there are, praised be God, pious Jews. Warsaw is a veritable ocean of people, but here

everyone is always rushing. No one has any time.
What is the hurry? And I want to ask a favor of you."

"What is it?"

"Can I leave some money with you? I always carry
the money on me, but for the Sabbath I can't keep it.
Usually I entrust it to the Rabbi of the town I happen
to be in and take it back when the Sabbath ends. It's
happened that I've been robbed. Once I was staying
in the charitable hostelry of a town, and a thief was
there for the night, too. I had the money in one of my
boots. Early in the morning he took his bundle and
disappeared. No use looking for him. How would I
have recognized him? An ordinary Jew with a beard
and earlocks. Even the Piosker thieves wear beards.
So, I'll leave the money with you. Till after the
Sabbath."

Father frowned. "To tell you the truth, I'm afraid.
This is Warsaw and there are many thieves."

"What are you afraid of? You are an unpaid
guardian, and as such you are not responsible for
theft or loss."

"True, but I don't want to be—God forbid—the
occasion for another's temptation."

"Don't worry, don't worry. Everything happens as
it is determined by Providence. I've been cheated and
robbed ever since I was born. My Sarah Mindl would
have been a grandmother by now if they had not
made me a pauper. But it is as heaven wills it. Can
you hide it somewhere?"

"Where could I hide it? I can only keep it in a
drawer."

"Nu..."

Quickly the white-haired stranger pulled a bundle
of banknotes from his breast pocket. Father looked at
them and said, "At least count it first."

"I can trust you without counting."

"No, count it."

Traitl began to count. He counted rapidly and I
thought that several times he counted two notes as
one. From time to time he moistened his fingers. I am

not sure now exactly how much money there was, but I believe it was several hundred rubles.

He turned to my father. "Put it away in the drawer."

"But it's not even Friday yet. Come here Friday afternoon."

"No, I want to go to the public bathhouse tomorrow. They don't heat it on Fridays."

"But...really, I'm afraid."

"Don't worry. Jews are generous—when they hear that the money is needed for dowering a bride, they give. In one town, I met a shoemaker who is surely one of the thirty-six hidden saints. He and his eight sons are all shoemakers. He gave me quite a bit of his own money, and then he went throughout the town to collect money for me. He is the best shoemaker in the entire province. All the Gentiles come to him. He wears a skullcap even in his workshop, and he can learn some Talmud, too. And in Ludmir there is a butcher who gives away all he owns to charity. Or perhaps he lives in Vladove? My memory is a bit muddled. Then there is one rich man who is so miserly that his wife has to bake the bread three weeks in advance—because fresh bread is eaten too quickly. He never gives a groschen for charity. You meet all kinds of people when you travel. But there is always someone who helps out. Once I have the dowries for all three of them, I'll get them married and I'll stop wandering. For myself, how much do I need? I can get along on bread and borscht. I could become a private tutor, or get a job as a slaughterer...."

The visitor talked far into the night. At last we pushed the benches in the study together and made up a bed for him. He went to sleep about two in the morning. At five o'clock he arose and left.

After my mother heard that we were safeguarding the stranger's money, she would not leave the apartment unwatched. Somewhere she found the key for the drawer and locked it. After all, Krochmalna

Street abounded with thieves. She scolded Father for assuming this responsibility. What would we do if—God forbid—anything were to happen to the money? Especially since it was money dedicated as the dowry for a poor bride. The week passed. On Saturday night we expected Traitl to return and relieve us of the burden. But he did not come. He came neither on Saturday night nor on Sunday, neither on Monday nor on Tuesday. He had disappeared as suddenly as he had come. Who could tell what might have happened to him? Perhaps he would return one day and claim more money?

We took the money from the drawer and stuffed it into a straw mattress. But even this new hiding place did not seem secure enough to my mother and she devised a new scheme: we would conceal the money amid the Passover dishes that were kept on top of the wardrobe with the carved lion's head and the wide cornice.

Weeks passed and there was no sign of Traitl. The summer had gone. Now it was already midwinter. One day, another Tomashov acquaintance visited us. Father asked him whether he knew anything of Traitl's whereabouts.

The man shrugged his shoulders.

"Traitl is not quite right in the head."

"You mean, not sane?"

"That's right."

"But he was here this summer. He wanders around collecting dowries for his daughters."

"What dowries? All his daughters are married."

"What?"

"It's a special kind of madness. Why, was he really here?"

"Yes. He left some money with us and disappeared, like a stone thrown into a lake."

"He's unbalanced...."

I do not remember how much later it was, but one day there was another knock on the door and Traitl entered. He was grayer and more shriveled. He dragged puddles of mud into the house with his heavy boots.

He turned to my father. "I left some money with you."

"But why did you disappear? How can you just go away and disappear for so long?"

"I had to visit a number of places."

"Do you at least know how much money you left here?"

"My memory is weak, but I trust you."

"All this time we couldn't leave the house because of your money. We were afraid that there might be a robbery, God forbid."

"I've been robbed many times before. I had almost reached my last crust of bread—but Jews are merciful souls. That I might only live to marry off my daughters. Sarah Mindl is forty already. Baile Broche is also past thirty. How much longer can they wait?"

"But you haven't been in Tomaszow all this time. Perhaps by now they're married?"

"Without dowries? Nonsense."

"It happens."

"Bah."

"At least, you should inquire."

"No!"

We pushed a table next to the wardrobe and placed a chair on top of the table. Then we took Traitl's money, carefully wrapped in paper, from the basket of Passover dishes. Traitl put the bundle in his pocket without counting it.

"Is Hinde Esther still living? She must be very old now...."

Father shook his head. The man was clearly unbalanced, but only in regard to one idea. Otherwise he told many interesting anecdotes, only interrupting himself from time to time with the refrain: "That I might only live to see my daughters married...."

I Become a Collector

AN UNOFFICIAL RABBI was supported by the people of his neighborhood. In need of his advice on matters of religious law, and knowing that he had to earn a living, they gave various sums each week to a collector. True, the collector made out receipts, but it was an easy matter for him to retain more than the twenty-percent commission that was his due.

Our first collector was an honest man, but he later married and became a ritual slaughterer. Each of those who followed was more of a thief than the last, and it ended with a collector who was taking most of the money himself. Every week he would turn in less and less money, with complaints: "I can't get them to pay!" or "There's a shortage, a crisis!" It was beneath my father's dignity to suspect another Jew.

Finally there wasn't a piece of bread in the house, and the storekeepers refused us credit. I no longer received a daily two-groschen piece for candy or chocolate. We could not pay the rent and the landlord threatened to take us to court and auction our furniture. When Father recited grace, "And let us not partake of the gifts of flesh and blood," he would look heavenward, sighing more deeply than usual. Was it possible to study the Torah and be a Jew if there was no Sabbath food?

One day when Father had been telling me his troubles, I said, "Let me collect!"

Stunned, Father looked at me, "But you're only a boy. You have to study."

"I'll study."

"What do you think Mother would say?"

"Why tell her?"

After deliberating awhile, he said, "Well, we'll try it."

I took the collection tickets to the necessary addresses, and notwithstanding the excuses made by my corrupt predecessor, donations were generous. Since we had discharged the collector, many people were several weeks behind in their payments and within an hour my pockets were full of copper and silver coins. In two hours, finding that both pockets were full, I began stuffing my breast pocket and my trousers.

The shame I had felt diminished. Everyone was so gracious, the men pinching my cheeks, the women blessing me and treating me to cookies, fruit, and candy. My father, they told me, was a godly man, a saint. I kept climbing stairs, knocking at doors. Krochmalna Street, which I had thought I knew, was now turning itself inside out for me. I found tailors, cobblers, furriers, brushmakers, and numerous artisans. In one house, girls were stringing coral, and colorful beads gleamed in piles on tables, chairs, and beds. It looked like an enchanted palace to me.

But when I opened the door of another apartment, I screamed. Dead animals were heaped on the floor. This tenant bought hares from a hunter and sold them to restaurants. In another apartment, girls were winding thread from spindles to bobbins, singing Yiddish songs while bits of thread flew into their disheveled hair.

In one place, people were playing cards, and in another an aged, white-bearded man planed a board while shavings and chips fell everywhere and a bonneted old woman prayed from a holy book. In a bookbinder's apartment I was horrified to find workers tramping over Pentateuchs and other holy books. Then in another apartment I found a female freak with a head that came almost to a point. She had huge calf's eyes and an extraordinarily broad body, and she grunted like a mute and made frightening sounds. Much to my surprise, I found that she had a husband.

Somewhere else I saw a sallow-faced, paralyzed man lying on a kind of shelf while a woman fed him and the food dribbled over his withered beard. His eyes seemed crossed. I shut that door almost as soon as I opened it. Up an incredibly filthy stairway I climbed to an attic, past barefoot scurvy children playing with shards and mud. One boy's skull had been shaved. He was pale, his ears were swollen, and he had long unkempt sidelocks. A girl spat at him and he cried out some kind of curse. Taking out a ticket, I asked, "Where does Yenta Flederbaum live?"

"In the *shtchunka*..."

In Warsaw this was the term for a dark hallway. I was inclined to be fearful, but that day I was somehow infused with great courage, as if I had been transformed. Stumbling along the dark corridor, bumping into baskets and crates, I heard a rustling noise, as if mice were about. Lighting a match, I discovered that there were no numbers or even latches on the doors. When I pushed one open, I was transfixed by what I saw. A corpse wrapped in a sheet lay on the floor, a pair of candles at its head and a woman beside it on a footstool, weeping, wringing her hands, and crying out. The mirror on the opposite wall had been draped. My ribs tingling with fright, I slammed the door and backed into the hallway, fiery spots before my eyes, my ears throbbing. I began to run but became entangled in a basket or crate. It was as if someone had clutched my coattail, drawing me backward; bony fingers dug into me, I heard a dreadful scream. In a cold sweat, I ran out, tearing my gabardine. There would be no more collecting for

me. I threw up, and shivered. The coins burdened me
as I walked. It seemed to me that I had grown old in
that one day.

I had no appetite, even though I hadn't eaten since
morning. My stomach felt swollen. I went into the
study house, deserted because it was midday, and,
like an old man, sat there, resting, with aching feet
and a pounding head. I looked at the sacred books
and felt estranged from them; I seemed to have
forgotten my studies.

Suddenly I realized that I had done something
wrong, and felt contemptuous of myself. I made a
resolution then to which I still adhere: never do
anything for money that goes against the grain, and
avoid favors and presents. I wanted to relieve myself
as soon as possible of the miserable job.

When I arrived home, Mother happened to be out
and Father, in his study, looked at me anxiously,
asking, "Where were you all day?" Then he blurted,
"I'm sorry about the whole thing. You've got to
continue studying..."

Emptying my pockets, I discovered that I had
collected more in a day than the collector had given
us in a month. Without counting the money, Father
shoved it into a drawer. I felt relieved.

"I can't do it any more," I said.

"God forbid!"

But the new collector also stole. Finally Father put
up a notice that no more money should be given the
collector. He tried to get along on his fees from
lawsuits, weddings, and divorces, but our situation
grew worse, and even though he took pupils they did
not remain with him very long. Mother went on a trip
to Bilgoray to get help from her father and stayed
there for weeks.

At home there was chaos. We lived on dry food and
there was no one to supervise me, but I suddenly felt a
great urge to study. I began in some inexplicable way
to "read" a page from the Germara by myself and

even to understand a commentary. I examined
Maimonides's *The Strong Hand* and other books that
I had not until then understood. One day in my
father's bookcase I found a book of the Cabala, *The
Pillar of Service* by Reb Baruch Kosower. Although I
missed the meaning of most of it, I did understand a
little. A part of my brain that had been sealed seemed
to be opening. I now experienced the profound joy of
learning...

My Sister

ALTHOUGH WE WERE not acquainted with Freud in
those days, it could be said that a Freudian drama
was occurring at home. My sister suspected my
mother of not loving her, which was untrue, but
actually they were incompatible. My brother Israel
Joshua took after my mother's family, but Hinde
Esther had inherited the Hasidic inspiration, the love
of humanity, and the eccentric nature of Father's
side. Had she lived in another era, she might have
become a female saint, or like the Baal Shem's
daughter, Hodel, who had danced with the Hasidim.
Our great-grandmother, whose namesake my sister
was, used to wear ritual fringes and visit the Belz
Rabbi like a man. My sister was akin to all the saintly
female Rebbetzins who fasted and made pilgrimages
to Palestine to pray at ancient graves. Hers was a life
of holidays, hymns, hope, and exultation. She was a

Hasid in skirts; but she suffered from hysteria and had mild attacks of epilepsy. At times, she seemed possessed by a dibbuk.

My father ignored her because she was a girl, and my mother could not understand her. In her spare moments Mother would read a book of moral instruction, scarcely glancing out of the window unless it was with a distant and dejected gaze. The rabble and the noise distressed her, she was interested only in thought. My sister, on the other hand, kept chattering, singing, and laughing all day long, expressing opinions that she should have kept to herself. Whoever she liked was praised excessively, and those she disliked received unrelenting abuse. She tended toward exaggeration, leaping when joyous, crying when unhappy, and sometimes falling into a faint. In her jealousy of my brother Israel Joshua, she made up numerous accusations, but then, regretting what she had done, she would want to kiss him. After weeping furiously, her spirit would suddenly soar, and she would begin to dance. We younger children were always being kissed and fondled by her.

Everything was momentous to her. A barber who worked across the street from us fell in love with my sister and sent her a mash note. My sister, immediately assuming that everyone knew about it and would gossip, became afraid to go into the street. It took a long time to convince her that other girls too received such notes and that no one would blame her for it.

One Sabbath, hearing her wailing in the kitchen, I ran in to find a fire burning in the stove. She had put into it the dried papers used to cover the Sabbath meal, and a spark had ignited them. It was only after we explained what had happened that she gave up her notion that a demon had stolen in there.

She wasn't the kind of a girl who could be married off easily, but she was pretty, and a match was proposed. A Warsaw man, Reb Gedaliah, managed the money collected for a yeshivah in Palestine. His sons had escaped the draft by going to Belgium, where they became diamond cutters. But his control over them was still so great that he even arranged their marriages from a distance. Hearing that my father had a daughter, Reb Gedaliah sent a matchmaker before he too visited us. Tall and heavy-set, with a fan-shaped beard and smoking a cigar, he showed us a photograph of his son, a handsome young man with a rounded beard but dressed in modern clothes. In Antwerp, where his son lived, Reb Gedaliah told us, he prayed daily, ate only kosher food, and studied the Talmud. Proof of his piety was the fact that he had let his father choose a bride for him. Like Eliezer, Abraham's slave, who had come to take Rebecca to Isaac, Reb Gedaliah came to us.

My father frowned, worried about sending his only daughter beyond the frontier. But Mother was pleased; it had become increasingly difficult to live with this erratic girl. My sister, who had already acquired some modern ideas, and read Yiddish newspapers and books, longed for a romance, not an arranged marriage. Sometimes she would put on a hat and walk with her girl friends in the Saxony Gardens. What decided things was that my father had no money for a dowry and Reb Gedaliah did not demand one. I remember the evening when, in our brightly lit apartment, the preliminary arrangements were written up and sent by express to the prospective bridegroom in Antwerp for his signature. In my father's study the table was set with refreshments, as though it were Purim. Smoking a cigar in an amber holder, Reb Gedaliah discussed Torah with my father. Then he presented my sister with a golden chain which he took from a jewelry box. His wife was a stout, large-bosomed woman, and his daughters had extraordinarily long hair. The daughters had to wait for this son to marry before they could take their turn. There was so much talk of the prospective bridegroom that I felt as if he were there. In an optimistic mood, my sister blushed, laughed, and thanked everyone for the presents, compliments, promises, and good wishes.

I heard Father ask where the wedding would be, and Reb Gedaliah answered, "In Berlin."

Father was astonished, but Reb Gedaliah said, "Don't worry. There are Jews everywhere. I've been to Berlin several times, and it has everything you'd want, houses of prayer, study houses, ritual baths. Berliners visit the Rabbi of Gur, and they are very generous in their donations."

"Praised be the name of god..."

"Antwerp," Reb Gedaliah continued, "is very Jewish too. I've been to Paris as well, and rode an elevator up a tremendous tower. I spoke to the Paris Rabbi, a genius. I have a letter from him. He speaks French."

Both Father and I were astounded that a Rabbi could speak French and live in Paris. But Father only clutched his beard silently, and Mother too was quiet at the women's table. She had no patience for their small talk about jewelry, clothes, shoes, food, and bargains. In contrast to these stylish women, my mother wore a dress that had been made for her wedding.

Following the sending of preliminary contracts, letters in a German Yiddish began to arrive from the groom-to-be. In my sister's answering letters, the first literary spark in our family became apparent. She wrote long, intelligent, even humorous letters, of which my father was unaware, but my mother was amazed that her daughter had acquired such command of words. How had it come about? Hinde Esther had only a little while before arrived from Leoncin and Radzymin. My mother herself was a marvelous storyteller, but not much of a writer. Her own letters all followed a formula and were brief.

Other strange and unexpected things began to happen at home. While still attending the study house, my brother Israel Joshua was beset with an urge to draw. Surreptitiously, he bought paper, pencils, charcoal, and paints, and began to paint landscapes, trees, flowers, cows, peasants, and huts with straw roofs and smoking chimneys. He also concealed from Father a Russian grammar textbook and Yiddish books, which he called "literature." He told us that in Palestine there were colonies where young Jews plowed the earth and herded sheep as in King David's time, and that in Russia there were revolutionaries planning to overthrow the Tsar and abolish money. In America, he said, there were millionaires richer than Rothschild, who had to be guarded against criminals called "The Black Hand." Everything he said was imbedded in my brain. Closing my eyes, I saw shapes and colors that I had never seen before, which kept shifting into new designs and forms. Sometimes I saw a fiery eye, brighter than the sun and with a weird pupil. To this day, when I try to do so, I can still see this radiant eye. My memory of those days is full of visionary flowers and gems. But at that time the visions were so numerous that sometimes I could not get rid of them.

A worldly excitement swept through our house as a result of my sister's engagement. A trousseau was prepared, the mother-in-law engaging tailors from the better streets, while Father borrowed money from a loan company. Our apartment was filled with silk, velvet, plush, pleated dresses, tape measures, and bed linen. Although usually in a good mood, my sister would sometimes become upset, telling my mother, "You're sending me away because you hate me!"

"Woe is me, you're driving me crazy!"

"It's true."

"Look. I'll call off the wedding!"

"No. I'd rather go into exile. I'll disappear. You won't know what happened to my remains...."

Before Mother could answer, my sister laughed and fainted, but she always did so in such a way that she would not get hurt. She swooned, blinked, and smiled. Yet, even though she seemed to be pretending, it was all terribly real.

I, too, was affected by modern ideas. I even began to write, in my own fashion. Taking sheets of paper from my father's drawer, I covered them with scribbles and freakish sketches. I was so eager to indulge in this infantile writing that I could scarcely wait for the Sabbath to terminate so that I could get back to it.

Mother, observing me, would say, "What do you think you're doing? Normal children don't act that way."

The Miracle

EVEN THOUGH we had moved to Warsaw, Father kept up his connection with the Radzymin Rabbi, visiting him occasionally and praying at the Radzymin study house in No. 12 Krochmalna Street.

A fellow worshipper there was Reb Joseph Mattes, or Reb Joseph Goosedealer, as he was called, since his wife was a goose dealer in Yanash's court. Only among Polish Jews could someone like Reb Joseph be found. Torah, Hasidism, charity, and good deeds occupied him constantly; he was always praying, studying, reciting the Zohar, or helping impoverished men. Heavy-set, with a blond beard and a ruddy face, he had eyes that emanated piety, good nature, and the delight of those who take pride in serving God.

The goose dealers in Yanash's court did not have the best of reputations, since the foul oaths and curses they uttered while making a sale were indispensable to their business. My mother, therefore, was afraid of having anything to do with them. They were capable of tearing the wig off a housewife who dared to haggle. Even before a customer approached to ask the price, a dealer might begin this kind of soliloquy:

"You think this is a goose? God in heaven, it's a calf! Look how the fat pours off—our enemies should only melt from envy. If this goose doesn't feed you for a week, may I get a fire in my belly, a heart attack; I shouldn't live to marry off my youngest daughter— dear God, she should stand beneath a black canopy! You think I'm making money from you? For every groschen profit you give me, I should get a plague. If I'm not losing money, let them put shards on my eyes. Someone offered me a ruble more, we should both live so long, but it's Thursday and I don't want to be stuck with the bird over the Sabbath. I don't keep meat on ice—may our enemies lie on the ground with boils and blisters on their heads, and poison in their blood..."

Some of the goose dealers were masters of the language, creating words and similes and adjusting their curses to fit the time of year. For the Great Hosanna they would wish the black seal, for Rosh Hashanah and Yom Kippur a death verdict. Reb Joseph Mattes's wife was one of the goose dealers whose mouth, even in Yanash's court, couldn't be matched.

A loud-mouthed shrew, she earned a fine living, and her husband, who never entered the store, gave half of it to charity. Of her children, the daughter assisted her mother in the goose business, and the

daughter's husband, a delicate young man, spent his
time being Jewish, and often visited Radzymin for
months. In that family the men all studied the
Talmud and the women provided for them. But there
was one tragedy: the daughter's children were all
stillborn, despite annual promises from the Radzymin Rabbi that she would deliver a living male child. It
was the opinion of doctors that she needed an
operation, for her own life was endangered more with
each stillbirth. Whenever Reb Joseph asked the
Radzymin Rabbi for advice, he would answer, "I hate
the knife!"

Finally, one year, the Warsaw obstetrician refused
to deliver the child and advised the woman to go
abroad, to Vienna. This meant she would have an
operation—a great blow to the Radzymin court. But
soon after her departure a telegram came saying that
she had borne a living child. The telegram had come
so quickly that it was assumed there had been no time
to operate.

It was during the Passover holiday, and Reb
Joseph had a party, which I attended. There was
dancing, singing, wines, and mead, and innumerable
delicacies served by the maid and her assistants, but
what I remember best is Joseph Mattes climbing on a
table, holding a huge matzoth pancake, and shouting, "Jews, this is the first chapter!"

The Hasidim tore the pancake into pieces. "This is
the second chapter!"

The Hasidim tore it into shreds. "This is the third
chapter!"

In less than a second, the pancake became nothing.

In the midst of the celebration, a Gentile Letter
carrier wearing an official's cap and brass buttons on
his uniform entered with a special-delivery letter
from Vienna. Reb Joseph climbed down, gave the
man a few kopecks' tip, and climbed back to the table
to read aloud what he supposed was a description of

the Radzymin Rabbi's miracle. But the longer he
read, the more distracted he grew, swallowing words,
stammering, pausing. His voice caught in his throat,
his beard tossed.

What had happened was that as soon as his
daughter was admitted to the Vienna hospital she
was operated on because both she and the child were
in danger. Only because of the operation had she
borne a living child.

I have seldom witnessed anything more dramatic.
The celebration came to a halt, and the Hasidim
stood there with disheveled beards, gaping eyes, and
pale faces. The entire Radzymin court was about to
totter. All the Hasidim in all the Warsaw study
houses already knew of the supposed miracle.

Suddenly Reb Joseph called out, "Jews, don't you
see—this is an even greater miracle!"

And beginning to dance, he stamped his feet so
vigorously that the table cracked beneath his weight.
As if the crowd had been waiting for this signal, they
took up the dance also, singing lustily. They were
determined not to be trapped by Satan, or by reason
or facts. Despite their terrible defeat and the way it
would be used by their enemies, the Radzymin
Hasidim, by turning that defeat into a victory,
showed that they still believed in their saint. Years
later I observed that political groups were familiar
with the trick, as one could tell by the way they
twisted facts and corrupted logic, but on the day of
the Mattes celebration I was totally confused. I
wished the dancing and noise would come to a halt so
that I could ask my father for an explanation. But the
excitement gained momentum, flourishing on more
wine and mead, pancakes, and matzoth brei. Drunk-
en Hasidim drenched in perspiration wriggled
around dancing and shouting hoarsely. Unable to
speak any longer, Reb Joseph jerked his body, moved
his mouth, raised his hands. Everyone seemed to be
saying, "To Radzymin we all remain true!"

The news spread rapidly through Warsaw, and the Alexandrower, Pulawer, and Skolower Hasidim had something to ridicule. They teased and vilified the Radzymin Hasidim—who made no effort to defend themselves. Why argue with enemies? In the Radzymin study house, no one dared ask questions. The Radzymin Rabbi, nevertheless, remained constant in his beliefs—or obstinate, refusing an operation years later and dying because of his refusal.

Whether or not my brother Israel Joshua attended this party, I don't recall, but he was certainly aware of what went on there, and it did nothing to strengthen his faith in Hasidism. As usual, my father came to the Rabbi's defense.

"It's possible for a saint to be incapable of miracles."

But my mother said, "How can a fool be a saint?"

"Go on! Corrupt the children!" Father said.

"I want my children to believe in God, not in an idiot," Mother replied.

"First it will be the Radzymin Rabbi, tomorrow all Rabbis, and then, God forbid, the Baal Shem himself," Father cried.

He was right. Even though my brother still dressed as a Hasid, he spent more and more time painting and reading worldly books, debating at length with Mother, telling her about Copernicus, Darwin, and Newton, of whom she had already read in Hebrew books. She had a predilection for philosophy and countered my brother's views with the kind of arguments religious philosophers still use.

Even though I was only a boy then and did not have the courage to comment, I was filled with questions, which I would take out to the balcony to ponder. Breaking a piece of lime from the wall, I crushed it between my fingers until it became granular. But it was still lime, and what would happen if it were ground even finer? How minute could it become? Was there a limit? Everything, I thought, could be made smaller, perhaps divided up endlessly.... If that is so, every speck of lime had an infinity of parts. But how could this be?

Even before I learned to read or write, I was obsessed by the paradoxes of time, space, and infinity, and moreover I was convinced that only I myself could reason out such enigmas, that no one could help me.

Once when I had brought home a herring for my mother I took the newspaper it was wrapped in out to the balcony and tried to determine what it was all about. I wondered if I would ever understand that Gentile language or the subjects with which it was concerned. For Father the answer to all questions was God. But how did he know there was a God, since no one saw Him? But if He did not exist, who had created the world, how could a thing give birth to itself? And what happened when someone died? Was there really heaven and hell? Or was a dead person no better off than a dead insect?

I do not recall a time when these questions did not torment me.

Reb Asher the Dairyman

THERE ARE SOME PEOPLE in this world who are simply born good. Such was Reb Asher the dairyman. God had endowed him with many, many gifts. He was tall, broad, strong, with a black beard, large black eyes, and the voice of a lion. On the New Year and the Day of Atonement he served as cantor of the main prayer for the congregation that met in our house, and it was his voice that attracted many of the worshippers. He did this without payment, although he could have commanded sizable fees from some of the larger synagogues. It was his way of helping my father earn a livelihood for the holidays. And as if this were not enough, Reb Asher was always doing something for us in one way or another. No one sent my father as generous a Purim gift as did Reb Asher the dairyman. When Father found himself in great straits and could not pay the rent, he sent me to Reb Asher to borrow the money. And Asher never said no, nor did he ever pull a wry face. He simply reached into his trouser pocket and pulled out a handful of paper money and silver. Neither did he limit himself to helping out my father. He gave charity in all directions. This simple Jew, who with great difficulty plowed through a chapter of the Mishnah, lived his entire life on the highest ethical plane. What others preached, he practiced.

He was no millionaire, he was not even wealthy, but he had a "comfortable income," as my father would put it. I myself often bought milk, butter, cheese, clabber, and cream in his shop. His wife and their eldest daughter waited on customers all day long, from early in the morning till late at night. His wife was a stout woman, with a blond wig, puffy cheeks, and a neck covered with freckles. She was the daughter of a farm bailiff. Her enormous bosom seemed to be swollen with milk. I used to imagine that if someone were to cut her arm, milk would spurt forth, and not blood. One son, Yudl, was so fat that people came to stare at him as at a freak. He weighed nearly ten pood. Another son, slight of build and something of a dandy, had become a tailor and gone off to Paris. A younger son was still studying at the heder, and a little girl attended a secular school.

Just as our house was always filled with problems, doubts, and unrest, so everything in Asher's house was whole, placid, healthy. Every day Asher went to

bring the cans of milk from the train. He rose at the
break of dawn, went to the synagogue, and then
drove to the railroad depot. He worked at least
eighteen hours every day, yet on the Sabbath, instead
of resting, he would go to listen to a preacher or come
to my father to study a portion of the Pentateuch with
the commentary of Rashi. Just as he loved his work,
so he loved his Judaism. It seems to me that I never
heard this man say no. His entire life was one great
yes.

Asher owned a horse and wagon, and this horse
and wagon aroused a fierce envy in me. How happy
must be the boy whose father owned a wagon, a
horse, a stable! Every day Asher went off to distant
parts of the city, even to Praga! Often I would see him
driving past our house. He never forgot to lift his
head and to greet whomever he saw at the window or
on the balcony. Often he met me when I was running
about the streets with a gang of boys or playing with
those who were not "my kind," but he never
threatened to tell my father, nor did he try to lecture
to me. He did not, like the other grown-ups, pull little
boys by the ear, pinch their noses, or twist the brims
of their caps. Asher seemed to have an innate respect
for every one, big or small.

Once when I saw him driving by in his wagon I
nodded to him and called out: "Reb Asher, take me
along!"

Asher immediately stopped and told me to get on.
We drove to a train depot. The trip took several hours
and I was overjoyed. I rode amid trolley cars,
droshkies, loading vans. Soldiers marched; policemen stood guard; fire engines, ambulances, even
some of the automobiles that were just beginning to
appear on the streets of Warsaw rushed past us.
Nothing could harm me. I was protected by a friend
with a whip, and beneath my feet I could feel the
throbbing of the wheels. It seemed to me that all
Warsaw must envy me. And indeed people stared in
wonderment at the little Hasid with the velvet cap

and the red earlocks who was riding in a milk wagon surveying the city. It was evident that I did not really belong to this wagon, that I was a strange kind of tourist...

From that day on, a silent pact existed between me and Reb Asher. Whenever he could, he would take me along as his passenger. Fraught with danger were those minutes when Reb Asher went off to fetch the milk cans from the train, or to attend to a bill, and I remained alone in the wagon. The horse would turn his head and stare at me in astonishment. Asher had given me the reins to hold, and the horse seemed to be saying silently: "Just look who is my driver now..." The fear that the horse might suddenly rear up and run off gave to these moments the extra filip of peril. After all, a horse is not a child's plaything but a gigantic creature, silent, wild, with enormous strength. Occasionally a Gentile would pass by, look at me, laugh, and say something to me in Polish. I did not understand his language, and he cast the same sort of dread upon me as did the horse: he too was big, strong, and incomprehensible. He too might suddenly turn upon me and strike me, or yank at my earlock—a pastime the Poles considered a great joke....

When I thought the end had come—any moment now the Gentile would strike me, or the horse would dash off and smash into a wall or a street lamp—then Reb Asher reappeared and all was well again. Asher carried the heavy milk cans with the ease of a Samson. He was stronger than the horse, stronger than the Gentile, yet he had mild eyes and spoke my language, and he was my father's friend. I had only one desire: to ride with this man for days and nights over fields and through forests, to Africa, to America, to the ends of the world, and always to watch, to observe all that was going on around me...

How different this same Asher appeared on the New Year and the Day of Atonement! Carpenters had put up benches in my father's study, and this was where the women prayed. The beds had been taken out of the bedroom, a Holy Ark brought in, and it had become a tiny prayer house. Asher was dressed in a white robe, against which his black beard appeared even blacker. On his head he wore a high cap embroidered with gold and silver. At the beginning of the Additional Service, Reb Asher would ascend to the cantor's desk and call out with the roaring of a lion: "Behold me, destitute of good works..."

Our bedroom was too small for the bass voice that thundered forth from this mighty breast. It was heard halfway down the street. Asher recited and chanted. He knew every melody, every movement. The twenty men who made up our congregation were all part of his choir. Asher's deep masculine voice aroused a tumult in the women's section. True, they all knew him well. Only yesterday they had bought from him or from his wife a saucepan of milk, a pot of clabber, a few ounces of butter, and had bargained with him for a little extra. But now Asher was the delegate who offered up the prayers of the People of Israel directly to the Almighty, before the Throne of Glory, amid fluttering angels and books that read themselves, in which are recorded the good deeds and the sins of every mortal soul.... When he reached the prayer "We will express the might," and began to recite the destinies of men—who shall live and who shall die, who shall perish by fire and who by water— a sobbing broke out among the women. But when Asher called out triumphantly: "But repentance, prayer, and charity can avert the evil decree!"—then a heavy stone was taken from every heart. Soon Asher began to sing of the smallness of man and the greatness of God, and joy and comfort enveloped everyone. Why need men—who are but passing shadows, wilting blossoms—expect malice from a God who is just, revered, merciful? Every word that Asher called out, every note he uttered restored courage, revived hope. We indeed are nothing, but He is all. We are but as dust in our lifetime, and less than

dust after death, but He is eternal and His days shall
never end. In Him, only in Him, lies our hope...

One year, at the close of the Day of Atonement, this
same Asher, our friend and benefactor, saved our
very lives. It happened in this manner. After the day-
long fast, we had eaten the repast. Later a number of
Jews gathered in our house to dance and rejoice. My
father had already put up the first beam of the hut for
the coming Festival of Tabernacles. Late that night
we had at last fallen asleep. Since benches and pews
had been set up in the bedroom, and the entire house
was in disorder, each of us slept wherever he could
find a spot. But one thing we had forgotten—to
extinguish the candles that were still burning on
some of the pews.

Late that night Asher had to drive to the railroad
station to pick up milk. He passed our house and
noticed that it was unusually bright. This was not the
glow of candles, or of a lamp, but rather the glare of a
great fire. Asher realized that our house must be
burning. He rang the bell at the gate, but the janitor
did not rush to open it. He too was asleep. Then Asher
set to ringing the bell and beating on the door with
such a furor that at last the Gentile awoke and
opened the gate. Asher raced up the stairs and
knocked on our door, but no one answered. Then
Asher the mighty hurled his broad shoulders against
the door and forced it open. Bursting into the house,
he found the entire family asleep while all around,
benches, prayer stands, prayer books, and holiday
prayer books were aflame. He began to call out in his
booming cantorial voice and finally roused us, and
then he tore off our quilts and set to smothering the
conflagration.

I remember that moment as though it had been
yesterday. I opened my eyes and saw many flames,
large and small, rolling about and dancing like imps.
My brother Moishe's blanket had already caught fire.
But I was very young and was not frightened. On the
contrary, I liked the dancing flames.

After some time the fire was put out. Here indeed something had happened that might well be called a miracle. A few minutes more, and we would all have been enveloped by the flames, for the wood of the benches was dry and they were saturated with the tallow of the dripping candles. Asher was the only human being who was awake at that hour and who was prepared to be so persistent with the ringing of the bell and who would risk his own life for us. Yes, it was fated that this faithful friend should save us from an infernal fire.

We were not even able to thank. It was as though we had all been struck dumb. Asher himself was in a hurry and left quickly. We wandered about amid the charred benches, tables, prayer books, and prayer shawls, and every few minutes we discovered more sparks and smoldering embers. We might all easily have been burnt to cinders.

The friendship between my father and Reb Asher grew ever stronger, and during the war years, when we were close to starvation, Asher again helped us in every way he could.

After we had left Warsaw (during the First World War), we continued to hear news of him from time to time. One son died, a daughter fell in love with a young man of low origins and Asher was deeply grieved. I do not know whether he lived to see the Nazi occupation of Warsaw. He probably died before that. But such Jews as he were dragged off to Treblinka. May these memoirs serve as a monument to him and his like, who lived in sanctity and died as martyrs.

The Lawsuit

THE ONLY YIDDISH WRITER whom I knew personally
when I was a child was the celebrated Simcha
Pietrushka, who translated the Mishnah into Yiddish. When Father was the head of the Radzymin
yeshivah, Pietrushka was his pupil. I often heard my
father speak of Pietrushka's genius; there was one
story he repeated many times. Pietrushka, it seems,
made a wager that he could commit to memory in the
space of a single summer's night the two treatises of
the Talmud called Zbachim and Minachot. These
treatises, which are notoriously difficult to understand, concern themselves with the temple, its rites,
and the vessels used for sacrifice. Many Talmudic
scholars do not bother to study them. Their texts are
too long even to be recited in several days. But
Simcha Pietrushka mumbled and flipped pages from
sundown to sunrise. In the morning, Father found to
his amazement, when he tested his pupil, that
Pietrushka knew not only the body of the text but
every footnote and gloss.

A skeptic might argue that Pietrushka had
already memorized the work, but this in itself would
have been a remarkable feat for a boy his age.
Pietrushka had almost total recall.

I knew one other prodigy, the son of the Rabbi who
lived at No. 11 Grzybowska Street. If I remember
correctly, the Rabbi's name was Reb Mayerl. His son,

though brought up piously, later went bad, as did
Pietrushka. Mayerl's son started to write his own
encyclopedia, keeping his notes in sacks which he
stored in the attic. People who read sections of this
never-completed encyclopedia said that there were
passages which could only have been written by a
genius. Reb Mayerl's son literally knew the Talmud
by heart.

When I was small, a Warsaw watch manufacturer
by the name of Reb Meir Yoel advertised that he
would give a watch to any boy who could prove that
he knew fifty pages of the Talmud by heart. These
watches had Hebrew characters on their dials and
bore the inscription "For excellence in studies." To
win such a prize (which was probably worth no more
than three or four rubles), a boy had to bring
affidavits from three Rabbis attesting that he knew
the required fifty pages. Meir Yoel's offer caused a
sensation in the Hasidic study houses, and hundreds,
maybe thousands of boys began to memorize the
Talmud. Our house was besieged by these ambitious
students; Rabbis paid by the community rarely had
time for such activities. Father would usher the boys
into his study and test them thoroughly; when now
and again one stumbled over a passage, Father
would supply the necessary word. Afterward he
would write an enthusiastic letter for each, and affix
his stamp to it. I always managed to be present when
these savants were tested. I myself was learning the
Mishnah; for every chapter I memorized, my father
gave me a kopeck. To this day I still remember a few
of the chapters I learned then.

My father, author of religious books, was in his
own fashion a "littérateur." Since I was curious
about what he wrote, Father confided his views to me.
He had his favorites among the commentaries, and
those which he considered incomprehensible. Assuming that when I grew up I too would write
religious books, he gave me the following advice. "Be
straightforward in your reasoning and avoid casuis-

try. None of the great scholars tortured the text. True, they dug deeply, but they never made mountains out of molehills."

Every morning before prayertime Father sat by a window that looked out onto the square, smoking his pipe and drinking innumerable glasses of tea as he studied and wrote. Before Father's eyes, thieves picked pockets, snatched bundles, and conducted their crooked lotteries. But Father, never having taken notice, was absolutely unaware of their existence. The neighborhood teemed with Zionists, socialists, territorialists, assimilationists. Yiddish and Hebrew secular literature already existed, but to Father, all of this non-Jewishness signified nothing.

One Sabbath evening we heard the screams of a woman. In a moment Krochmalna Street was black with people. From every doorway, there ran boys and girls. Father walked out onto the balcony and inquired of our neighbor Reb Haim what had happened.

"It's nothing for you to worry about, Rabbi. Some girl's been raped."

The word Reb Haim used was not actually "raped" but a gutter equivalent. Embarrassed, Father went inside and ordered the windows to be shut. Just a few feet away from him, abominations were being committed. Only a thin wall separated his study from the forces of evil.

Another time a revolver showed up in our house.

It happened this way. Suddenly the street door swung open, admitting several tough-looking characters. They wore light-colored jackets, wide trousers, and gleaming hightop boots. With them came the smell of alcohol and something else dissolute and unkosher; they were talking excitedly in coarse voices. Accompanying them was a stooped, wrinkled little man with a patchy beard, wearing a short gabardine that was neither the costume of a Jew nor the dress of a Gentile. It was hard to determine whether he was prematurely old or seriously ill. He had bushy brows and pouchy eyes beneath which hung what looked like violet moss. Though Father was frightened, he asked the group to be seated. "What can I do for you?" he inquired.

"Rabbi, we want you to settle a suit."

"Well, all right—who is suing whom?"

"We're suing him, Rabbi." The most arrogant of the men pointed to the old fellow.

"Since you're the plaintiff, you speak first."

"Rabbi," the hoodlum shouted, "we've been dealing with this wretch for years. He's already made several fortunes off of us. He's nothing but a filthy bloodsucker. He's robbed us, Rabbi, fleeced us out of thousands. We believed him, Rabbi. We trusted him like our own father. Rabbi, this man is no Jew; he doesn't have a Jewish heart. We were dumbbells, Rabbi, and he made fools of us. If I'm lying, may I never live to see my daughter under the wedding canopy."

"Calm yourself, please. What sort of dealings did you have with him?" Father asked.

"What difference does that make? We did business together."

"In a lawsuit, one has to know these things."

"We bought all sort of things from him: horses, oats, sometimes even a carriage. He supplied us with whatever we needed. We trusted him like a brother and thought of him as one of us. You might say that it had to do with confidential matters. But he swindled us, Rabbi. He tried to make out that he was giving us everything just a little above cost. He robbed us. We demand that we get back what we overpaid him. Twenty thousand rubles."

"Do you have any records of the transactions?"

"We don't keep records. We do everything with a handshake. We're not bookkeepers. A man's word with us is as holy as the Torah. We didn't haggle; everything was done over a glass of beer. We'd have knifed anyone who said a bad word about this man. But now, Rabbi, we've found out that he is a usurer.

We want our money back, or else..." The speaker
broke off and banged his large fist on the table.

The old man opened his toothless mouth as if to
speak, but no words came out. He began to creak like
an old clock before it rings. His mangy beard
trembled and twisted; his entire body shook jerkily.
Then suddenly the old fellow found his voice and
began speaking with great firmness. "Rabbi, do you
know what this bunch is and why they don't keep
records? They've been in and out of jail so often they
never learned to write. If I didn't help out their wives,
the poor women would starve to death. They don't
keep records, Rabbi, but I do. I write down everything
in my ledger—every ruble, every groschen. Here,
Rabbi, I've brought the book."

And with a wizened hand the old man drew from
his pocket a book that looked as ancient and wrinkled
as he did. The pages were frayed at the edges. Inside
the book, the various transactions were written in a
faded, half-obliterated script; the entries were so
dense, one line crept into the next.

"Here, Rabbi, just take a look. See for yourself."

Taking the book, Father leafed through it. Then he
handed it back. "I can't read accounts."

"Let them pay a bookkeeper to look through them.
Everything is marked down."

"We don't need a bookkeeper. Give us back our
money."

"What you'll get from me is a boil on your
backside," the old man said, raising his brows and
looking out at the men as if from a deep cave.

One of the gang drew a revolver. It was the first
time I had ever seen this instrument of death. Father
paled and I caught my breath. The old man
snickered. "Go ahead and shoot, you blockheads. Do
you think you can scare me with a gun?"

Father suddenly began to speak in a hoarse voice.
"Men, in this room the Law is sacred. If you want to
act in violence, you must leave here."

"Don't be afraid, Rabbi, we won't hurt you."

"People come to me with lawsuits, not with weapons. No good can come from such things."

"Put away the gun."

The curses, shouts, and recriminations continued for an entire hour. The thugs alternated between threats and entreaties, pounded their breasts and swore powerful oaths. They mentioned the wonderful times they'd all had together in various restaurants and taverns. The old man gave back as much as he received, called his accusers apes, mongrels, jailbirds, scum. He lashed them unmercifully with his tongue. Father looked on, bewildered. Occasionally he stared at me quizzically. At times even the slight trace of a smile appeared within the thicket of his beard. The old, apparently moribund man more than held his own against these brutish, almost incomprehensible people. In the end, nothing was resolved. They continued to argue and fight until they got up and left.

Oddly enough, the old man's courage and stubbornness had captured my father's imagination. He spoke about the incident for a long time afterward. Even among the worldly rabble, force wasn't everything. The power of the word here had been stronger than that of the revolver. It brought to mind the story of David and Goliath.

There was one thing Father didn't know: this little man was an important member of the underworld, and had his own gunmen. Father related the incident at the Radzymin Hasidic study house and learned that the old man was well known there. He was a notorious fence, a buyer of stolen goods, and a kind of "Rabbi" to the thieves.

To the Wild Cows

IN ALL THE YEARS that we lived in Warsaw, I never
left the city. Other boys used to talk about their
vacations. People went out to Falenica, to Miedzes-
zyn, Michalin, Swider, Otwock—but for me these
were only names. No trees grew on Krochmalna
Street. Near No. 24, where I used to go to heder, there
was a tree, but No. 24 was far from our house.

Some of the neighbors had potted flowers, but my
parents considered this a pagan custom. I, however,
had an inborn love of nature. In the summertime I
would sometimes find a leaf still attached to the stem
of an apple, and such a leaf would arouse both joy and
longing in me. I would sniff at it and carry it around
with me until it withered. Mother brought home a
bunch of carrots, parsley, red radishes, cucumbers—
and every fruit and vegetable reminded me of the
days in Radzymin and Leoncin, where I was
surrounded by fields and orchards. Once I found a
full ear of corn in my straw mattress. This ear of corn
awakened many memories. Among other things it
reminded me of the dream of Pharaoh, wherein the
seven lean ears of corn devoured the seven fat ones.

Many different kinds of flies used to alight on the
railing of our balcony: large, small, dark, green-gold.
Once in a while a butterfly would stray there. I would
not try to catch it, but would hold my breath and stare

at it in wonder. The little fluttering creature was for me a greeting from the world of freedom.

But Mother Nature did her work even on Kroch-malna Street. In the winter the snow fell, in the summer the rains came. High over the rooftops the clouds passed—dark ones, light ones, some like silver, some in the shapes of fish, snakes, sheep, brooms. Occasionally hail fell on our balcony, and once, after the rain, a rainbow stretched above the roofs. Father told me to recite the blessing "Who remembereth the Covenant." In the evening the moon shone and the stars appeared. My mother and my older brother said that every star is larger than our earth. But how could a star be larger than the earth? It was all a great mystery.

My friend Boruch-Dovid was always talking about the fields and wastelands that lie beyond Warsaw, and about the wild cows that graze there. I began to demand he take me there. He delayed as long as he could and put me off with various excuses. But finally it reached the point where he had to make good on his promises, or our friendship would end.

One Friday in the summertime I arose very early, so early that the sky was still glowing from the sunrise. To my mother I made some pretext or other, put a few slices of bread and butter in a paper bag, took a kopeck that I had somehow saved from my meager allowance from its hiding place, and went off to meet Boruch-Dovid. I had never been up so early in the morning, and everything looked cooler, fresher, and somehow like a fairy-tale landscape. Here and there a stone was damp and Boruch-Dovid said it was because of the dew. This meant, then, that there was dew even on Krochmalna Street. I had thought that dew fell only in the Land of Israel, or in the biblical portion "Give ear, ye heavens," where it is written: "My speech shall distil as the dew ..."

Not only the street, but the people too looked fresher. I discovered that early in the morning

various peasant wagons came to our street. Gentiles
from the surrounding villages brought vegetables,
chickens, geese, ducks, and freshly laid chicken eggs
(not the limestone eggs one could buy in Zelda's shop).
On Mirowski Place, behind the market halls, was the
wholesale fruit market. The abundance of all the
orchards around Warsaw was brought hither: apples,
pears, cherries, sour cherries, gooseberries, currants.
Here too were traded strange fruits and vegetables
that most Jewish children had never tasted and
thought forbidden: tomatoes, cauliflowers, and green
peppers. Inside the market halls proper, one could get
pomegranates and bananas. These were bought only
by grand ladies, whose shopping baskets were
carried by servant girls.

Boruch-Dovid and I walked quickly. As we walked,
he told many strange tales. His father, he said, had
gone on foot from Warsaw to Skierniewice and on the
way he had met a wild man. I was very curious about
the appearance of the wild man and Boruch-Dovid
gave me a detailed description: black as shoe polish,
with long hair reaching to the ground and a horn
growing in the middle of his forehead. For breakfast
such a creature always ate a live child. I was panic-
stricken and I asked: "Maybe a wild man will attack
us?"

"No, they are far from Warsaw."

I was already a grown boy and should not have
been so gullible. But I always believed everything
that Boruch-Dovid told me.

We passed through the Nalewki and the Muranow,
and from there the way led to the open country. I saw
broad meadows covered with grass and all sorts of
flowers, and mountains of a kind I had never known
to exist. At the top they were indeed mountains, but at
the bottom there were brick-red walls with small
sunk-in windows covered by iron grates.

"What is that?" I asked.

"The Citadel."

A feeling of dread came over me. I had heard of the

Citadel. Here were imprisoned those who had tried to overthrow the Tsar.

I had not yet seen any wild cows, but what I had seen already was wonderful and strange. The sky here was not a narrow strip as on Krochmalna Street, but broad, spread out like the ocean, and it descended to the earth like a supernatural curtain. Birds flew overhead in swarms, with a twittering, a cawing, a whistling—large birds and small birds. Two storks were circling above one of the hills of the Citadel. Butterflies of all colors fluttered above the grass: white, yellow, brown, with all kinds of dots and patterns. The air smelled of earth, of grass, of the smoke of locomotives, and of something more that intoxicated me and made my head reel. There was a strange stillness here, and yet everything murmured, rustled, chirped. Blossoms fell from somewhere and settled on the lapels of my jacket. I looked up at the sky, saw the sun, the clouds, and suddenly I understood more clearly the meaning of the words of Genesis. This, then, was the world God had created: the earth, the heavens, the waters above that are separated by the firmament from the waters below.

Boruch-Dovid and I climbed up a hill and below us we saw the Vistula. One half glittered like silver, the other half was green as gall. A white ship sailed past. The river itself did not stand still—it flowed, it was headed somewhere, with an eagerness that hinted at miracles and the coming of the Messiah.

"That's the Vistula," explained Boruch-Dovid. "It flows all the way to Danzig."

"And then?"

"Then it flows into the sea."

"And where is the Leviathan?"

"Far away, at the end of the earth."

Then the storybooks did not tell lies, after all. The world *is* filled with wonders. One need merely pass through the Muranow and one street more, and

already one was in the midst of marvels. The end of
the earth? Was not *this* the end of the earth?...

Locomotives whistled, but no trains could be seen.
Gentle breezes were blowing, and each brought with
it a different fragrance—aromas long forgotten or
never dreamed of. A honeybee came from somewhere,
alit on a flower, smelled at it, hummed, and flew on to
the next flower. Boruch-Dovid said: "She wants to
collect honey."

"Can she bite?"

"Yes, and she has a special poison."

He, Boruch-Dovid, knows everything. Were I
alone, I could not find my way home. Already I have
forgotten even the direction toward Warsaw. But he
is as much at home here as in his own courtyard.
Suddenly he starts to run. He pretends to run away
from me. He throws himself down and is hidden by
the tall grass. Boruch-Dovid is gone! I am alone in the
world—a lost prince, just like in the storybooks.

"Boruch-Dovid!"—I began   to   call—"Boruch-
Dovid!..."

I call, but my voice rebounds from somewhere.
There is an echo here, like in a synagogue, but it is
thrown back from a great distance and the voice is
changed and terrifying.

"Boruch-Dovid! Boruch-Dovid!..."

I know that he is only playing a joke on me. He
wants to frighten me. But though I know it, I am
afraid. My voice is breaking with sobs.

"Bo-r-uch Do-v-id!..."

He reappears, his black eyes laughing like a
gypsy's, and begins to run about in circles like a
young colt. His coattails fly. His prayer vest billows
in the wind. He too has become like a wild creature in
the lap of nature.

"Come on, let's go to the Vistula!"

The path leads downhill, and we cannot walk—we
run. Our feet seem to be running by themselves. I had

to hold them back lest they run even faster and jump right into the water. But the water is further away than I had thought. As I run, the river becomes broader, like an ocean. We come to heaps of pebbles and moist sand, long and marked with lines, like giant cakes made by children playing in the sand. Boruch-Dovid takes off his boots, rolls up his trouser legs, and wades into the water up to his ankles.

"Ouch, it's cold!"

He tells me to take off my boots. But I am embarrassed. Walking barefoot is not in my nature. Only rowdies and Gentile boys go barefoot.

"Are there any fish here?"

"Yes, lots of fish."

"Do they bite?"

"Sometimes."

"What will you do if a fish bites you?"

"I'll grab it by the tail..."

Compared to me, Boruch-Dovid is a country boy, a peasant. I sit down on a rock and everything inside me flows, gurgles like the waters of the Vistula. My mind sways with the motion of the waves and it seems to me that not only the Vistula, but everything around me—the hills, the sky, I myself—is swaying, flowing away into the distance, toward Danzig. Boruch-Dovid points to the other shore and says: "Over there is the Praga forest."

This means that near me there is a real forest, full of wild animals and robbers.

Suddenly something extraordinary happens. From the left side, where the sky and the waters meet, something floats on the water, but it is not a ship. At first it appears small, enveloped in a haze. Soon it grows larger and more distinct. It is a group of rafts made of logs. Men lean against long poles and push them with all the weight of their bodies. On one of the rafts there is a little hut—a small house in the midst of the water! Even Boruch-Dovid stares in open-mouthed wonder.

It takes a long, long time for the rafts to come close

to us. The men yell something to us. I notice someone
who looks like a Jew. He has a beard. I think I can
even make out a Jewish cap. From my reading of the
parables of the Preacher of Dubnow I know that
Jewish merchants make voyages to Danzig and to
Leipzig. I have even heard that timber is shipped by
water. But now I see it with my own eyes—a tale of
the Dubnow Preacher brought to life! For a while the
rafts are near us. A dog stands at the edge of one of
the rafts and barks directly at us. Woe to us, if he
could jump across the water! He would tear us to
shreds. After a while, the rafts move on. Time has
passed, the sun has already reached the middle of the
sky and is now moving into the West. Only after the
rafts have disappeared beneath a bridge do we start
to go back, not the way we came, but in a different
direction. I remember the wild cows and am about to
ask Boruch-Dovid where they are, but suddenly I see
a new scene.

A youth and a girl are lying in the grass. A sheet of
some kind is spread beneath them. The girl is
uncovered in an unseemly way. I catch sight of a pair
of heavy feet and white legs that cast a strange dread
over me. For a while I stand still as though paralyzed.
Then I begin to run, to run without knowing whither.
Something inside me wants to cry out. My throat is
tight. Boruch-Dovid runs after me and calls out to me.
After a while I stand still. Boruch-Dovid catches up
with me, panting, his black eyes glisten and twinkle
and shine, and are filled with a kind of pagan
pleasure.

"Fool, why did you run away?"

I feel embarrassed, before him and before myself. I
had seen something that it was not fitting for a
Hasidic boy to see. I feel that I myself have become
impure, unclean. Something inside me is crying. How
can anyone do such a thing—and here, of all places,
where everything is so beautiful and radiant and
fragrant like the Garden of Eden!

But there is no more time to stand here. The sun is reddening. At home Mother is surely beginning to worry—she is so nervous. Soon it will be time to take the Sabbath *cholent* to the baker, and who will be there to carry it? We begin to walk quickly, each sunk in his own thoughts, while above our heads the birds play, and the windows of the Citadel glow red and gold in the sunset.

I think of those who lie inside in chains because they tried to overthrow the Tsar. I seem to see their eyes, and suddenly everything is filled with a Sabbath Eve sadness and eeriness.

The Divorce

SOME ODD DIVORCES were granted in our house, but the one I'm about to describe was the oddest of all. One day the front door opened to admit the owner of a haberdashery and dry-goods store located in the neighborhood. He was about forty and had a beard so black it looked almost blue. His eyes were not shifty or cunning but instead seemed to be gazing into the distance. I have since met Italians and Spaniards who had the same dark eyes. He was dressed like a Hasid, but an exceptionally neat one. Everything he wore glistened—his alpaca capote, his cloth hat, his soft collar with the black silk tie. His name was Mordecai Meir.

"Good morning, Rabbi."

"Good morning, Reb Mordecai Meir. Welcome. Please be seated. What can I do for you?"

Mordecai Meir uttered something akin to a grunt. "I want a divorce now."

"So?"

"Rabbi, I'm not doing this for frivolous reasons."

"What is wrong, then?"

"Rabbi, I'm very ill," he said calmly. "The doctors have given me up. We don't have any children; when I'm gone my wife will have to be released from a levirate marriage.[1] My only brother lives in America. So it's better to get a divorce now."

"What is wrong with you?"

The man whispered something to my father, who paled.

"The doctors are sometimes mistaken," he said after a moment. "It's all a matter of Providence."

"I'm not a *Kohen*. If I live, I'm allowed to remarry."

"I see. But what is your hurry?"

"Why wait?"

"Why not? You should consult someone else. Perhaps a specialist. There are some wonderful doctors in Vienna."

"I know. I've seen them already."

Father suddenly noticed me. "Out!" I went to another room, upset and frightened by the words I had overheard from this man who sold us thread, buttons, and other such items. I knew what the problem was: the wife of a Jew who had died childless must be released from a levirate marriage. Mordecai Meir was willing to divorce his wife and live out the final months of his life alone to spare his wife the hardship of being forced to have dealings with her brother-in-law. But how could a man speak so calmly of such matters? Tears came to my eyes, and I feared this man, who seemed to me now almost a walking corpse.

---

[1] A law obliging the brother of a man who died, leaving a widow but no children, to marry the widow.

Mordecai Meir soon left the house. My father took my mother aside and told her what had happened. Hearing their whispers and sighs, I went outside and walked past Mordecai Meir's store. I wondered about his wife. Was she crying? Not at all. She stood behind the counter measuring a length of sacking with a wooden rule. As she went about her work, she smiled and talked with the customer. Dark like her husband, with a rounded figure, plump cheeks, and a high bosom, she still kept the customary amiability and decorum of a shopkeeper and matron. Her face showed not the slightest trace of concern. With great deliberation she counted the money she had just received and placed it in the cash drawer. "But this is impossible," I said to myself. "After all, it's her husband. She must know that he's going to die."

It was very odd; I, a stranger, was suffering while she, his wife, appeared unmoved. Later in life I was to have this same experience many times: to lose sleep over people that I hardly knew, though their closest relatives remained indifferent. I learned for the first time that there are people so stolid that no misfortune can affect them. They trudge on toward the grave, their minds on food and the trifles of the day. Even when they must look directly into death, they remain preoccupied by the pettiest ambitions.

But to return to Mordecai Meir. From that time on, I became more and more curious about him and his wife. At every opportunity I strolled past their store. And just like his wife, he continued to chat with customers, to display and sell his goods as usual, to count the day's receipts, or work on his accounts. But as he went about his business, he sometimes stared off into the distance as if he could see beyond the houses, across the roofs, and over the clouds. As the weeks passed, his face grew pale and then green, as though he had undertaken a long fast; his pallor made his beard seem even blacker.

Then one day in our house the divorce was granted. The scribe wrote out the terms with his quill pen. The two witnesses practiced their signatures.

Mordecai Meir faced the scribe; his wife sat on a
bench. A single tear fell from her eye and lingered on
her cheek. The look on her face expressed the
acquiescence of a simple woman who is dealing with
matters beyond her comprehension. She knew how to
sell thread, buttons, safety pins, how to handle a
maid and clean house, but how to behave to a
husband who was about to die bewildered her. I saw
that her mind was wandering, and for a time she
seemed to be counting the fringes on her shawl. Then
suddenly she turned and twisted her wedding ring.
Father sat leafing through a holy volume. He bowed
his head and covered his eyes with his hand. Not for
one moment did he doubt that what was happening
had been ordained by Providence; but why had
Providence denied Mordecai Meir his full comple-
ment of years? He was, after all, a decent fellow. Yet
who dared question the ways of the Almighty?

Finally, Mordecai Meir's wife stretched out her
hands and was given the bill of divorcement. Only
then did she begin to wail. Father said what he
always did on such occasions: the divorced woman
could not remarry for ninety days. This caused a
fresh rush of tears.

What subsequent arrangements were made by
Mordecai Meir and his wife, I do not know. According
to the law they were not permitted to sleep under the
same roof. I forgot about them or, rather, forced
myself to forget.

One day I saw a procession. It was Mordecai Meir's
funeral cortege. His widow walked with uplifted
arms, weeping and moaning. Behind her came a
number of men, who were chatting as they walked.
Their manner seemed to say: "Mordecai Meir is
Mordecai Meir, and we are we. He's a corpse, but
we're alive. He's about to be buried, but we must pay
our rent and our children's tuition. We no longer have
anything in common."

Perhaps six or nine months later, I entered
Mordecai Meir's store to buy thread, and found a
strange man there. How different he was from
Mordecai Meir. Mordecai Meir had been slim and
delicate while this man was burly, with a large head,
a flat nose, and a wide, thick beard. Hair sprouted
from his long ears and wide nostrils; a little beard
grew from every finger. He spoke in a rattling voice.
His unbuttoned capote was spotted. It was the second
husband. He had taken over everything: Mordecai
Meir's wife, his home, his store. He opened the cash
drawer and casually took out a handful of coins,
shuffled over the account books and papers, addressed his wife as though they had been married for
years. It was as if there had never been such a person
as Mordecai Meir.

In time, Mordecai Meir's wife had a child, which
was just as husky and slovenly as its father. She
played with the baby, she clucked and cooed: "A-
cuckoo, cuckoo."

That is not quite the end of the story. During the
First World War an epidemic of typhus ravaged
Warsaw. More people died on Krochmalna Street
than in any other section of the city. Among those
who were taken was Mordecai Meir's widow. A
neighbor lamented to my mother: "Such a young
person, a mother of small children, and as lovely as a
rose. Woe is us."

Mother, her matron's wig askew, nodded at this
new episode in the timeless catastrophe to which one
never becomes accustomed. It was only additional
proof to her that life was a dream and it was useless to
sin against one's Maker. Perhaps one should never
have been born....

But what was one to do if one was born?

A few months passed and in Mordecai Meir's store
a strange woman could be seen.

Wolf the Coal Dealer

ALTHOUGH MOTHER AND FATHER were not much alike, both were revolted by vulgarity, boastfulness, conniving, and flattery. There was a family understanding that defeat was preferable to viciousness, that one's achievements must be gained honorably. We were the inheritors of a heroic code not as yet described in Yiddish literature, the essence of which was an ability to endure suffering for the sake of spiritual purity.

But all around us seethed a rabble who did not share our ideals. The one who was most affected by these people was my mother, who was compelled to cope with the everyday life of Krochmalna Street.

We had no servant and Mother had to do the shopping herself. Each time she went to market, she returned humiliated. The butcher served her last or made her the butt of some coarse joke; the fishmonger, knowing that Mother could afford to buy no more than a pound, snatched the fish from her. Mother's reserved, slim figure and melancholy air annoyed the blowsy wives of Krochmalna Street, who considered her snobbish.

Whenever Mother returned from a shopping tour, she took out one of the volumes that taught one how to be humble and forgive the insults of others, such as the *Duty of the Hearts,* or the *Beginning of Wisdom.* Often she would blame herself. "Maybe I have put on airs? Why can't I get along with such people and be like them?" But nothing she did helped. She was offended by both their abuse and their compliments. She was unable to weep unrestrainedly at funerals, and carry on at weddings. Her character and the tradition which she had inherited condemned her to an isolation from which there was no escape.

Even when she was in her own home, she was not safe from the rabble. There was constant squabbling among those who congregated in our house for Sabbath services. To satisfy their egos, all sorts of honorary titles were created; there wasn't just one warden, but wardens for the first, second, and third quorum. Although these were meaningless titles, they were fought for by rival factions. In the middle of prayer, violent quarrels would break out; then everyone would make up and peacefully assemble for some celebration or other.

On the Ninth Day of Ab, both the Book of Lamentations and the Book of Threnodies were read in our house. For my mother, the destruction of the Temple was a living reality. On the seventeenth day of the month of Tammuz, which is the anniversary of the beginning of Nebuchadnezzar's siege of Jerusalem, Mother would fast the entire day, although she was anemic and frail. The three weeks, the Nine Days were for her, because of the destruction of the Temple and the exile of the Jews, a time of sorrow. One evening (it was the Ninth Day of Ab) Mother, having removed her shoes, seated herself on a low bench in anticipation of hearing the Lamentations read. But the men of the congregation, having a quite different conception of the meaning of this anniversary, arrived with their pockets stuffed with thistles, which they proceeded to toss into each other's beards. When they ran out of thistles, they ripped the plaster from the walls and threw it. Winking and laughing, ignoring my father's admonitions, by the light of a single candle they carried on as though they were still recruits in the army, and the room in which they sat, a barracks. Suddenly the door was flung open, admitting my mother, who entered in stocking feet, with a kerchief on her head.

"Men, have you no shame?" she cried, her voice quivering with emotion. "Don't you know the significance of the Ninth Day of Ab? This is a day of mourning. This was the day on which the walls of Jerusalem fell. It's the day on which our troubles began. All over the world Jews weep, but you have nothing better to do than rip plaster from walls. Are you babies? Don't you know that we Jews are in exile?"

The congregation became still. I remember sitting there trembling with fear. My mother, normally quiet and reserved, had pushed her way into a room full of men to make serious accusations. Her face turned as white as the lime on the wall.

No one said anything for quite some time. At last Yossel the warden broke the silence. "Rebbetzin, what's wrong with their having a little fun? After all, they make good livings."

"Does a good living produce indifference to the destruction of the Temple?"   •

Among those in the congregation was a man known as Wolf the coal dealer, a fellow who was as husky and swarthy as a gypsy and whose occupation had made his dark complexion even darker. A coarse person, he was at least half savage. Occasionally I bought coal from him, ten pounds at a time. Having weighed out the coal, he would throw it into my basket, and grunt, "*Jadza*...off with you."

That was the way he spoke to both children and adults. My mother never went back to him after receiving this treatment.

Rather like a lump of coal himself, he remained from early morning until late at night in his store, where coal and coke were piled almost to the ceiling. In daylight he looked like a chimney sweep, the only white parts of him being his eyeballs, but at night, when the only illumination in the shop was a small

kerosene lamp, he resembled a devil. He kept wetting
down the coal to prevent it from heating up too much
and from weighing too little. He had a voice that
sounded more like a dog's bark than any other I have
heard. A primeval darkness, a kind of black sorrow,
emanated from his face. He treated everyone inso-
lently. The day before the Sabbath he would wash
and soap himself vigorously, but the water never
made him any lighter. The white shirt that he wore
on the holiday accentuated the blackness of his face
and hands.

Wolf the coal dealer lived on the ground floor in a
room in back of his store. He liked to nap after the
Sabbath dinner. But how could one sleep with all the
noise coming from the courtyard? Boys would be
teasing some lunatic, or throwing rocks, or just
making a general commotion. Out of his house would
run Wolf in his underdrawers—strangely white
against his black flesh—to chase after the disturbers
of his sleep. Wolf's sorties were not limited to the
courtyard. Often in the street one would see a black-
skinned man, barefoot and in his underwear, chasing
a band of pale-faced urchins. Wolf's pursuits were
always unsuccessful, the boys being faster than he.
But hopeless though his efforts were, each time he
was awakened, Wolf the coal dealer sprang from his
bed and pursued his tormentors. At times he would
hurl a broom or a piece of coal at the retreating boys.
"Wolf," the pious Jews would say, "not on the
Sabbath."

"Go stick your heads in the mud," Wolf the coal
dealer would reply. "Break yourselves on the wheel."

He acted as savagely in our house as he did at the
store. Sometimes he would complain that he had not
been called up to read from the Torah. From time to
time he had the urge to be a warden. He spat on the
ground, wiped his nose on his sleeve. For my mother
he symbolized the rabble. She was restricted to a
small portion of the world. He could go everywhere,
felt at home in the barracks, in the factories, the

mines, the poorhouses, the prison. Everyone, even the old, was "thou" to him.

Wolf the coal dealer's wife, though a woman of the people, had an aristocratic spirit. Childbirth had deafened her. The louder Wolf barked, the less she understood what he was saying. She was seldom seen in the store; she slaved away in the back room. At times she would bare her heart to my mother.

"Rebbetzin, I can't take it any longer. Dear lady, I'm losing my mind."

"What does he expect of you?"

"He jumps around like a cat on hot bricks, swearing and fussing. He's tearing me apart."

"Why don't you put him in his place?"

"As soon as he opens his mouth, I black out. He beats me, too."

"Don't you have any relatives?"

"No one. I'm as solitary as a stone."

The woman's deafness seemed to have an emotional basis, for she began to hear singing voices. "Dearest Rebbetzin, listen. Put your ear close to mine. Can't you hear, it's the Kol Nidre."

"I hear nothing."

"Someone's singing, I tell you, a cantor with a magnificent voice."

"Why don't you consult a doctor?"

"I've been to three doctors already. None of them knows the difference between a foot and an elbow."

One day during Pentecost the congregation banqueted at our house, although my father was away in Radzymin visiting the Rabbi. The guests, among whom was Wolf the coal dealer, sat drinking beer and munching nuts. Wolf had washed and dressed more carefully than usual but remained his black, ungainly self.

"Who'll cover my bet?" he barked.

"What are you betting about?"

"Look, I'll pour a few drops of beer into your glass and fill mine to the top. My money says that I'll finish my beer and put the glass back on the table before you do."

"How can you do that?"

"That's none of your business. It'll cost you ten rubles to find out."

"Fine. Let's shake on it."

Wolf and some other fellow shook hands. Then Wolf poured a few drops of beer in the fellow's glass and filled his own glass to the brim.

"All right, drink up."

Wolf's opponent emptied his glass in a single gulp and set the glass down. Wolf, dipping his black mustache in the foam, slowly sipped until there was no beer left; then, having raised the tablecloth, he placed his glass down on the bare wood.

"I win," Wolf said. "You didn't put your glass on the table but on the tablecloth."

"What do you mean, I didn't put it on the table? The tablecloth's on the table, isn't it?"

They began to argue and bicker.

"But the glass was on the tablecloth."

"What's the difference?"

"A great deal."

Soon they were fighting. Wolf struck first and received a punch in return. His beard glistened with red. Once again Mother intervened.

"Men, have you no shame? This is a holiday."

Pale and frightened, she faced them. Anger and respect mingled in the glances that they gave her. Wolf opened his mouth to bark out something, but was restrained by the others. He gave my mother a baleful look.

At that time I was studying the Pentateuch and may even have begun reading the Talmud. I had already placed who Wolf was; he was the mixed multitude mentioned in Exodus. The quarrel between him and my mother had had its beginning at the time of Moses.

And what of the Messiah? The Messiah would not come until Mother became like Wolf the coal dealer or Wolf the coal dealer like Mother.

Descendants

A FEW DOORS away from us, at No. 14, dwelt a tiny little man, a Rabbi who would have been a person of great significance if family were everything. His father's father was Reb Moshe, who had had in turn as his father the great Kozhenitz Rabbi. Our neighbor, Reb Berele, was already in his eighties when I knew him. One of the reasons he was not a Hasidic Rabbi was his inability to study. He could barely struggle through a chapter of the Mishnah. It was his fate to go through life known as the grandson of the great Kozhenitz Rabbi, but himself only a Rabbi for women. But he was a man of breeding, having inherited the gentility of his distinguished ancestors. A small man with a full white beard, he wore an outergarment of silk, a sable hat, stockings, and half shoes. His beadle accompanied him wherever he went. So slowly did he walk that it took him half an hour to get from our house to his. He had such a pronounced stoop that all one could make out was a white beard, a sable hat, and a small bundle of silk.

As he passed, the market women blessed him. Gentiles stared at him uncomprehendingly. Reb Berele lived a life of near-perfect serenity. Once I watched him put on his phylacteries. His hands scarcely moved. It took him almost an hour to wind the thongs round his arm. The tranquillity in his eyes was of a variety men have almost forgotten. This

midget of a man was a hearty eater and a brandy
drinker as well. He always wore a joyous, holiday
look of contentment on his florid face.

Every Purim, as a token of his affection, Reb
Berele sent my father a fish which had been cooked in
sweet-and-sour sauce. Whenever the two met on the
street, he chided my father for not visiting him more
often; my father only went to Reb Berele's when
someone in our building died. Being a Kohen, that is,
of priestly descent, Father was not permitted,
according to Mosaic law, to remain in a house which
contained a corpse.

Whenever Father went to Reb Berele's, he took me
with him. The only thing Reb Berele liked to do
besides praying was to recite the Zohar. It is doubtful
whether he understood the Aramaic in which the
book is written. But what difference did that make?
Since the Zohar deals with various celestial secrets
such as the hierarchy of angels and the sacred names
of God, the mere act of enunciating the words
elevates the soul. Actually Reb Berele didn't quite
speak the text, but mumbled it with that sort of
exuberance that comes from having led a pure and
blameless life.

By the time I knew him, Reb Berele was tended by
a servant, as his wife had died. Women came to ask
him to pray for their sick children, to give them his
blessing for continued good health, or to intercede
with heaven in their behalf when they were pregnant
or about to go into labor. Reb Berele, taking a pinch of
snuff from his bone snuffbox, promised the best for
everyone. He had two sons who were also Rabbis of
small importance but were otherwise unlike their
father.

He was small; they were large. He was slow; they
were speedy. Those sons were so alike you would have
thought them twins, and perhaps they were. For
them to have sat around and waited for women to
consult them would have been a waste of time. They
were obliged to rush about the city in search of

wealthy patrons who were willing to give a hand up
to the great-grandsons of the Kozhenitz Rabbi. As
they hurried about, their predatory eyes scanning the
upper stories of houses, they, like their father, wore
silk gabardines and sable hats. At times I felt that the
force that propelled them was so great that they
would suddenly spread their coattails and soar off
over the rooftops. Between Reb Berele's sons and the
rest of the city of Warsaw there existed an undeclared
war. The city was determined to give these cunning
men nothing. "Let them work for a living like
everyone else," the city seemed to say. "Why don't
they go peddle herring in the market place?" Reb
Berele's sons, having wives and children to support
and being unwilling to take no for an answer, rushed
off to the back door when the front door of a house
was slammed in their faces. They were always
thinking up some new scheme by which they could
promote themselves a few more rubles. For them it
was merely a matter of being sufficiently alert and
enterprising.

And Reb Berele's wellborn sons always managed
to get what they were after.

One day Father was delighted to find that the old
man had come to visit us. Imagine having the
grandson of the Kozhenitz Rabbi in our house! For a
full hour Father and he discussed Jewish affairs,
current events, their respective lives, and the unique
customs of Kozhenitz and Lublin. Finally Reb Berele
explained why he had come; he wanted to get
married.

Soon, in walked the bride-to-be, a woman of about
seventy and a Rabbi's widow. She was at least two
heads taller than Reb Berele. A stout woman, she
wore a fur coat and a peaked bonnet, and spoke in a
loud voice. Yiddish didn't suffice her; she sprinkled
her conversation with Hebrew. A notorious sponger
in her own right, she was busy collecting money to
subsidize an edition of a commentary that her late

husband had written. That was how she had happened to meet Reb Berele. One remark had led to another and finally to the betrothal.

Though Father was surprised that so old a man should be planning to get married, he recognized that such things do happen. Mother was shocked, maintaining that the marriage was wrong for both parties. But no one can interfere in such matters, and Father did want to earn the money for performing the ceremony.

I attended the wedding because I was one of those who carried the four-pronged wedding canopy that was stored near the stove in our apartment. Reb Berele's spacious home was alight with candles and lamps. Reb Berele's face was also aglow as he and his bride took their places under the canopy. But, unlike the groom, the bride didn't seem happy, and kept looking about her as if perplexed by something. She was wearing a new cape and a holiday bonnet. One could read in her face a refusal to suffer and a determination to snatch from life all that it had to offer. Reb Berele was not the proper mate for her; she needed a mightier man. But when one is seventy, one can't afford to be picky. Better Reb Berele than no one.

During the wedding supper, the newly coined Rebbetzin began accusing the maid of mismanaging the household. It was obvious that the two women would not remain long under the same roof. And sure enough, a few days later Reb Berele's housekeeper came to our house to complain to my mother. She had just been discharged. This was only the beginning. The new Rebbetzin was evidently insane with ambition. Why should Reb Berele be the insignificant Rabbi he was, when he came from such important stock? She was determined to correct that situation and circulated stories among the women about the miraculous acts of her saintly husband. Whether she was at the butcher's, or the grocer's, or the dairy

store, she sang Reb Berele's praises. But people know
how to estimate each other. The women remarked,
"This is a loudmouth."

At the same time that she was trying to advance
Reb Berele's career, she continued collecting money
for her first husband's book. After all, what did one
thing have to do with the other?

Eventually friction developed between her and her
stepsons. The new Rebbetzin took up the fight with
her usual vigor. Fed up with the whole mess, Reb
Berele retired to his bed with a lung inflammation.
He lay there as calm and serene as ever, coughing
and smiling. When it was time for him to put on his
phylacteries, he would sigh softly and tie them to his
arms with characteristic slowness. Women still came
to see him, and he continued to pray for their good
health and the health of their children, or whatever
they wanted. He still liked to nibble on a piece of cake
and wash it down with a little brandy.

One day he sighed deeply and gave up his soul. The
Hasidim who while he lived had only rarely thought
of Reb Berele flocked to his funeral. There were a host
of Rabbis at the ceremony. After all, he was the
grandson of the Kozhenitz Rabbi. At the open grave,
the sobbing Rebbetzin spread out her arms and
delivered a eulogy of her own, although one had
already been given. The sons of the dead man, now in
their sixties, recited the Kaddish and studied the
crowd in search of possible benefactors.

The sons observed the period of mourning with
their stepmother, but apparently made her life
miserable, for she packed up and left the house as
soon as she could. Eventually she showed up at our
place to complain about her stepsons. That was when
I first learned that one bully can't bear another. The
weeping Rebbetzin cleared her nose and bewailed her
marriage. She had lived fifty years with her first
husband, blessed be his memory. What need had she
of this second marriage? She had thought she could
find somewhere to lay her head, but it had been

ordained otherwise. Now she would know no peace
until her first husband's book was published.

Mother, a keen judge of people, listened to her in
silence, with a look that seemed to say, "I know all
your fiendish tricks." Father, however, pitied her.
She spoke to him about learned matters, making
incredible blunders as she did, boasted about her
forebears and complained about her health, demand-
ing that Father take up a collection to send her to a
health resort for the cure of arthritis. As she rambled
on, she kept on drinking tea and munching cookies.
Looking at my mother, she said, "How old are you,
may the evil eye spare you?"

Mother told her.

"Ach, if I were only your age again!"

"What would you do?"

"I would move mountains."

The Satin Coat

IT WAS OUR CLOTHES that made our poverty apparent.
Food was cheap, nor were we big eaters. Mother
prepared a soup made with potatoes, browned flour,
and fried onions. Only on Passover did we eat eggs.
True, a pound of meat at that time in Warsaw cost
twenty kopecks, but it produced a lot of broth. Flour,
buckwheat, chickpeas, beans were not expensive.

But clothes were dear.

My mother would wear a dress for years and take
such good care of it that it still looked new. A pair of

shoes lasted her three years. Father's satin capote
was somewhat frayed, but so were the capotes and
skullcaps of most of the congregation at the Hasidic
study house where he prayed. It was worse for us
children. My boots wore out every three months.
Mother complained that other children were careful
but I messed up everything.

At the nearby Radzymin study house, on the
Sabbath, boys wore satin or silk gabardines, velvet
hats, polished boots, and sashes. I went about in a
gabardine that was too small for me. Now and again
I did get a new piece of clothing, but not until what
I had was nothing but rags.

But there was one time just before Passover when
suddenly we struck it rich.

This was a good period of the year for us, for Father
always sold to a Gentile—our janitor, to be exact—
people's hametz, that is, all those items such as
unleavened bread, flour, kneading boards, and
rolling pins which are not permitted in a Jewish
household during Passover. There was a certain
element of the spurious in this transaction because
immediately after Passover all this property reverted
to its original owners.

From listening to those who came to sell their
hametz, I learned how little we had in comparison to
them. They had to dispose of whisky, ark, cherry
brandy, preserves; we, nothing but a few pots and
pans. Occasionally someone listed a stable with
horses, although I am uncertain how a horse can
possibly be considered a hametz. But, then, horses do
eat oats. There was one man whose son was traveling
with a circus and who felt it necessary to declare as
hametz the entire menagerie.

Why was this particular Passover a lucky one for
us? To begin with, we had received a host of fine gifts
on Purim, which precedes Passover by only four
weeks. But best of all, Jonathan, a tailor from
Leoncin, where my father had once been Rabbi, had

moved to Warsaw. Jonathan, a tall, slender man with a pockmarked face, a spare beard, and brilliant eyes, dressed like a Hasid, not like a tailor. On the Sabbath he wore a satin capote; he took snuff, went to visit the Radzymin Rabbi on holidays, and was, in fact, a learned man. Now that he was in Warsaw he visited my father to discuss erudite matters. Seeing me, Jonathan offered to clothe me on credit. We could pay for the material at our convenience.

What a stroke of luck! As he measured me, he beamed proudly, treating me as though I were a member of his family. He had, as a matter of fact, been present at my circumcision. Noting my various measurements in chalk, he remarked to my mother, "Oh, Rebbetzin, how the years do fly."

Jonathan apparently had no other work at the moment, for almost immediately after taking my measurements he had me down to his house for a fitting, testing me on my Hebrew at the same time, and appreciating the opportunity to use a few Hebrew phrases of his own and discourse in a scholarly way. Although he was only a tailor, he had a great love for Judaism and savored every Hebrew word. At the time of his marriage he was familiar only with the required prayers, but later he studied the Scriptures in Yiddish, learned the Mishnah with a teacher, and made inquiries among students. Ridiculed in Leoncin for his aspirations, he proved despite this that it was never too late to learn. Father had helped Jonathan transform himself into a scholar, and the tailor was eager to show his gratitude.

His house was alive with girls, noise, and the odors of cooking food. The girls, who had known me since early childhood and now saw me being outfitted like a man for a satin capote, could not keep from making observations. With their mother, they argued about whether the capote was the right length. My mother, in a lavish gesture, had also ordered new boots for me from Michael the cobbler. I was to look completely done over when I entered the study house on Passover.

Although I had no great passion for clothes at that time, I soon acquired one, becoming more intrigued with each new addition to my wardrobe. New shirts were being sewn for me by a seamstress, and my new velvet hat already lay in a box in the closet. I had visions of entering the study house triumphantly on Passover Eve, and amazing all the boys there. Previously, my clothes had made me feel inferior to them, even though I was more informed than they, knew about Zionism, socialism, the weight of air, and the origin of coal—having learned it all from my brother and an almanac. But now they would see that I could also have a new outfit for the holiday. Most tailors did not keep their word about having things ready for a holiday, but Jonathan was different.

All the same, I felt a premonition of disaster, for how could things go as smoothly as the way I dreamed them? But, on the other hand, what could go wrong, and why was I so apprehensive? Yes, of course, Jonathan might burn the cloth while pressing it, or it could even be stolen. From *The Rod of Punishment,* as well as from my own experience, I knew that the material world was full of snares. I had become too enamored of its pleasures.

Even so, things kept going smoothly. True to his promise, Michael the cobbler delivered a pair of boots that gleamed as though lacquered. The satin capote hung already in our closet. Shortly before Passover, people began coming to our house to sell their hametz, and standing behind Father's chair, I watched the ceremony, which wasn't terribly complicated. The person selling the articles was told to touch the tip of a handkerchief, signifying that he agreed to sell his things to a Gentile. The bill of sale was begun, as follows: "The hametz of Reb so-and-so..." and in a mixture of Yiddish and Hebrew all the items were listed. I was sure I could do the job myself, if I had the chance.

The men would chat, sign, and talk about other Passovers. My father asked a deaf man if he had any alcohol to declare.

"Yes. A little wheat flour."

The others shouted into his ear, "Alcohol! Brandy!"

"Oh. Why didn't you say so? Of course I have alcohol."

A widow who came to sell her hametz didn't know how to sign her name, and Father told her to touch the pen, but she couldn't understand what he meant. Father repeated, "Just the shank of the pen, for a second."

She didn't know what the shank of the pen was. Efficient though she was in her stall at the market place, she was bewildered by Father's study and all the men there. Mother, entering, explained what had to be done, and the woman was greatly relieved, and said, "Rebbetzin, I have no trouble understanding you..."

And she touched the pen.

Then, unknotting a kerchief, she counted out several copper coins. "Have a good Passover," she said to Father.

"May you live to see the next," he replied.

Suddenly, over her wind- and sun-ravaged face, the tears gushed, and everyone grew silent. After she had left, Father said, "Who knows who is best-loved by God? She may be a saint..."

Mother reentered the study looking flushed and grimy, as she had come from stoking the stove to remove all traces of hametz. In the bedroom, the ordinary matzoth was suspended in sheets from the ceiling. The two portions of matzoth baked with extra care, and to be eaten only by the most devout, had been put aside for Father and Mother. Mother, a Rabbi's daughter, was granted this privilege usually reserved for men. Everything went according to ritual. The night preceding Passover, Father searched the house in the traditional manner for hametz to be burned the next day. One was allowed to

eat hametz until nine the next morning—and after
that until sundown, neither hametz nor matzoth.
From mashed potatoes, eggs, and sugar, Mother
prepared for us children a pancake that was
indescribably delicious.

At sunset Passover began. Nothing so far had
gone wrong. I washed, put on a new shirt, new
trousers, new boots, new velvet hat, and the satin
capote that glistened festively. I had become a boy
from a wealthy family, and I walked downstairs with
my father. Neighbors, opening doors to look at me,
spat to ward off the evil eye, and girls who sat on
thresholds grating the traditional bitter herb, horseradish, laughed and wept as I went by. Girls my own
age, who had so short a time before shared toys and
pebbles with me, looked on with approval. Now that I
was a young man and they themselves were almost
mature, they were too shy to speak to me, but their
glances were reminiscent.

My father and I went to the Radzymin study
house, climbed the stairs, and tried the door. It was
locked, and a notice hung there: "Gas out of order.
Closed until after the holiday."

Closed on Passover Eve? The Radzymin study
house? Incredible! We didn't know what to do, and
remained there, confounded. The *Rod of Punishment*
had been right. One should not depend on the
comforts of the material world; there was nothing in
it but disappointments. Only service to God mat-
tered, and the study of the Torah. Everything else
crumbled...

At the Minsk study house, where we went to pray,
no one knew me or cared about my new outfit. There
were a few boys that I recognized, but, as strangers,
we all huddled near the exit.

It was a harsh blow and a lesson not to get
involved in worldly vanities.

A Boy Philosopher

MY BROTHER ISRAEL JOSHUA, because of his emancipated views, found it difficult to speak to my father, whose only response was, "Unbeliever! Enemy of Judaism!" On the other hand, my brother would have long talks with my mother, and often, in my presence, they would discuss me.

"What's to become of him?" my brother would argue. "Must he marry and open a store or become a teacher in a heder? There are too many stores already and too many teachers. If you glance out the window, Mother, you can see what Jews look like—stooped, despondent, living in filth. Watch them drag their feet as they walk...Listen to them speak. It's no wonder everyone else thinks of them as Asiatics. And how long do you think Europe will stand for this clump of Asia in its midst?"

"Gentiles have always hated Jews," Mother said. "Even if a Jew wore a top hat, he'd be hated, because he stands for truth."

"What truth? Does anyone know what the truth is? Every religion has its own prophets and holy books. Have you heard of Buddhism? Buddha was just like Moses and he performed miracles too."

Mother made a face as if she had some bad-tasting thing in her mouth. "How can you dare to compare them—an idol worshipper to the patriarch Moses? Woe is me! What my own flesh and blood says..."

"Listen, Mother. Buddha was no idol worshipper, but a very profound thinker. He agreed with our own prophets. As for Confucius..."

"No more! Don't speak of those heathens in the same breath as our saints. The Buddha came from India...I remember that from *The Paths of the World*. They burn widows there and kill aged parents while everyone celebrates."

"You don't mean India?"

"Who cares? They're all beasts. A cow, to them, is a god. The Chinese, on the other hand, throw away their extra daughters. We Jews alone believe in one God; all the others worship trees, snakes, crocodiles, everything you can think of...They're all wicked. Even while they say, 'Turn the other cheek,' they murder each other and go on sinning. You want to compare them to us?"

"If we had our own country, we'd be involved in wars also. King David wasn't such a compassionate man..."

"Shush! Watch what you say! May God have mercy on you! Don't touch our anointed. King David and Solomon were both prophets. The Talmud says it is wrong to consider David a sinner..."

"I know what it says. But what about Bathsheba?"

Since that was my mother's name, every time I heard about Bathsheba I felt that Mother was somehow implicated. Mother's face flushed.

"Sh! You read idiotic books and repeat everything! King David will live forever and those trashy books aren't worth the paper they're printed on. Who are the authors? Loafers."

These discussions intrigued me. I had already discussed the subjects with my brother. I had no inclination to be a storekeeper or Talmud teacher nor have a "slovenly wife and a bunch of brats," as my brother put it. Once he said, "He'd better become a worker."

"With God's help he'll be a Rabbi, not a worker. He takes after his grandfather," Mother said.

"A Rabbi? Where? Everywhere there are Rabbis. Why do we need so many?"

"And why so many workers? A Rabbi, no matter how poor he is, is still better off than a shoemaker."

"Just wait until the workers unite."

"They'll never unite. Each one wants to steal the other's bread. Why don't soldiers unite and refuse to go to war?

"Oh, that will come too."

"When? There's so much unnecessary killing. Every Monday and Thursday there's a Turkish crisis. The world is full of evil, that's all there is to it. We'll never find peace here—only in the other world."

"You're a pessimist, Mother."

"Wait, my soup is burning!"

How often I listened to discussions of this sort, with each side effectively destroying the arguments of the other! But when it came to proving the case, what was relied on were easily disputed quotations. I remained silent, with opinions of my own. The Gentiles were idol worshippers, true, but King David actually had sinned. And when Jews lived in their own country, they too had killed. And it was true that each religion had its own prophets, but who could say which ones had spoken to God? These were questions that Mother did not seem able to answer.

"What kind of trade appeals to you?" my brother asked.

"How about becoming an engraver and carving letters on brass and copper?"

"Good."

"Or a watchmaker?"

"Too hard."

"You can learn it. How about a doctor?"

"Let him be. What do doctors know? They take money for nothing. Jews will always be Jews and they'll always need Rabbis."

"In Germany, Rabbis attend universities!" my brother announced proudly.

"I know those reform Rabbis," my mother said.

"They can find a way to permit eating meat with milk dishes, but how can they justify shaving, when it's contrary to Mosaic law? What kind of Rabbi defies the Torah?"

"They use a kind of powder for shaving, not a razor."

"Are they ashamed of beards because they want to look like Gentiles? If their Rabbis are like that, I can imagine what the rest of them are like."

Suddenly Father appeared from his study. "Let's end these discussions once for all," he called out. "Tell me—who created the world? All they see is the body and they think that's all there is. The body is nothing but a tool. Without the soul, the body is like a slab of wood. The souls of those who gorge themselves and swill are evil and wander about in the desert, tortured by devils and hobgoblins. They've learned the truth too late. Even Gehenna is closed to them. The world is full of transmigrant souls..." Father cried out, "When a soul leaves a body unclean, it is returned to earth to wander about again, as a worm or a reptile, and its grief is tremendous...."

"Then, according to you, Father, God is wicked."

"Enemy of Israel! God loves man, but when man defiles himself, he must be cleansed."

"How can you expect a Chinaman to know the Torah?"

"What's a Chinaman to you? It's just as necessary for Gentiles to exist as for birds or fish. When I open a holy book I sometimes see a mite smaller than a pinpoint walking about. It too is a wonder of God. Can all the professors in the world get together and create one mite?"

"Well, what does it all add up?"

After Father left and Mother went out to buy something, I asked my brother, "Who did create the mite?"

"Nature."

"And who created nature?"

"And who created God?" my brother rejoined.

"Something had to come from itself, and later everything developed out of its original matter. From the energy of the sun, the first bacteria were created at the edge of the sea. Conditions happened to be favorable. Creatures fought among themselves and the strongest survived. Bacteria formed into colonies and a division of the functions began."

But where did it all come from in the first place?

"It was always like this; no one knows. But you can be sure of one thing—one needn't put on the phylacteries of Rabbi Tam. It's all fabricated. Every people has its own rites. There was the Rabbi, for example, who said you mustn't urinate in the snow on the Sabbath because it resembles plowing...."

Although later in my life I read a great deal of philosophy, I never found more compelling arguments than those that came up in my own kitchen. I even heard at home the strange facts that are in the province of psychic research. And after such discussions I would go outside to play, but as I went through the games of tag, hide-and-seek, and cops-and-robbers, my imagination was at work. What if I found the kind of water that made one wise and a party to all secrets, or if the prophet Elijah arrived to teach me all the Seven Wisdoms of the World? And what if I found a telescope that saw directly into heaven? My thoughts, which were not the thoughts of other boys, made me both proud and lonely. And always there was the final question: What was right? What must I do? Why did God remain silent in the Seventh Heaven? Once a man came up to me and asked, "What's the matter? Why do you think so hard? Are you afraid the sky will fall on you?"

Uncle Mendel

IT WAS ONLY when other boys spoke of their relatives that I became envious. "Grandpa gave me Hanukkah money...Grandma bought me a hat...Uncle is taking me to Falenica...I went for a droshky ride with Auntie..." So they spoke of cousins, great-uncles, and great-aunts. But at home there was only my immediate family. Three days' journey away, in Bilgoray, I had relatives. From Warsaw, one had to go to Bilgoray by way of Rejowiec. In Tomaszow, which is as far as Bilgoray from Warsaw, my paternal grandmother, Temerl, lived, and the rest of my family were in Galicia and Hungary. They were not real to me; they lived only in anecdotes and legends. No one gave me Sabbath fruit; there were no family parties. My own sister was elsewhere, having married and moved to Antwerp.

But family stories were plentiful.

For example, there was Uncle Mendel and my mother's sister Aunt Taube—five years older than my mother. They lived in the town of Gorshkov, near Izhbitze, in an extremely impoverished manner.

Although his father, Isaac Gorshkover, had been wealthy, Uncle Mendel was so smart, so stubborn, and so conservative that he professed the belief that if men lived only according to their strictest needs, most of the world's ills would be eliminated. Neither did he believe that one should suffer from pride. Even a scholar and son-in-law of the Bilgoray Rabbi could tote a sack of buckwheat on his shoulders, drive a cow to pasture, and do heavy labor. And if one was to avoid becoming a swindler, he said, one must dress in coarse patched clothing.

Short and slight, with a scraggly yellow beard, Uncle Mendel kept his erudition to himself, considering knowledge a possession that placed one in superior relationship to the poor. Having ennobled poverty to the point of holiness, this son of a wealthy family had nearly pauperized himself.

Aunt Taube suffered, for at the time of her marriage she had been greatly respected in town, being, after all, daughter of the Bilgoray Rabbi, and married to Reb Isaac Gorshkover's son. But his eccentricities had degraded her.

To make it worse, Uncle Mendel presented the family with a tendency to consumption. His eldest, Notte, was tubercular, presumably from having drunk a glass of cold water while he was overheated. But he wasn't the only child in the family to spit blood.

Aunt Taube wept. Hidden away in little Gorshkov, she had become simple enough to supplicate minor Wonder Rabbis.

One day our door opened and in walked a sumptuously dressed Uncle Mendel with Notte. Mother was astounded.

It was part of Uncle Mendel's creed to dress well for a journey or holiday. Even though one wore rags in Gorshkov, in Warsaw things had to be different. He seemed haughty and affluent. Already a man, and betrothed, Notte was tall, broad and handsome, deceptively ruddy. Uncle Mendel was taking him to a doctor.

This stranger-uncle studied me keenly, and asked, "Do you study?"

"Yes."

"Well, you can't eat the Torah," Uncle Mendel said sarcastically. He had the sharpness of a Kotzker Hasid.

Although Father welcomed his brother-in-law graciously, Mother nursed a resentment against him; however, this was not the time to settle accounts. Notte played the part of a prospective bridegroom.

His watch was nickel-plated. He peeled an apple with a pearl-handled pocket knife. His clothes were new and stylish.

"What's new in Gorshkov?" Mother asked.

"Nothing's ever new there," Uncle replied.

"How's Taube?"

"Taube is Taube."

"And the other children?"

"They're in Gorshkov. What else?"

It seemed to him, he said, that all Warsaw was in such desperate haste that one was almost prevented from crossing streets. Where were they all rushing and why did they scream so much? What commotion!

Uncle Mendel bought a twenty-five-ruble ticket and took Notte to a specialist, who prescribed three spoonfuls of cognac a day.

Many people offered advice. Some said a stay in Otwock would save his life, there was no air like Otwock air, even if Gorshkov, too, was surrounded by pine-tree forests. A rather credulous man said that one of his relatives who had been dying of tuberculosis had eaten pork on the advice of a doctor. The Rabbi, he said, had permitted the relative to do so, since it was a matter of life or death. Someone else mentioned a person who had spat out his lungs and later grew new ones...I think the doctor suggested that Notte refrain from marrying.

For me, Uncle Mendel's visit was a big event. Mother kept him up late, asking about people she knew. Uncle Mendel's replies were sharp.

"Him? His house burned down. He's in great need. That one? Dead."

"When? How?"

"Does it matter?"

Before leaving with Notte, he gave me some money, but he left us feeling depressed. Not long afterwards, we learned of Notte's death.

Notte's sister, now wealthy, lives in Flint, Michigan. Her son, an American officer, was killed in the war against Japan.

Then there was Uncle Eli. He was really a cousin, but since he had a son my age, we called him Uncle. Moshe, his father, my Aunt Sarah's first husband, had been considered a saint, on intimate terms with God. He was so preoccupied with Torah and lofty thoughts that he barely spoke. But he too died of consumption, leaving three children, and Aunt Sarah married a grain dealer named Israel.

Tall, blond-bearded, and noble-looking, Eli had an unusual gold and saffron complexion. The sun apparently shone more brightly in Bilgoray, which was to the south. As if Bilgoray belonged to the Holy Land, Eli's complexion had an Oriental warmth. Eli, who was a storekeeper, and looked more like a Rabbi, wore two capotes, one over the other. His wife came from Rowna. Mother asked about his son Moshe, a year or two older than I.

"He studies alone already and helps out at the store as well."

"The store? At his age?"

"He speaks and writes good Polish."

Glaring at me reproachfully, Mother asked, "Did he have a tutor?"

"Yes, but he learned by himself. He's good at arithmetic too."

Mother didn't even have to glare this time. Her brow was eloquent.

"What's new on our side?" She was referring to my grandfather's house and courtroom at Bilgoray. Eli wasn't the talkative kind, and Mother had to drag the words out of him. Uncle Joseph and Uncle Itche were at odds. Aunt Rochele, the daughter of Rabbi Isaiah Rachover, the famous author, couldn't get along with her sister-in-law, Sarah Chizha, Uncle Joseph's wife. The argument concerned Grandmother's preference for her youngest son, Itche, whom she favored with marzipan and roasted doves. Uncle Itche, his wife Rochele, and their two sons had been boarding with Grandfather, Itche himself having been in that position for almost twenty years, and Joseph was

wild with jealousy. Rochele, moreover, instead of
showing gratitude to Grandmother, acted haughtily
and made nasty remarks about her. Everyone
maligned everyone else. Recently, because of a
government order that Bilgoray would have to select
a Russian-speaking Rabbi (which Grandfather was
not), Uncle Itche had asked to be considered, but
Joseph, the Assistant Rabbi, did not approve.
Meanwhile, an outsider named Kaminer, who had
followers in town, was also asking to be selected.
There was considerable turmoil, with the Turisk
Hasidim backing Uncle Itche, and the Gorlica
Hasidim for Kaminer, who was an enlightened man.
Kaminer, or one of his followers, had sent the Lublin
governor a letter denouncing Uncle Itche. Grandfather, locked in his study and detached from it all,
read his holy books and took a daily drink of brandy.
With his hair completely white, he looked like an
angel of God.

Mother, recognizing an eternal truth, nodded her
head and grew pale, "I hope it all turns out well!"

Anyone who fooled around with Grandfather, she
knew, was playing with fire; anyone who spoke to
him arrogantly was sure to be punished. He had the
power of heaven behind him. They'd better watch
out!

"May God forgive the fools!" Mother said.

But she too had a grudge against Itche because he
could get anything he wanted out of Grandmother.
And as for Rochele, what if she was Isaiah Rachover's daughter? He might be a pious Jew and a
scholar, but he was no genius. What genius published
a volume in Yiddish for women each year? He was an
ordinary dilettante, certainly not Grandfather's
equal. When Itche was staying with his father-in-law
in Rachev, Mother said, he had been served hard-
boiled eggs with the soup. What a small-town custom!
And to make it worse, she added, Rochele's mother
had insisted that Itche wash his hands just before
she took the rolls from the oven: Mother implied that

Reb Isaiah Rachover was nothing but a provincial Rabbi living in a miserable settlement whose customs dated back to the time of King Sobieski.

I sat there spellbound, my imagination aflame. This wasn't mere gossip, but what my brother would term food for literature. I felt that I knew Tomaszow and Rachev, and generations of my family lived through my mother's speech.

The Strong Ones

THE HEDER, too often described as a place where innocent children suffered at the hands of a sloppy, ill-tempered teacher, was not quite that. What was wrong with society was wrong with the heder.

There was one boy who with constantly clenched fists kept looking for a chance to hit someone. Assistant bullies and sycophants surrounded him.

Another boy, for whom it was not practical to use violence, acted the little saint, smiling at everyone, doing favors, and all with an expression that implied immeasurable love. But in his quiet way he schemed to acquire things, to taste something wonderful for nothing. Pious though he was, he showed friendship for the bully while feigning sympathy for his victims. When his friend the bully decided to give someone a bloody nose, the little saint would run to the victim with a handkerchief while gently admonishing the bully, "You shouldn't have done that..."

There was another boy who was interested only in

business, trading a button for a nail, a bit of putty for
a pencil, a candy for a roll. He was always losing out
on bargains, but in the end he got the best of
everyone. Half the heder was indebted to him, since
he lent money on interest. He and the bully had an
arrangement whereby anyone who reneged had his
hat snatched off.

Then there was the liar who boasted that his
family was rich and famous and that Warsaw's elite
visited his home. Promising us dates, figs, St. John's
bread, and oranges from theoretical weddings and
circumcisions, and a projected summer vacation, he
demanded advance presents from all of us.

Then there was the victim. One day the bully drew
blood from him, and the next day he gave the bully a
present. Smiling with sly submissiveness, the victim
indicated another boy who required a beating.

From my seat in the heder I saw everything, and
even though the bully had punched me, I presented
him with neither smiles nor gifts. I called him an
Esau and predicted that his hereafter would be spent
on a bed of nails. He hit me again for that, but I didn't
weaken. I would have nothing to do with the bully,
the priggish saint, the money lender, or the liar, nor
would I pay them any compliments.

I wasn't making out too well. Most of the heder
boys had grown hostile, informing against me to the
teacher and tutor. If they caught me in the street, they
said, they'd break my leg. I realized my danger. After
all, I was too small to take on the entire heder. But I
couldn't even pretend to be friends, so how could I
make peace?

The trip to heder each morning was agonizing, but
I couldn't complain to my parents—they had their
own troubles. Besides, they'd probably say: "That's
what you get for being different from everyone
else..."

There was nothing to do but wait it out. Even the
devil had to weary. God, if He supported truth and
justice, must inevitably side with me.

The day came when it seemed to me impossible to go on. Even the teacher, in that hellish atmosphere, opposed me, though I knew my Pentateuch. The Rebbetzin made malicious remarks about me. It was as if I were excommunicated.

Then, one day, everything changed. The bully miscalculated the strength of a new boy, who just happened to hit back. Then the teacher hurled himself at the bully, who already had a lump on his head. The bully was dragged to the whipping bench, his trousers were pulled down, and he was whipped before all of us. Like Haman, he was punished. When he tried to resume his reign of terror, he was repulsed in favor of the victor.

The moneylender also met his nemesis. The father of one boy who had paid out too much interest appeared at the heder to complain. A search of the moneylender's pockets proved so fruitful that he too was whipped.

The saint's hypocrisy was recognized at last, despite his whispered secrets and his flatteries.

Then, as if in response to my prayers, the boys began speaking to me once more. The flatterers and the traders offered me good will and bargains—I don't know why. I might even have formed a group of my own, but I wasn't inclined that way. There was only one boy whose friendship I wanted, and he was the one I chose. He was a fine, decent person without social ambitions. We studied from the same Pentateuch, walked with our arms about each other, and learned to write Yiddish. Others, jealous, intrigued against us, but our friendship remained constant. We were like David and Jonathan ...

Even after I left the heder, this friendship persisted. I attended several heders, and from each one I had retained a friend. Occasionally, in the evenings, we would meet near the markets, and walk along the sidewalk, talking, making plans. Their names were Mottel Horowitz, Mendel Besser, Abraham something-or-other, Boruch-Dovid, and others.

More or less their leader, I would tell them things my
older brother had told my mother. There was a great
feeling of trust among us, until one day I had the
impression that they resented me. They grumbled
about my bossiness; I had to be demoted a little. They
were preparing a revolution and I saw it in their
faces. And even though I asked how I had offended
them, they behaved like Joseph's brothers and could
not answer amicably. They couldn't even look at me
directly. What was it they envied? My dreams... I
could actually hear them say as I entered their
domain, "Behold this dreamer cometh... Let us slay
him and cast him in some pit... Let us sell him to the
Ishmaelites..."

It is painful to be among one's brothers when they
are jealous. They were good to me, they praised me,
and then they were mean. All at once they grew
angry. Turning away as I approached, they whispered...

Friendships with me are not casual; I cannot make
new friends easily. I wondered if I had sinned against
them, or deceived them. But if so, why hadn't they
told me what was wrong?

I could not recollect having harmed them in any
way, nor had I said anything against them. And if
someone had slandered me, why should my friends
believe it? After all, they were devoted to me.

There was nothing to do but wait it out. My kind
has to become accustomed to loneliness. And when
one is alone there is nothing to do but study. I became
a diligent scholar. I would spend whole days in the
Radzymin study house and then pore over religious
works at home. Purchasing books from peddlers, I
read constantly. It was summertime and the days
were long. Reading a story of three brothers, I
imagined that I could write too, and began to cover
both sides of a sheet. "Once there was a king who had
three sons, one was wise, one foolish, and one
merry..." But somehow the story didn't jell.

On another paper I began to draw freakish

humans and fantastic beasts. But this too wearied me, and going out to the balcony I looked down at the street. Only I was alone. Other boys were running, playing, and talking together. I'll go mad, I thought—there was too much happening in my head all the time. Shouldn't I jump from the balcony? Or spit down on the janitor's cap?

That evening, at the Radzymin study house, a boy approached me, acting as a go-between. He spoke tactfully, suggesting that my friends were eager for an understanding, but since I was the minority, it was up to me to make the first move. In short, he suggested that I submit a plea for truce.

I was infuriated. "It wasn't I who started this," I said. "Why should I be the one to make up?"

"You'll regret it," he warned.

"Leave!" I commanded.

He left angrily. His job as a trucemaker had been spoiled. But he knew I was adamant.

Now that they had sent an intermediary, I knew that my friends were remorseful. But I would never give in to them.

I grew accustomed to being alone and the days no longer seemed interminable. I studied, wrote, read stories. My brother had brought home a two-volume book called *Crime and Punishment*. Although I didn't really comprehend it, it fascinated me. Secluded in the bedroom, I read for hours. A student who had killed a crone suffered, starved, and reasoned profoundly. Coming before the prosecutor, he was questioned ... It was something like a story-book, but different. Strange and lofty, it reminded me of the Cabala. Who were the authors of books like this, and who could understand them? Now and then a passage became illuminated for me, I understood an episode, and grew enthralled by the beauty of a new insight.

I was in another world. I forgot about my friends.

At evening services in the Radzymin study house, I was unaware of the men among whom I stood. My mind was wandering when suddenly the intermediary approached.

"Nothing you have to say can interest me," I said.

"Here's a note," he told me.

It was like a scene from a novel. My friends wrote that they missed me. "We wander about in a daze..." I still remember what they said. Despite this great triumph, I was so immersed in my book that it scarcely seemed important any more that they wanted to make amends. I went out to the courtyard, and there they were. It reminded me of Joseph and his brothers. They had come to Joseph to buy grain, but why had my friends come to me?

Nevertheless, they did come, ashamed and somehow afraid—Simon, Levi, Judah.... Since I had not become Egypt's ruler, they were not required to bow down to the earth. I had nothing to sell but new dreams.

We talked together late and I spoke of my book. "This is no storybook, this is literature..." I said. I created for them a fantastic mélange of incidents and my own thoughts, and infected them with my excitement. Hours passed. They begged me to forgive them, confessed that they had been wrong and never would be angry with me again...

They kept their word.

Only time separated us. The rest was accomplished by the German murderers.

The Shot at Sarajevo

FOR A LONG TIME our family had discussed the possibility of moving from our flat at No. 10 Krochmalna Street, where we used a kerosene lamp because there was no gas and shared an outhouse in the courtyard with everyone else in the building. This outhouse was the bane of my childhood. It was dark there all the time, and filthy. Rats and mice were everywhere, overhead as well as on the floor. Many children, because of it, were stricken with constipation and developed nervous disorders.

The staircase was another plague because certain children preferred it to the outhouse. Worse still, there were women who used it as a garbage dump. The janitor, who was supposed to light lamps along the staircase, seldom did so, and when he did, we were deprived of them by ten-thirty. The tiny, smoke-stained lamps gave so little light that the darkness seemed to thicken around them. When I used this murky staircase, I was pursued by all the devils, evil spirits, demons, and imps of whom my parents spoke to prove to the older children that there was a God and a future life. Cats raced along beside me. From behind closed doors, one often heard a wailing for the dead. At the courtyard gate a funeral procession might be waiting. I was breathless by the time I reached my door. Nightmares began to come to me, so horrifying that I would wake from sleep drenched in sweat.

We found it hard enough to pay the twenty-four rubles a month rent for a front apartment and balcony; then how could we afford to move to No. 12 Krochmalna Street, a new house with gas lights and toilets, where the rent would be twenty-seven? However, we decided that changing our place would change our luck....

It was the spring of 1914.

The newspapers had for years referred to the explosive situation in the Balkans and the rivalry between England and Germany. But there were no newspapers in my home any more. It was my brother Israel Joshua who brought them there, and he had moved out after an argument with my father.

Everyone told us to change apartments. The No. 12 landlord, Leizer Przepiorko, was an Orthodox millionaire. Reputedly stingy, he had all the same never evicted a Jew. The house manager, Reb Isaiah, was an old Kotzk Hasid, my father's friend. Since No. 12 had a gate that led to Mirowski Place, to the bazaars, Father would be Rabbi for both Krochmalna and Mirowski streets. Also, many lawsuits, weddings, and divorces were scheduled at that time, meaning extra money for us. We decided to move.

Freshly painted, the new apartment faced a bakery, and the kitchen window looked out on a wall. There were five or six stories over us.

No. 12 was like a city. It had three enormous courtyards. The dark entrance always smelled of freshly baked bread, rolls and bagels, caraway seed and smoke. Koppel the baker's yeasty breads were always outside, rising on boards. In No. 12 there were also two Hasidic study houses, the Radzymin and Minsk, as well as a synagogue for those who opposed Hasidism. There was also a stall where cows were kept chained to the wall all year round. In some cellars, fruit had been stored by dealers from Mirowski Place; in others, eggs were preserved in lime. Wagons arrived there from the provinces. No.

12 swarmed with Torah, prayer, commerce, and toil. Kerosene lamps were unheard of. Some apartments even had telephones.

But it had not been an easy move, even though Nos. 10 and 12 adjoined. We had to load our things in a wagon, and some of them broke. Our wardrobe was unbelievably heavy, a fortress with lion heads on oaken doors, and a cornice covered with engravings that weighed a ton. How it had been dragged from Bilgoray is beyond me.

I will never forget lighting the two-jet gas lamp for the first time. I was dazzled and intimidated by the strange radiance that filled the apartment and even seemed to penetrate my skull. Demons would have a hard time hiding here.

The toilet delighted me. So did the gas oven in the kitchen. It was not necessary any more to prepare kindling for tea or bring in coal. One only had to strike a match and watch the blue flame ignite. Nor would I have to drag jugs of kerosene from the store, since there was a gas meter, where one inserted a forty-groschen piece to get gas. And I knew many people here because it was in this courtyard that I always prayed.

For a while, our predicted good luck came about. Father's lawsuits were numerous. Things went so well that year that Father decided to enroll me in a heder once more. I was past heder age, being able to learn a page of Talmud by myself, as well as some of the Commentaries. But at No. 22 Twarda Street there was a special heder for older boys where the teacher lectured instead of studying with his pupils. Some of my friends from other heders attended this one.

I was at that time reading forbidden books and had developed a taste for heresy; it was rather ridiculous, therefore, that I was attending heder again. My friends and I made fun of the teacher, who had a yellow beard and bulging eyes, spoke with a ridiculous accent, ate raw onions, and smoked stinking tobacco in a long pipe. He was divorced and matchmakers came to whisper secrets in his hairy ears...

Suddenly there were rumors of war. The Austrian Crown Prince had been shot, they said, in Serbia. Newspaper extras appeared, printed only on one side, and with huge headlines. Discussing politics, we boys decided that it would be preferable for Germany to win—what would be gained from Russian rule? German occupation would put all Jews into short jackets, and the Gymnasium would be compulsory. What could be better than going to worldly schools in uniforms and decorated caps? At the same time we were convinced (much more than the German General Staff) that German's strength could never match the combined forces of Russia, France, and England. One boy speculated that because of a shared language it was only natural that America should step in to help England...

My father began to read newspapers. New words were prevalent—mobilization, ultimatum, neutrality. The rival governments sent notes. The kings wrote letters one to the other and called themselves Nicky and Willy. The common people, workers, porters, met in groups on Krochmalna Street to discuss conditions.

Suddenly it was the Ninth Day of Ab—the Sunday which is the postponed fast day. It was also the beginning of the war.

Women were everywhere, buying up food. Small though they were, they carried huge baskets of flour, groats, beans, and whatever else they could find in the stores, which were closed half the time. First the storekeepers rejected crumpled bank notes, then they demanded silver and gold instead of paper. They began hoarding their stock in order to increase prices.

People were in a festive mood as if it were Purim. Women weepingly trailed their husbands, bearded Jews with tiny white pins in their lapels, indicating

that they had been called up for military service.
Annoyed and amused at once, the men strutted along
while children behind them carried sticks on their
shoulders and called out military commands.

Running home from the Radzymin study house,
my father announced that he had heard the war
would be over in two weeks. "They have cannons that
can kill a thousand Cossacks at one blow."

"Woe..." cried my mother. "What is the world
coming to?"

Father consoled her, "Well, there won't be any
more rent to pay..."

My mother went on, "And who will want lawsuits?
Where will we get the money to eat?"

We were in trouble. There were no more letters from
my sister in Antwerp, and my twenty-one-year-old
brother Israel Joshua had to report for conscription
in Tomaszow, my father's home town. We had no
money with which to stock up on food, as our
neighbors did. Knowing how hungry I was going to
become, I experienced an extraordinarily gnawing
appetite. I ate insatiably. Mother would come in
flushed from outside, moaning about the food shortage.

Now, for the first time, I began to hear unflattering
bits of gossip about other Jews on the street. Jewish
storekeepers, just like the Gentiles, were hiding
goods, raising prices, trying to capitalize on the war.
Moshe the paper dealer, who lived in our courtyard,
boasted in the study house about his wife's purchase
of five hundred rubles' worth of food. "Thank God,"
he said, "I have provisions for a year. How much
longer can the war last?" And he smilingly stroked
his silver beard.

There was considerable confusion. Young men
with blue tickets were able to study the Talmud, but
pale and concerned, the green-ticketed ones tried to
lose weight to avoid the draft. Men who sold flour and
groats were lucky, but not so the now unemployed
bookbinders, teachers, and scribes. The Germans

captured Kalisz, Bedzin, and Czestochowa. I felt the burden of maturity and expected a mysterious catastrophe. It seemed to me that if only we had accepted the lack of toilets and gas in No. 10, we might have been spared all this...

This was the war between Gog and Magog, Father said. And every day he discovered new omens proving that the Messiah was soon to come....

The Recruit

MY BROTHER ISRAEL JOSHUA was supposed to appear for conscription in Tomaszow immediately after the Feast of Tabernacles. Difficult as this would have been for my parents in normal times, now it seemed like assigning him to the furnace. Had he remained a Hasid, a wealthy father-in-law would have ransomed him. At the most, he might have wounded himself a little. Poland was full of malingerers with punctured eardrums, extracted teeth, and amputated fingers. Why serve the Tsar? But, influenced by modern ideas, my brother found it necessary to offer himself to the army.

My brother, who was painting and writing a little and educating himself, lived with another family and would come to visit us dressed in modern clothes. Father was shamed and humiliated by him, and occasionally so angered that he would order my brother out of the house. But he didn't want his son to die at the front.

Mother prayed and wept, while Father tried to induce my brother to wound himself.

"Haven't we enough cripples already?" my brother asked. "The whole body of Jews is one big hunchback..."

On the side of enlightenment, he spoke sharply and with great clarity, joking despite his dilemma. It was hard to know exactly where he stood. Although opposed to piety, he was aware of the faults of worldly existence. Hadn't worldliness itself caused the war? Inclined toward socialism, he was at the same time too skeptical to have that much faith in humanity. My father summed up my brother's point of view with, "Neither this world nor the world to come...."

But in Father's eyes a berth with a wealthy father-in-law was to be preferred to secluding oneself in an attic, wallowing in heretic literature, painting indecent pictures, and participating in a Gentile war. There was still time, my father said; it was still possible to find an affluent bride. But my brother's views were not mercurial. What he decided was what he did. Despite my youth, I understood his problem— he had deserted the old, but there was nothing in the new that he could call his own. Despite his divorce from Jewish ways, he would remain a Jew to the Gentiles on the draft board, and therefore, as were all Jews, was suspected of spying.

Traveling to Tomaszow was dangerous in trains filled with soldiers, recruits, bullies, and anti-Semites. The Tsar's uncle had driven the Jews out of villages, and an occasional Rabbi or pious Jew was hanged for supposedly selling military secrets during the ceremony of blessing the new moon. In Warsaw, provincial Jews roamed from one study house to another, eating at soup kitchens. Tearing at her cheeks, my mother begged my brother to stay. But if he failed to report he would be imprisoned as a deserter.

Having made up his mind, he left, promising to write immediately. But days and weeks went by without a letter. It was a black period in my life. Mother, who stopped eating and sleeping, wept and prayed all day long. Father said nothing. What was God's will? There were no more marriages, divorces, lawsuits, and we had no means of livelihood. Cold weather followed the Feast of the Tabernacles, but coal had become a luxury. Having moved into the apartment during the summer, we now discovered in the wet fall that the tile oven smoked.

My father went on studying as usual. He covered sheets of paper in defense of Rashi in whose Commentary Rabbi Tam had found contradictions. Sucking watery tea through a bit of sugar, he would now and then fall into deep thought. He sent me out for newspapers and read with difficulty the stories in journalese about massacres, pogroms, savagery. He kept asking me what was a machine gun, a grenade, mines...They were always described as if they were inventions of enormous value.

Father would cry out, "Woe is us...dear God above. How long, how long? We are already up to our neck..."

We were convinced that something had happened to my brother, for after all he would have written even if he had been drafted. Had he been murdered on a train? Or—God forbid—he could have committed suicide...

There was a lot of rain and a kind of perpetual dusk. Someone had stolen our storm windows before we could install them, and consequently the window-panes rattled. Austria had occupied Bilgoray and Tomaszow, and had been driven out again by Russia. What had happened to Grandfather, Grandmother, the family? The war was no longer being fought in distant places, Serbia, Manchuria—it had come home to us, and synagogues were being burned. German cannons were audible in Warsaw, roaring all day and thundering at night. Strangely enough, the Hasidim in the Radzymin study houses looked up from the Talmud and divided their sympathies, some for Russia, the others for Germany, just as if they were Gentiles.

I was constantly hungry, but Mother no longer cooked. Her son was lost among the wicked and she lay awake listening to the sounds of cannon, rain, and the wind whistling through our apartment. The Almighty, as only the Almighty can, remained silent to her beseeching prayers, her vows to give to charity if my brother would be saved. This all-powerful Father who sat in Seventh Heaven on the Throne of Glory, surrounded by angels, seraphim, and cherubim, and allowed Rabbis to be hanged began to annoy me. How much more would Israel have to endure? I could only conclude that He did not exist. What was there, then? How had everything been created?

One night as we huddled fearfully in our beds we heard a knock at the door. Mother got up, asking, "Who is it?"

"Joshua..."

She gasped.

Father lit the gas, and my brother, whom we had given up for lost, entered, casting an enormous shadow, dressed in modern clothes despite a blond beard. Wearing a derby, tall and imposing, he seemed altered, had grown older and more important-looking, as if he had just come back from a journey in a foreign land. "Put out the light," he said. He had deserted, he told us, and would be executed if they caught him.

Sitting with us in the bedroom, he told us what had happened. Grandfather, the Bilgoray Rabbi, had taken a trip to try to get my brother exempted, but had been unsuccessful. Then he had hesitantly advised desertion. Somehow my brother had acquired a false passport and now used the name of Rentner. The description on the passport was so unlike him that he was always in dread of police examination. He had been traveling in trains, wagons, freights, and on foot, and dared not remain

at home because they might start searching for him
any day. But he had no place to go, and would have to
make a decision in the morning. There was a kind of
pride behind what he said.

He was intoxicated with fatigue. He lay down in
the bed my father had given up for him, and fell
asleep immediately. My parents continued whispering long afterwards. Every time the gate bell rang, we
were terrified. At one time it had been possible for us
to forget that there were such things as police,
soldiers, and the laws of Gentiles, but no longer...

In the morning, my father gave my brother a set of
phylacteries and he wound the thongs about his arm,
mumbled, and promptly unwound them again. He
ate a crust of bread and left, promising that we would
hear from him soon.

To us, it seemed as if we had been dreaming. At the
Holy Ark, Father leaned his head against the curtain
and prayed in silence. Mother paced back and forth.
My brother's return had been miraculous, but he was
still in danger. Would Mother's intercession in
heaven keep him safe? Perhaps even now he was
being arrested.

"We must have mercy..." Mother said.

"The Almighty will help," Father promised.

A few moments before my brother appeared,
Mother said, she had fallen asleep and been awakened by a verse from the Psalms. But this was not
unusual. Every night she woke up with a verse, at
times not even knowing where it came from. Later
she would locate it somewhere in Ezekiel or the
Twelve Minor Prophets....

After the rains there was snow. In the papers we
read that the Germans were retreating, "leaving
behind many dead and wounded." But for us this was
bad news, since the German capture of Warsaw
would have meant my brother's freedom.

My mother was back at the stove, my younger
brother Moishe at the heder, while I, in the Radzymin

study house, read the Gemara. From somewhere in
hiding, my brother sent word. I had become a
frequent reader of the newspapers, accustoming
myself to the unfamiliar Yiddish, and I absorbed
everything, even the serials, the humorous articles,
and the jokes. Although infuriated with Germany,
the papers sided with her in a sly way ... Incongrui-
ties were many. Beside an article praising the
Hasidim, the Baal Shem, the Kotzker Rabbi, there
was a story of a veiled countess riding in a coach to
meet her lover. There were stories for the Jews and
against them, pious articles and heretic ones.
Snatching the paper from me, and scanning it,
Mother said, "All they want is your pennies ..."

Well, and what did the Tsar's uncle want? Or
Kaiser Wilhelm? Or old Franz Josef? And—to beg the
comparison—what did the Emperor of everything,
the Creator of Heaven and Earth require? That He
could go on watching soldiers fall on battlefields?

"The Lord is good to all and His mercies are over
all His works ..."

Was this so? Or did I mouth a lie two times a day? I
must find an answer, and I must do so before the time
of my *bar mizvah* ...

The Studio

THE STRANGE NEWS reached us that my brother had
moved into an artist's studio, where he lived with a

false passport and painted—apparently unsuccess-
fully. Mother sent me there one day carrying a basket
of food.

The studio, which I think was at No. 1 Twarda
Street, belonged to the famous sculptor Ostrzego who
years later carved the monument over Peretz's grave.
After climbing five flights of stairs, I entered a
fantastic hall with a large skylight and landscapes,
portraits, and nude paintings on the wall. Statues
covered with moistened sacks were in the center of
the room. I was reminded of a greenhouse which I
had once seen, and of a Gentile cemetery. A Hasidic-
looking person, small and stooped as a yeshivah boy,
happened to be removing one of the sacks, exposing a
surprisingly lifelike woman, a kind of female golem
who would perhaps shortly perform miracles
through the power of the Cabala. Frightened and
ashamed, I remained at the door, my mouth open.
Walking up to me, the small man said, "You are
Joshua's brother?"

"Yes."

"I recognized you right away. The same facial
structure. Your brother is in the next room."

As if the statues were shrouded corpses, I walked
between them in fear of contact. The man opened the
door and I found my brother in the midst of other
young men and girls. "Look, a guest!" my brother
called out.

They examined me with the curious penetration of
artists. I heard them murmur, "Interesting..." I was
introduced to a painter named Felix Rubinlicht.

Speaking both Yiddish and Polish, they behaved
as no other young people I had ever seen. It seemed to
me that they were all somehow related, not only to
each other, but to the student, Raskolnikov, about
whom I had been reading. My gabardine and
sidelocks embarrassed me, although my brother did
not seem discomfitted by them.

He asked what I was studying. Ostrzego questioned me about the Talmud; he could still recite

sections from memory. The sacred words sounded
odd coming from the lips of a hatless man in such
surroundings. The girls smiled wearily. Finally,
Rubinlicht asked me to pose. When I sat down, he
held his hand before him to measure the proportions,
frowned, and began to sketch. Others gathered
around him, commenting. Finally the drawing
appeared, myself translated into line, tone, and
shadow, looking like something I might become some
day, or have been in a former existence.

Quibbling about the resemblance of the drawing to
the original, the artists made me feel important, as I
had once before felt in a clinic where several doctors
poked my belly, back, and ribs. No one, in my Hasidic
background, had ever mentioned my red hair, white
skin, and blue eyes, but here the body was respected;
there was more to a boy than the ability to study. But
awareness of my body shamed me. Yet I began to see
that others had physical characteristics also.

My brother asked what Father was doing.

"Studying."

"Studying? How long will that go on? The world
goes to pieces and they still ponder the egg laid on a
holiday."

The door swung back and forth incessantly as
other men and girls came in, among them a young
man in a velvet jacket and a bobbed-haired girl with
unusually black eyes. All acquainted, speaking
wittily, they seemed far beyond me in wisdom and
knowledge; their eyes were worldly, intelligent. A boy
entered who did not seem much older than I, but who
had the manner of an experienced person, an
appearance of strength. I believe he was the painter
Haim Hanft. Later, when I came to know these
people, I spoke to them as an equal, but at that time
they appeared like beings from a superior world.

I visited my brother several times, but each visit
startled me all over again. I was fascinated by the
thought of being in a room with a glass roof. Through
the skylight I could glimpse blue sky, sun, and birds.

Passover had come and gone. The paintings and statues were spangled with light. Every time I came, Ostrzego would have to lift the moist sacks again so that I could see the statues, which became more and more real for me, as if the hunchback had breathed a soul into them.

I was astonished at the sight of naked breasts on the figures of young and pretty girls, for I had assumed that breasts were solely the property of slovenly women who nursed babies in public. I had been brought up to believe that only a lecher observed such things, but I came to realize that artists looked at them differently.

The ways of the intelligentsia became more familiar to me. They neither prayed nor studied from holy books nor made benedictions. They ate meat with milk, and broke other laws. The girls posed nude with no more shame than they would have about undressing in their own bedrooms. In fact, it was like the Garden of Eden there, before Adam and Eve had partaken of the Tree of Knowledge. Although they spoke Yiddish, these young people acted as freely as Gentiles.

This was quite a change from my father's studio, but it seems to me that this pattern has become inherent to me. Even in my stories it is just one step from the study house to sexuality and back again. Both phases of human existence have continued to interest me.

Even though Germany had been compelled by the Russians to retreat in the fall of 1914, the Germans were once more advancing, and we heard the cannons again. But we had become accustomed to the war. Soldiers were dying in battle, but the sun shone on us, and as long as the Russians were in possession of Warsaw we didn't starve, even though food was expensive and scarce. In the courtyard of the house where the studio was, there was a market where one could buy many things. The city was full of refugees and soldiers, many of them unfamiliar, like Circassians with huge *papachas,* chests bulging with daggers and cartridges. There were Kalmucks, and other savage people, all in their own uniforms, some leaving for the front, others returning. The barracks were jammed. Wagons full of wounded rode by, like mobile hospitals, the men within swathed in bandages and the gloom of death.

In the study houses and houses of prayer, one came upon the strange sight of homeless people, dreary mothers with children, cooking utensils, and bedding. Nothing was as it should have been, and perhaps because of this I grew accustomed to my brother's studio.

The Russians, who had been so victorious during the winter were now on the run, having been driven out of Galicia, the Carpathians, and Königsberg. The "brave" Cossacks and Circassians of the communiqués had become frightened peasants fleeing before the German and Austrian armies. But how had the generals who had been so brilliant in the winter turned so stupid in the summertime?

Questions were endless. Of all the journalists who tried to explain matters, one Itchele tried hardest, spicing his political discussions with quotations from the Talmud and Midrash. My father, each time he read Itchele, would remark, "How clever!"

There were only two writers whom my father would acknowledge, Peretz and Itchele. Of the two of them, he preferred the Talmud-quoting Itchele, although he hadn't read Peretz. But having been informed in the Radzymin study house that Peretz ridiculed the Jewish way of life, he cursed this writer with, "May his name be blotted out!"

After the war, however, Father never looked at a newspaper again. He must have heard that my brother and I were writers, but he decided that we were in the newspaper business. "Do you still deal in newspapers?" he asked the last time we saw him. Perhaps being in the newspaper business was in his eye preferable to writing. After all, as long as one sold something, what difference what the product was?

Hunger

IT TURNED OUT that the German occupation of
Warsaw did not result in the Jews wearing modern
dress and all boys being sent to gymnasiums. Jews
remained in their gabardines and boys continued to
attend heder. Only the German constables in blue
capes were new, and Polish and Jewish militiamen
carried rubber truncheons in the streets. But the
shortage of goods increased, the stores became more
depleted, the women peddling fruit and provisions in
Yanash's bazaar and the markets had almost
nothing left to sell, and hunger began to be felt
everywhere. German marks now mingled with
Russian money, and the feature writer from the
Yiddish paper *The Moment* left off praising the Allies
and began to vilify them. He prophesied the German
occupation of St. Petersburg.

People came to worship at our house for the High
Holy Days, but most of the women were unable to pay
for pews. When Asher the dairyman rose to recite,
both men and women began to wail. The words
"Some will perish this year by the sword and some
from starvation, some by fire and some by flood" had
become grimly vivid. One felt that Providence was
preparing something terrible. Our Rosh Hashanah
meal was meager, even though one is supposed to eat
well on a holy day and especially at the beginning of

the New Year. Father had not been called in very often for lawsuits, weddings, or divorces, but he was often consulted on questions of religious law, for which he received no payment.

Nevertheless, the Germans did bring us one bit of luck in the form of my brother Joshua's freedom. He no longer had to hide under an assumed name. He could visit us, but every time he did so, there was a quarrel. My father could not accept his smooth chin and modern clothes.

My brother and his worldly books had sown the seeds of heresy in my mind. We Jews with our belief in a God whose existence could not be proved had neither country nor land to work, nor had we devoted ourselves to the study of trades. Storekeepers with nothing to sell now roamed the streets.

At No. 10 Krochmalna Street we had shared a booth with poor neighbors during the Feast of Tabernacles, but at No. 12, with families better off than we, the contrast between our food and theirs was all too evident. I especially remember my mother serving me a broth in which there was nothing "under the broth," as the saying goes. Reb Isaiah the superintendent, noticing this, threw in a pretzel, much to my consternation. All the same, I was grateful that he had been so considerate.

The war demonstrated for me how unnecessary Rabbis were, my father among them. From all the towns and villages, Rabbis and other ecclesiastics converged on Warsaw, dejectedly walking the streets in their silk gabardines looking for a piece of bread. Thousands of matchmakers, brokers, and small businessmen had no way of earning a living. Starving men dozed over their Talmud volumes in study houses and houses of prayer. The winter was cold and there was no fuel for the ovens.

In the house of prayer, some Jews explained that when Esau is stuffing himself, Jacob can find a small bone somewhere; but when Esau goes to war and

suffers, it's the end for Jacob. If only God would take
pity on Israel and send help! But heaven at that time
was apparently not thinking of Jews.

I would like to tell about Joseph Mattes, who
devoted himself to religious matters while his wife
sold geese. Even before the German occupation, the
cost of a goose had risen to twenty-five rubles. Who on
Krochmalna Street could afford such luxury? Joseph
Mattes, his wife, daughters, and their husbands had
been left penniless. While other goose dealers had
managed to put something aside, Joseph Mattes had
given his whole fortune to charity and the Radzymin
Rabbi.

The extent of his poverty was not known by those
in -the study house, and besides, the war had
intensified individual selfishness. Men with full
pantries worshipped alongside those who had
nothing, but seldom thought of helping them. There
wasn't actually that much food to share. Fear of the
future haunted everyone. No one any longer thought
the war would end soon.

I became personally acquainted with hunger, and
I noticed that the skin hung loosely on Joseph
Mattes's pale face. But his son-in-law, Israel Joshua,
was even paler and more emaciated. The young man,
tugging at a barely sprouting beard, hovered over the
holy books, sighing and stealing glances beyond
them. The delicate young man suffered from shame
as well. He yearned to serve the Almighty, but hunger
tormented him. Sinking ever more deeply into the
Hasidic books, he twisted his sidelocks incessantly.
What could he do about it, I wondered, this son-in-law
living on his father-in-law's bounty and starving?
Timid and weak, prematurely round-shouldered, he
could do nothing but study and pray, and look into
the *Grace of Elimelech* or *The Holiness of Levi....*

One Friday evening, Joseph Mattes, who had
given his fortune toward Hasid banquets and the
support of the Radzymin Rabbi, slammed his fist on

the table, shouting, "Men, I don't have the bread to usher in the Sabbath!"

His words were an indication of the times. Bread had had to be substituted for the Sabbath wine when making the benediction.

For a moment there was silence, and after that, tumult, confusion. Reb Joseph's sons retreated into corners, dreadfully ashamed of what their father had said. Israel Joshua became chalk-white. Despite the collection of bread, fish, and Sabbath loaves that was taken up that night, nothing, essentially, changed. Paupers remained paupers, and benefactors were few. I felt terribly afraid the same thing might happen to my father.

Like most of the Rabbis, the Radzymin Rabbi had moved to Warsaw, where he owned property. He was reputedly wealthy, but this was dubious, since real estate had ceased to provide income. I do not know whether he helped the Hasidim or not. Nevertheless, we were so much in need that Father paid a visit to the Radzymin Rabbi's wife—who was partially responsible for my father's loss of position as head of the yeshivah. This so-called "young Rebbetzin," however, was not to be envied, for even though medical opinion blamed her husband for their lack of children, the Rabbi insisted it was his wife's fault and demanded a divorce. Although she did not object to a divorce, the Rebbetzin asked a 25,000 ruble settlement, which the Rabbi was unwilling to pay. He was constantly tormenting and disgracing her, she told Father, taking her to Wonder Rabbis and doctors, refusing to give her sufficient household money. Unable to lend Father anything, she begged him to accept her diamond ring and pawn it. Father protested, but the Rebbetzin swore: "By my life and health, take it!" showing him, at the same time, a Talmudic passage that prohibited the wearing of jewelry while others starved.

When Father in his shame returned home carrying

the ring in a box, Mother made a face, perhaps from
jealousy. But when Father pawned the ring, we
bought flour, bread, and groats. Meat was too
expensive. We began to use cocoa butter, which could
be eaten with both meat and milk dishes.

The most difficult thing to bear at that time was
the cold, and we could not afford to heat the
apartment. Our pipes froze and it was impossible to
use the toilet. For weeks, frost patterns decorated our
windows and icicles hung from the frames. When I
was thirsty I broke off an icicle and sucked it.

At night the cold was unendurable. No amount of
covering sufficed. The wind, rustling through our
apartment, made me think of goblins. Huddled in
bed, I had fantasies of treasures, black magic,
incantations that would help my parents, Joseph
Mattes, and everyone else who suffered. I imagined
myself Elijah, the Messiah, and whatnot... Like the
biblical Joseph, I filled storehouses with food and
threw them open in the seven years of famine. A word
from me made whole armies tremble, as well as their
generals and the emperors behind them. I gave the
Radzymin Rebbetzin a basketful of diamonds.

It was too cold to get out of bed. Mother and we
children never arose until late in the day, but Father
forced himself to dress. The water for his ablutions
froze. He rubbed his hands on the windowpanes and
placed a pan of ice on the stove. He had learned to use
the gas jet, but the meter still required a forty-
groschen piece. Tea was his one luxury, although it
consisted almost entirely of hot water with just a
pinch of tea leaves. Sugar was unavailable and he
detested saccharin. Wrapped in a padded gabardine,
he drank his tea and studied, writing with frozen
fingers. In *The Face of Joshua* everything was as it
had been, and the *Roar of the Lion* asked the ancient
questions: Is the reading of *Shema* based on Mosaic
or rabbinic law? Is one obliged to repeat all of it,
according to Mosaic law, or only the first verse? Or

the first section? Only there did Father feel comforted.

Before the war I used to buy him several packs of cigarettes a day, and he also used to smoke a pipe. But now that cigarettes cost so much, he would fill his pipe with a peasant type of tobacco called Majorka. Smoking, drinking weak tea, he studied endlessly. What else was there but the Torah?

In desperate straits again, my brother Israel Joshua was living at home, sleeping on a table in my father's study, where the cold was worse than it was outside. My mother covered him with whatever she could find.

In spite of the terrible frosts, mice invaded our apartment, attacking books and clothes, leaping about at night with suicidal abandon. Mother obtained a cat, but it observed their activities indifferently, its yellow eyes implying, "Let them run. Who cares?"

Her mind seemed to be far away, she was always dozing, dreaming. "Who knows?" Father said. "She might be a reincarnation...."

Father took care of her respectfully. Wasn't it possible that she might have the soul of a saint? After all, a saint who sins is returned to earth for a while. The earth was full of transmigrant souls sent back to correct a single transgression. When Father ate, he would call the cat to him, and with an air of majesty she would allow herself to be coaxed, eating slowly and discriminatingly. Then she would look up gravely, as if to say, "If you knew who I am, you would feel honored to have me here...."

How could she go after mice?

Vain Hopes

AFTER SUCCESSIVE GERMAN VICTORIES it seemed
evident that Warsaw would become part of Germany
just as Bilgoray had been annexed by the Austrian
Empire. Two head Rabbis appeared out of Germany,
a Dr. Carlbach and a Dr. Kohn, and it was rumored
that they wished to turn us all into German Jews.
Even though they studied the Talmud, they spoke
German and were friendly with generals. An orthodox man, Nahum Leib Weingut, sought them out
with the intention of uniting the German and
Warsaw rabbinates, but community leaders were not
too enthusiastic about this. After all, it was still
wartime, and if one sided with the Germans now,
what would happen if the Russians suddenly
overcame them? When the rabbinate decided to
remain neutral, Weingut determined to use unofficial
Rabbis for his purpose, and called a meeting at which
he promised them official status and salaries if only
they permitted him to become their spokesman.

Unofficial Rabbis, who had seldom come to our
house before, began to visit us. It was summer, and
our apartment looked better. Previously there hadn't
been much for one unofficial Rabbi to say to another,
but now they formed an association and a federation,
elected a committee, and chose a president. My father
attended the meetings. Every time there was a knock
at the door, it opened to a man in silk gabardine and

velvet hat. Our neighbors watched respectfully the
line of Rabbis asking for our apartment. Mother
served tea and Father turned down the place of honor
in favor of white-bearded Reb Dan. Our apartment
had become festive, a gathering place for the Sanhedrin.

Worldly matters were discussed as well as the
Torah. They agreed that if God willed it, Weingut's
plans would materialize, but meanwhile one had to
go on making a living. A fierce-eyed Rabbi with pitch-
black hair protested that he approved neither the
council nor the leaders. What if an alliance were
formed to force out impractical members?

"Why should they, God forbid?" Father said.

"These days," the other Rabbi said, "everyone
does what he alone thinks is right."

"But the world hasn't gone completely mad,"
Father replied.

"The evil spirit," said the Rabbi from Kupiecka
Street, "isn't cowed by a satin capote."

"Then it is the end of the world!" Father cried.

As the discussions went on, one Rabbi stroked his
beard, another his skullcap, a third his high
forehead, while a fourth wound the ritual fringe
around his index finger. How differently, I thought,
all these unofficial Rabbis looked and behaved! Over
the belly of one fat Rabbi the sash pressed like a hoop;
the mouth under his beard was round and fleshy, and
his eyes popped. He smoked a cigar, sent me out to get
seltzer, took a few coins from his pocket for my
brother Moishe to buy him cookies. Running to the
window, he wheezed, apparently from asthma.

Another Rabbi remained beside the bookcase,
ignoring everything, frowning into a book as if to
imply: None of this chatter means anything. Only
the holy words are important...

An aged Rabbi, to whom no one but Father
listened, quoted a saying from Reb Isaiah Moskat, or
Prager, as he had been called.

A youthful Rabbi with stringy sidelocks and a

sketchy beard sat there moodily, and finally took an old envelope out of his vest, scanned it, and wrote down a few words. He seemed not only skeptical of the plan but sorry to be in the company of such dreamers. Later I heard that he had a beautiful wife and a wealthy father-in-law who wanted him to go into business. The Rabbi from Kupiecka Street whispered to my father that he was afraid there was nothing in this whole venture but talk.

"Why not?"

"We were meant by Providence to be poor ..." And smiling wisely, he offered my father some snuff.

One day, the unofficial Rabbis were informed by Weingut that they were to meet and be addressed by a great leader with a Von in front of his name, at city hall. To go to the city hall and speak with a lord? My father was terrified. Also, he couldn't see the sense in combing out his beard and wearing his best clothes, as Weingut had advised. Why should he mingle with Germans? He had refused to be tested by the Russian governor—then why should he see a German official? Mother was annoyed. "What are you afraid of? No one will ask you to dance with the ladies...."

"I don't understand German...I'm afraid...I don't want..."

"What's there to lose—your poverty?"

Other unofficial Rabbis, as intimidated as he, came to call. The Kupiecka Street Rabbi asked Father's opinion.

"What if they just want to convert us?"

"But Nahum Leib Weingut is a Hasidic Jew."

"Is he in charge of our affairs?"

"What could a German have to say to us?"

"God forbid, maybe we'll be exiled from Warsaw..."

The Kupiecka Street Rabbi was pessimistic and apparently even more timid than Father, because Father became stronger in the other man's presence.

"In wartime it might prove just as dangerous not to go as to go..."

"We could say we're sick..."

They decided finally to go. The preceding day, Father went to the ritual bath, and soaked his beard. Mother prepared a clean shirt and breeches for him, removed as many stains as possible from his gabardine, sewed, and patched. Father prayed and sighed that morning, having little inclination to study. Since it was Monday, he recited the confession, pleading, "Lean your ear toward me, God, and listen... open Your eyes and observe the abominations and the city whose name is profaned... God, hear, forgive and save before it is too late..."

Then he put on his satin gabardine and polished boots, went out to meet the other Rabbis, and accompanied them to city hall.

That night he told us that they had entered a hall full of police and high officials, and were ushered into a room where there was a portrait of Kaiser Wilhelm. The German Rabbis greeted them, and a nobleman, a military doctor in epaulets, lectured them on the need for cleanliness. Although he spoke German, they understood a little of what he said, especially when he showed them a much enlarged picture of a louse and said that it was the cause of typhoid fever. Begging the *Herren Rabbiners* to spread the word about cleanliness, which was also in accordance with their religion, he bowed and left the room.

"And what else?" Mother asked.

"Nothing."

"No positions? No wages?"

"Not a word."

"That's something they'll never talk about," she said.

"But they called us to city hall, so they must consider us official Rabbis."

"Hah!"

"Well, at least I lived through it. To tell you the truth, I didn't sleep a wink last night," Father said.

The following Sabbath he spoke of cleanliness in a synagogue while the congregation yawned and

shook their heads. If a cellar leaks, how can you keep
it clean? And how can you yourself stay clean
without an extra shirt, clothes, or even a piece of
bread? But they knew Father had received orders to
lecture them.

Mother was right, nothing came of it. The
unofficial Rabbis were forgotten by the Germans,
and Nahum Leib Weingut started an Orthodox
newspaper. Now it was journalists he needed instead
of Rabbis. My brother was now a writer, having
forsaken painting, and Weingut sent for him, asking
if he had a sketch about Jewish life with an Orthodox
angle....

My brother did have a sketch and it was published.
It was a humorous tale of a spinster. I recall that he
received eighteen marks for it.

Briefly, afterwards, the unofficial Rabbis met and
discussed various goals. It was thought that the
newly organized Orthodox Party would help them,
but the party was unable to do so and my father had
no faith in it. The outlandish name Orthodox did not
appeal to him and he was disturbed by their
newspaper, which employed modern language in
articles by unpious journalists. Perhaps this would
be instrumental in keeping young people from
becoming heretics, but to him the news items and
descriptions sounded too worldly.

My brother, on the other hand, started his career in
this newspaper, publishing a series of stories in it,
and translating a novel by the German author
Lehman, a history of Rabbi Joselman.

I began to read that newspaper, along with
Dostoevsky, Bergelson, and detective stories about
Sherlock Holmes and Max Spitzkopf. The detective
stories seemed like masterpieces to me. A sentence
from one of them remains in my memory, a caption
under a drawing showing Max Spitzkopf and his
assistant Fuchs, guns in hand, surprising a robber.
Spitzkopf is crying out, "Hands up, you rogue. We've
got you covered!"

For years these naïve words ran like music through my mind.

The Book

AS USUAL IN TIMES OF TROUBLE, the days passed slowly, but as I look back on them now, it seems that everything happened fast. We lived through the severe winter on half-frozen potatoes, with an occasional piece of cabbage browned in cocoa butter. On Saturdays our meal was *parve,* neither meat nor dairy, and we almost forgot the taste of meat and fish. For a while, my brother Israel Joshua repaired a bridge for the Germans (later describing the experience in a novel, *Blood Harvest*). He returned bearded and carrying the largest loaf of bread I have ever seen. Big as a wheel and almost as flat, it lasted us for weeks. He couldn't have brought us anything better. But the work had been too difficult and dangerous for him and he did nothing for a while except play chess with another boy and sing:

"My brothers and I were nine...
We plied a trade in wine..."

The chaos of the period and our desperate situation interrupted the fights between my father and brother, but they did not speak to each other. My brother, wearing modern clothes but unable to pay a barber to shave his beard, would put on phylacteries in the morning and then look out of the window instead of praying. Since there was little chance of my father's being consulted on a lawsuit, he would leave the house early, to study the holy books in various study houses.

One day as Father was writing a commentary he was frightened by the sudden appearance of a young officer who approached and asked in German, "Are you Pinhos-Mendel?"

Trembling, Father replied that he was.

"Uncle," said the young man, "I am Isaiah's son..."

Paling and then flushing with joy, Father greeted him profusely. This was the son of his deceased eldest brother, Isaiah from Galicia. Wealthy Uncle Isaiah had been a devout Belz Hasid, but his son was educated, sophisticated. An officer in the Austrian army, whose outfit was then passing through Warsaw, he had decided to visit his uncle. I had never before met a cousin from my father's side and I was surprised at his lack of resemblance to our family. Tall, erect, regally clothed, in boots with spurs and carrying a sword, he seemed very handsome and gay and just as grand as other young German officers I had seen strolling the streets of Warsaw. But this officer with epaulets and medals was the grandchild of Temerl and Reb Samuel—his ancestors were our ancestors. "Are you sure you're still a Jew?" Father asked.

"I certainly am."

"Well, may the Almighty protect you and bring you back safely so you may live as a Jew," Father said, "and never forget your ancestors."

My cousin told Father he had no money with him but he would write home and ask them to send us some. Father told Mother to prepare some tea and even mentioned sending out for refreshments, but the young man had no time. Kissing Father's hand, bowing to Mother, he clicked his heels, said goodbye, and left. After he left, the whole episode seemed unreal to us, but a short time later we received a money draft.

In connection with this draft, for fifty marks, I have a story to tell. Mother wasn't home when it arrived, and Father called me to him, asking, "Can you keep a secret?"

"Definitely."

He told me confidentially that for a long time he had wanted to publish his book on the treatise of vows, and that even though the fifty marks would be appreciated at home, why throw it away on food? He wanted to tell Mother he had received only twenty marks and use the additional thirty as a down payment on his book. Justifying himself, Father said this was a white lie for the sake of peace, because Mother would start a quarrel if she knew the truth. Now it seems to me that Father acted like any writer who wants to see his work in print. Of all the manuscripts he had written, only one thin volume had been published. According to Father, nothing was more estimable to God than the publication of a religious book, because it kindled the author's desire for the Torah and stimulated others to do the same.

I agreed to keep Father's secret, and he took me to Landau's bank to cash the draft, and then to Jacoby's printing shop on Nalewki Street. Never before had I seen a print shop, with its type cases and matrix stacks. A boy selected type, and Jacoby sat at a table investigating a dusty newspaper. A typical Lithuanian Jew, both pious and enlightened, he wore a tiny skullcap, and his grayish beard seemed to have been trimmed. Showing him the manuscript, Father explained what he wanted done with it. Jacoby scanned a page and shrugged, "Someone needs this?"

"What's the matter with you? The world hasn't gone completely to the dogs. Jews still study and still need religious books."

"There are too many already. I set up books for Rabbis who don't even come to take out the matrices."

"With God's help I'll pay for the matrices too,"

Father said. "But meanwhile I want the typesetting started."

"Well, if that's what you want... You'll get as much as you pay for..."

Father gave the thirty marks to Jacoby, who promised to set up thirty-two pages of manuscript and send Father the galleys.

The twenty marks proved very useful at home, and I detected Father's shame for what he had done in the frequency with which he told me what a privilege it was to publish a religious book. "God will bless us for this good deed," he said. "You'll see."

But what I saw was that when the twenty marks went, we became hungry once more. Father corrected his galley proofs, which Jacoby had sent in a hurry, but there was no possibility of a second installment, and the matrices remained in the shop with those of other authors who had been unable to redeem them.

My brother Moishe became ill with typhus during the epidemic of the summer of 1916, and we could not keep him at home because doctors had to inform the police about any cases. The carriage came to take him to the hospital for epidemic victims, on Pokorna Street, and we knew what would follow. Gentiles in white aprons would spray the house with carbolic acid and take everyone they found at home to the disinfecting station on Szczesliwa Street. We decided that my father and older brother would hide while Mother and I allowed ourselves to be taken away.

They did come and spray the house, and the air was filled with poison. Mother and I went off with a policeman, Mother carrying the few things she had been permitted to pack. In a strange house full of male and female guards, another boy and I had our hair cut. I saw my red sidelocks fall and I knew this was the end of them. I had wanted to get rid of them for a long time.

"Strip!" a woman guard commanded.

The idea of undressing before a woman appalled me, and I showed my reluctance, but she had no patience with me. Tearing off my capote, shirt, and breeches, she left me standing there naked as the day I was born. The other boy undressed himself, and I saw that he was as swarthy as I was fair. Together in the bathtub we giggled as the woman's soaping us tickled. We were given a shower as well and then dressed like hospital patients in bathrobes, slippers, and white trousers. I could not recognize myself in the mirror. Divested of sidelocks and Hasidic garments, I no longer seemed Jewish.

I was taken to my mother again and found her wearing strange clothes also, her head bound in a kerchief. We were brought upstairs, where there were two halls, one for men, one for mothers and children, with an open door between the two sections. The room was full of beds, including ours. Children ran about everywhere, and mothers screamed in Yiddish and Polish. Outside the window I could see the Gesia Street cemetery.

Although Mother had decided to eat nothing here but dry bread, she did not expect me, a boy of twelve, to get along for eight days on dry food only. We were not served meat, but I ate the non-kosher groats that Mother had hoped I would take the initiative of refusing. Nevertheless, she did not want to forbid me to eat, because I had grown pale and wasted, had developed a dry cough, and she was worried about my health. How could her conscience allow her to watch a boy grow so weak during an outbreak of typhus and the other calamities of the time?

I ate double portions, Mother's and mine, savoring the non-kosher taste. Mother shook her head over me, having hoped that I would be at least a little reluctant, but corruption had begun in me long before. I couldn't see any difference between these groats and those Mother made, for actually these too were fried in cocoa butter and the only thing that wasn't kosher would be the utensils in which they had been cooked.

The eight days of my stay there were full of

observation. Men whispered indiscreetly to the
women guards, women changed their clothes in front
of us, and boys and girls played together frivolously.
Exhausted from eating only dry bread, Mother could
barely stand and spent the entire time in bed. She
was also worried about Moishe, who was in the
hospital, and it had been years since she had heard
from my sister, who had fled to London from Belgium
during the invasion.

But for me the experience was novel, an introduc-
tion to a non-Jewish world. Between Ostrzego's
studio and the disinfecting station, the heder,
Father's courtroom, and the study house lost their
attraction for me...

The Visa

I HAD GROWN old enough to begin using phylacteries.
In Russia the revolution had taken place. I saw in the
newspaper that Tsar Nicholas, now under house
arrest, amused himself by chopping wood and that
Jews were permitted to live in Petrograd and
Moscow. For Father these events were additional
omens of the coming of the Messiah. How else could
one account for the dethroning of so great a
monarch? What had happened to the Cossacks?
There was only one possible answer: heaven had
ordained Nicholas's overthrow. The Jews were rising
in the world as their enemies lost power.

That summer my brother Israel Joshua informed

us that it was now possible to obtain a visa to Bilgoray from the Austrian consul in Warsaw.

My urge to travel—and particularly to Bilgoray, where my grandfather was the Rabbi—was now stronger than ever. I had been no place since we had moved from Radzymin to Warsaw. Even a ride in a droshky or trolley was an adventure for me. I continued to long to go on lengthy trips to far-off lands. Our situation was such that we could no longer remain in Warsaw. Since the summer of 1915, we had been constantly hungry. Father was again writing and had become the head of a yeshivah which was under the jurisdiction of the Radzymin Rabbi (who had returned to Radzymin), but his salary wasn't large enough even to buy bread. For us the winter of 1917 was one continuous fast. We ate only frozen potatoes and farmer cheese. Our hunger was made particularly excruciating by the fact that our next-door neighbor was a baker. In those days, bakers made fortunes. Though food was rationed, they indulged in various illegal practices, since bread sold on the black market for high prices. At Koppel the baker's, they never stopped counting the profits. Meats and puddings whose existence for us was only a memory were cooked in that house. Koppel's apartment was on the same stairway as ours, and the odors drove us crazy.

Before describing our trip to Bilgoray, I must say a little about Koppel. I have already mentioned his daughter Mirele who used to sit inside the house gate selling bread, rolls, and Sabbath loaves, and kept her money in her stocking. Koppel had several sons, all of whom were bakers also. Mirele was Koppel's only daughter and the youngest of his children. Koppel, short and stout, had surgery done on his large belly a number of times. He had a round face ringed by a trim, gray beard. Talkative and boastful, he was forever swearing and had one favorite oath which he repeated at every opportunity, "If I'm lying, may I not live to see my Mirele under the wedding canopy."

He adored the girl. The young men of Krochmalna
Street dared not touch her for fear that Koppel and
his sons would knife them.

Like her father, Mirele ran more to breadth than
height. She had huge breasts, massive hips, and
thick ankles. At seventeen, she was already overma-
ture. Her entire body seemed to cry out, "I'm ready."
Koppel informed the matchmakers that only the
most exceptional young man would be considered as
a husband for his daughter. At last they found this
paragon, a young bookkeeper. Whether he really was
a bookkeeper or only what was called a bookkeeper
on Krochmalna Street, where any literate person was
given that name, I don't know.

Mirele's fiancé was evidently an orphan, for as
soon as the engagement was announced he moved
into Koppel's flat. He was a tall dandy with rounded
limbs and curly hair, attributes which were considered attractive on Krochmalna Street—a perfect
mate for Mirele. It didn't take him long to get
accustomed to the rich dishes served in his new home.
When he needed money he helped himself to
whatever was around, picking it up from the tables,
or searching for it in the drawers, or even under the
mattresses. The assumption was that Koppel would
inevitably turn over to him at least half of his fortune.
Young men in the neighborhood couldn't help but
envy him; he had everything—rolls, Sabbath loaves,
meat, money—and Mirele, to boot. What could be
more delicious?

Then, suddenly, in the middle of the wedding
preparations Koppel became ill, was rushed to a
hospital, and was operated on. But he was already
past help. Before he died, he gave as his last wish that
Mirele's wedding take place immediately following
the period of mourning.

On Krochmalna Street it was said that Koppel had
sworn his favorite oath once too often.

But let me return to our journey.

In 1917, both typhus and typhoid fever were

rampant in Warsaw. Nor was it surprising that they
should be, since people were keeping themselves alive
by eating potato peelings and rotten chestnuts. The
Germans began to compel everyone to take baths in
the public bathhouses. A cordon of soldiers would be
thrown around a courtyard and the inhabitants
driven off to the municipal bath. The beards of the
men were shaven off and the girls' hair cut. People
were afraid to go into the streets. Sanitary commis-
sions inspected the houses, looking for dirt. Hunger,
sickness, and fear of the Germans made life unbearable.

On Szczygla Street, a narrow thoroughfare that
led from Kracow Boulevard, or the so-called New
World, to the Vistula, stood the Austrian consulate. It
was a time when people waited in lines for bread,
potatoes, kerosene, and whatnot. But nowhere was
the line so long and broad as on Szczygla Street. Tens
of thousands of Warsavians and out-of-towners
waited to go to that part of Poland now occupied by
the Austrians. There, in the smaller towns, there was
more to eat. The rumor was that in those places one
could stuff oneself and forget about the war. But we
had also heard that with the Austrian army had
come cholera and that thousands of people were
dying in that region.

Mother had received no letters from Bilgoray since
the outbreak of hostilities, but somehow or other she
had ascertained that her father was no longer alive.
How had she learned this? From a dream. She had
awakened one morning and said, "Father is dead."

"What are you talking about? How do you know?"
we inquired.

Mother informed us that in a dream she had had of
Grandfather his face had flowed with the radiance of
one who has passed over to the other side. Though we
tried to minimize the significance of this dream,
Mother remained firm in her belief that her father,
the Bilgoray Rabbi, was no more.

Father was reluctant to cease being the Rabbi of

Krochmalna Street, nor did my brother want to give
up his newspaper work. He was already involved
with the girl who was to become his wife. It was
decided that, for the present, only Mother and the
younger children—my brother Moishe and I—would
go to Bilgoray.

But to get there one needed a visa and to obtain a
visa one had to stand in line. For how long? For
weeks or possibly months. Incredible though it may
seem, people stood on line night and day, waiting for
visas. Large families arranged it so that each
member took his turn on line. Queues generally
advance, but not the visa line, the reasons being that
the Austrian consul vigorously resisted issuing visas
and that the German soldiers who kept the line in
order sold places on it. Those who paid got to see the
consul; the others waited forever. Since the guards
were constantly being changed, one bribe was not
sufficient. The soldiers were free with both their rifle
butts and their abuse; the words most commonly
heard were *"Verfluchte Juden,"* damned Jews.

Our family took its place in the line. Mother, my
older brother, and I took turns waiting, but never got
any closer to the consulate door. Women whispered
that visas were being given only to harlots, and
cursed these whores. I recall that while I stood on line
I studied an old German textbook which was filled
with all sorts of stories and poems. Two phrases from
that text have stuck in my mind: *"Es regnet—Gott
segnet"* (It rains and God blesses). For me, German
had one virtue; because it was similar to Yiddish, it
was easy to understand.

We had already abandoned hope when one day my
brother returned home bearing my mother's passport, in which were visas for her, my brother Moishe,
and me. My brother had somehow scraped together
thirty marks and had bribed a German guard to
obtain the visas.

I will never forget that day, which must have been
a late July or an early August one. Our family,

though half dead from fatigue, hunger, and despair,
came to life. The apartment took on a new appearance. Mother's face lost its gloom. The sun shone
brightly. The day became airy and joyous. A stamp
on a piece of paper admitted us to a world from which
we had previously been barred, a frontier had been
opened, a pathway to green fields, to food, to kinsmen
we had never met. To us children, Bilgoray symbolized the coming of the Messiah, the miraculous.
There we had uncles, aunts, cousins. Bilgoray was
our special land of Israel from which Jerusalem was
only a step away.

I frolicked and danced. I was to travel on a train.
My mother smiled, though for her this was no
carefree adventure. Then she sighed. First of all,
Father must be left all by himself. True, he would not
be in Warsaw but in Radzymin with the Rabbi, but he
would be away from the family. Moreover, Joshua
was staying in Warsaw. How could she run away
when Father and Joshua were still in danger?
Mother promptly announced that she was acting
sinfully. The family should not separate during such
perilous times. But my father and brother argued
that not to go would be to put the lives of the children
in jeopardy. Was she willing to be responsible for
something like that?

I was too young and giddy to understand Mother's
self-recriminations and doubts. It seemed to me that
she was intent on dampening my hopes and robbing
me of my greatest pleasure. I was furious with her.
The urge to go was so great in me that I could think of
nothing else but sitting in a train and looking out the
window. It is an urge that still remains with me.

The Journey

THINGS WERE GOING WELL; I had said goodbye to my
friends and was ready to leave, but my shoes were in
bad condition and I went to the cobbler in our
courtyard to get them resoled.

The day was bright but the steps leading to his
cellar room were dark, the corridor damp and moldy;
I entered a tiny room littered with rags and shoes.
The ceiling was crooked and the window small, the
dirty panes patched with cardboard. I had thought
that conditions were bad enough at home, but at least
we had a spacious apartment with furniture and
books. Here there were two beds full of soiled bedding
and on one of them, in the midst of its own filth, lay a
newborn baby, wrinkled, bald, and toothless, like a
miniature hag. The mother fussed at a stove that kept
smoking, and a young red-bearded man with sunken
cheeks and a high forehead—yellowed like some of
the leather about him—worked at the cobbler's
bench.

Waiting while he resoled my shoes, I coughed from
the dust and foul odors, and remembered what my
brother had said about those who wore themselves
out while idlers thrived. I was overcome with a sense
of the injustice in the world, of young men going off to
die or be wounded, of people whose constant work
would not earn them a piece of bread, a shirt, or a
baby crib. The cobbler, I knew, could not continue to

struggle indefinitely. Sooner or later he would come down with typhus or consumption. And how could the baby flourish amid the smoke, dust, and stench?

It was my brother's opinion that there should be no rulers at all—that not only Nicholas, but Wilhelm, Karol, the English king, and all the rest should be ousted and replaced by republics; wars should be abolished in favor of popular rule. Why until now had this never been done, and why were monarchs despotic?

When my shoes were repaired and I was once more in the sunlight, I felt guilty. Why should I be going on a wonderful trip while the cobbler was confined to his cellar? Today he still represents, in my mind, the ills of society. Although I was only a boy, I sympathized with the Russian revolutionaries. Nevertheless, I still pitied the Tsar, who was then being forced to chop wood.

My brother Joshua accompanied us in a droshky to the Danzig Station, which was at that time called the Vistula Station. He bought tickets for us, and we walked to the platform to await the train. It seemed strange to be leaving all the familiar places and friends. But before long the huge locomotive, coughing and hissing steam, was ready for us, the awesome wheels dripping oil, a fire blazing within. Few people were traveling, and we found ourselves in an empty car. The German-Austrian border was only four hours away, at Ivangorod, or Deblin, as it was later called.

With a screeching of whistles, the train began to move. On the platform, my brother Joshua seemed to grow smaller.

Buildings, benches, and people moved backwards. It was thrilling to watch the world glide away, houses, trees, wagons, entire streets revolving and drifting apart as if the earth were a huge carousel. Buildings vibrated, chimneys rose out of the earth, wearing smoky bonnets. The towers of the Sobol, the famous Russian church, loomed over everything, its

crosses glittering like gold in the sun. Flocks of
pigeons, alternately black and gold, soared above the
spinning, whirling city. Like a king or a great wizard,
I rode through the world, no longer fearing every
soldier, policeman, Gentile boy, or bum. What I had
dreamed of for years was coming true.

As we rode over a bridge I glimpsed tiny trolleys
down below, and people resembling locusts, the way
the spies during Moses' time must have looked to the
giants. Beneath us, on the Vistula, a ship sailed, and
in the summer sky there were clouds resembling
other ships, beasts, and piles of down. The train
whistled again and again. Mother took cookies and a
bottle of milk from a satchel.

"Say the benediction..."

Eating the cookies and drinking the milk, I forgot
war, hunger, and illness. I was in a paradise on
wheels. If only it would last forever!

Even my friend Boruch-Dovid would not know
about the existence of the parts of Warsaw and its
environs that I now saw. I was amazed to find a
trolley. If trolleys came this far, I could have gone
there myself. But it was too late now. We passed a
cemetery that seemed like a tombstone metropolis.
I'd faint with fear, I thought, if I had to walk here at
night...or even during the day. But why fear the
dead when one is on a moving train?

In Warsaw everyone was hungry, but the world we
traveled through was beautiful and green. Mother
kept pointing out the wheat, barley, buckwheat,
potatoes, an apple orchard, a pear orchard—still
unripe. She had been raised in a small town.
Peasants mowed hay; women and girls, squatting
among the furrows, dug out weeds, whose roots,
Mother said, spoiled the grain. Suddenly I saw a
phantom-like, faceless creature, with arms out-
stretched. "What's that?" I asked.

"A scarecrow to frighten the birds."

My brother wanted to know if he was alive.

"No, silly."

I saw that he wasn't alive, nevertheless he seemed
to be laughing. In the midst of the field he stood, like
an idol, while birds circled about him and screeched.

At dusk, a conductor appeared, punched our
tickets, exchanged a few words with Mother, and
observed with fascination what to him was our
strange, un-Gentile appearance—still bewildered, it
seemed, despite the generations before him that had
lived alongside the Jews.

In the fading light, everything became more
beautiful, blossoms seemed more distinct, everything
was green, juice-filled, radiant with the light of the
setting sun, and aromatic. I recollected the Pentateuch verse: "The odor of my son is like that of a field
that the Lord has blessed."

It seemed to me that these fields, pastures, and
marshes must resemble the land of Israel. The sons of
Jacob were herding sheep nearby. Before Joseph's
stacks of grain, other stacks bowed down. The
Ishmaelites would arrive soon, riding camels, their
asses and mules loaded with almonds, cloves, figs,
and dates. The Plains of Mamre were visible behind
the trees. God was asking Abraham: "Wherefore did
Sarah laugh? Is anything too hard for the Lord? I will
return unto thee and Sarah shall have a son...."

Suddenly I saw something and asked Mother what
it was.

"A windmill."

Before we could get a good look, it vanished, as if
by magic. But then it appeared again behind us, its
blades spinning to grind flour...

We saw a river, but Mother said it was not the
Vistula. Then there were cows, red, black, spotted,
grazing. We saw sheep. The world seemed like an
open Pentateuch. The moon and the eleven stars
came out, bowing before Joseph, the future ruler of
Egypt.

Evening came and lights were lit at the Ivangorod
Station when we arrived. We were at the border,
beside a kind of highway, and Mother said, "We're in

Austria." The station was full of soldiers who were not as tall, erect, or stiff-backed as the Germans. Many were bearded and seemed Jewish; they wore shoes and puttees. The tumult reminded me of a second holiday night at the Radzymin study house. The men talked, smoked, and gesticulated, and I felt at home. "Let's play chess," I suggested to my brother. We did not know how long we would have to remain there.

As soon as we had unpacked the chess set and sat down at a table to play, we were surrounded by soldiers and noncommissioned officers. Jewish soldiers asked us, "Where are you from?"

"Warsaw."

"And where are you going?"

"To Bilgoray. Grandfather is the Bilgoray Rabbi."

A bearded soldier said he had been to Bilgoray and knew the Bilgoray Rabbi.

One soldier stood beside me and showed me where to move, while another soldier helped Moishe. Finally it was the soldiers who played while we moved the pieces. Mother watched us with anxious pride. The soldiers were Galician Jews who probably wore fur hats and mohair coats on the Sabbath. Their Yiddish had a somewhat flatter sound than what was spoken in Warsaw. One soldier allowed my brother to hold his sword and try on his cap.

I do not remember how we spent that night, but the following day we rode to Rejowiec in another half-empty car.

In Rejowiec, where there was a Russian prisoner-of-war camp, I saw unarmed Russians with unkempt hair and shabby uniforms digging under Austrian guard. Austrians and Russians crowded the depot commissary, which was kept by a Jew with a trimmed beard. Besides my mother, his young wife was the only woman there, and the men stared at her eagerly. Smiling and blushing, looking up slyly, she drew beer into mugs. Her husband seemed surly and dour and everyone knew what was bothering him: jealousy.

Twisting their tongues to speak German, the Russians sounded as if they were speaking broken Yiddish. Certain Jewish soldiers among them did speak Yiddish.

The Russian prisoners had built a new track from Rejowiec to Zwierzyniec, and continued working at it as we rode. While Nicholas chopped wood, Cossacks were learning Yiddish. For all anyone knew, the Messiah *was* on his way.

Bilgoray

WE RODE PAST evidence of the Russian retreat—charred forests in which an occasional half-burned tree still sprouted green leaves and twigs. Despite three days' travel by train, I continued to watch everything with avid love and curiosity: fields, forests, gardens, orchards, and villages...One tree with uplifted branches seemed to be begging for a gift from heaven; another, bowing low, appeared to have abandoned all hope from anything but the earth itself. Still another, completely black, was a victim, with everything gone but its roots. Whether it hoped for anything more or was merely involved in dying, I could not determine. My thoughts sped on with the wheels, stimulated by every tree, shrub, and cloud. I saw hares and squirrels. The redolence of pine needles mingled with other scents, both exotic and recognizable, although I did not know from where. I wished that like some hero in a storybook I might leap from the moving train and lose myself amid green things.

Recently a short track had been laid between the villages of Zwierzyniec and Bilgoray, and although it was not finished, it was in use. Our train was a small, toylike locomotive with minute wheels, and in the low flatcars there were benches where Bilgoray passengers sat.

Everyone in the car looked sunburned, their clothes had a sunfaded appearance. Many of the people had red beards, the men were dressed in gabardines, and I felt related to them all.

"Bathsheba..." someone called. "The Rabbi's Bathsheba..."

Although I knew this was my mother's name, I had never heard her called anything but "Listen here—", which was my father's method of gaining her attention since the Hasidim did not approve of addressing a woman by name. Bathsheba, for all I knew, was merely a biblical name that no one actually used, and although the heder boys often mentioned their mothers' names, I was ashamed to mention that of mine, for it seemed to me too suggestive of King David's sin.

Here they were calling her Bathsheba and "thou," the women embracing and kissing her. Although a dream had convinced her of her father's death, no one had confirmed it; yet now she asked them, "When did it happen?"

After a silence they began to tell her not only about her father but also about her mother and sister-in-law, Uncle Joseph's wife, Sarah. Grandfather had died in Lublin, Grandmother a few months later in Bilgoray. Sarah and a daughter, Ittele, had died of cholera, and two cousins, Ezikiel and Itta Deborah, the son of Uncle Itche and the daughter of Aunt Taube, had also died.

In this sun-drenched day, in the midst of pine woods, in this green paradise, the terrible news came to her, and Mother began to cry. I too tried to cry, feeling it appropriate, but the tears would not come. I cheated, wetting my eyes with saliva, though no one was looking at me, nor did they care whether I wept or not.

Suddenly everyone shouted; the rear cars had jumped the track. There was a long wait while the cars were set back on the track with poles. That Sabbath, everyone agreed, a prayer of thanks would have to be offered. Other passengers, less fortunate than we, had been known to perish on this makeshift railroad.

Between Zwierzyniec and Bilgoray, the scenery was beautiful. We rode through forests and meadows, and passed an occasional straw-roofed hut or a whitewashed house with a shingle roof. The train kept halting to give one person a drink of water, to allow another an interlude in the bushes, or the engineer would deliver packages or chat with the various peasants living beside the tracks. The Jews treated the engineer as casually as if he were the Gentile who entered Jewish households on the Sabbath to light the ovens, and they asked him to make various stops for them. Once, during one of the prolonged halts, a barefoot Jewess in a kerchief came out of a shack with a gift of dewy blackberries for my mother. Having heard that the Rabbi's Bathsheba was coming, she had brought the berries as a present. Mother had no appetite, but my brother Moishe and I ate it all, with consequent stains on our lips, tongues, and hands. The years of starvation had left their mark on us.

Though Mother had praised Bilgoray, it was even prettier than her descriptions. The pinewoods our rounding it looked from a distance like a blue sash. The houses were interspersed with gardens and orchards, and before them massive chestnut trees stood such as I had never seen any place in Warsaw, including the Saxony Gardens. There was a sense of serenity in the town that I had not encountered, a smell of fresh milk and warm dough. Wars and epidemics seemed far away.

Grandfather's house, an old wooden loghouse

painted white, with a mossy roof and a bench beneath the windows, was near the synagogue, ritual bath, and poorhouse. The family came out to welcome us, the first to run up being Uncle Joseph, who had inherited Grandfather's position. Uncle Joseph always ran, even though he was thin and bent, with a milky beard, a beaked nose, and bright, birdlike eyes. He was dressed in rabbinical gabardine, wide-brimmed hat, and low shoes with white stockings. Without kissing Mother, he cried out, "Bathsheba!"

A stout woman, Aunt Yentel, his third wife, waddled after him. His second wife had died a year and a half before in the cholera epidemic, and his first had died when he was sixteen. Aunt Yentel was as stout and relaxed as Uncle Joseph was narrow and agile. She seemed more the Rebbetzin than he the Rabbi. A horde of redhaired children trailed behind them. I who had fiery red hair myself had never seen so many redheads at once. Until then my red hair had made me a novelty in the heder, study house, and courtyard; it had seemed exotic, like my mother's name, my father's occupation, and my brother's talent. But here there was a whole bevy of redheads, and the reddest among them was my uncle's daughter Brocha.

I was taken into Uncle's large kitchen, where everything seemed novel. The oven was as big as one in a bakery, and Aunt Yentel was baking bread. Over the stove there was an open chimney, and on the stove there was a tripod on which a pot boiled. On the table, flies crawled over a huge lump of sugar. The scents of leavening and caraway filled the air. My aunt offered us some prune cake, which tasted heavenly. My cousins, Avromele and Samson, took me into the courtyard, which was actually a garden with trees, tall nettles, weeds, and wild flowers of all colors. There was also a sleep-in porch; I sat down on the straw-mattress bed, and it seemed to me I had never known such luxury. The sounds of birds, crickets, and other insects rang in my ears, chickens wandered about in the grass, and when I raised my head I could see the Bilgoray synagogue and beyond it fields that stretched to the forest's edge. The fields were all shapes and colors, squares and rectangles, dark green and yellow... I wished I could stay there forever.

The Family

FOR A WHILE I could not grow accustomed to my suddenly acquired family, the aunts, uncles, and cousins I had never known before. But finally I did, and I would like to describe them.

The most significant person was Uncle Joseph, the Bilgoray Rabbi, ten years older than my mother but only fifteen years younger than his father. He and his father had grown gray together, and the symptoms of age had almost seemed more apparent in the younger man than in the older one; Uncle Joseph became stooped at an early age. Thin, weak, and sprightly, he was nevertheless known to be passionate, a scholar and mathematician, if somewhat undignified. Although his second wife, Sarah, was of common stock, he had fallen in love with her and had sent a matchmaker to arrange things. Now, soon after her death, he was married again. Although he seemed deep in thought all day long and had what is considered a high intellectual forehead, his remarks were usually inane, such as, "How much does Moshe the bath attendant earn?" or, "What is the wheat-eating capacity of a goose during its lifetime?"

Grandfather, who had once loved him, had later disapproved of this older son who was potentially a great Talmudic scholar but had persistently refused to study. On the other hand, he enjoyed gossip, shouted at his family, and abused them. But he was devout all the same, and whenever one of his children became ill, he paced through his study for hours, praying in a sobbing chant. But fundamentally he was a skeptic, wise to the devious ways of businessmen and skilled in dealing with their courtroom problems. Though a disappointment to Bilgoray after Grandfather, Uncle Joseph made fewer enemies, had more insight into practical things, and was capable of compromise.

Yentel, his third wife, and the only one of his wives whom I knew, had also been married twice before. She was a simple old-fashioned woman who could have been set down easily in some previous century. Her great tragedy was barrenness. When she was young, she kept going from one Wonder Rabbi to another, believing in the promises that would lead to fulfillment. Despite Uncle's mockery, she treated him with great respect, only occasionally defending herself, knowing that she was no match for his wit. She would say about him, "I wish him long life, but he's torturing me...."

His eldest daughter, Frieda, by his first wife had become a kind of legend since she had remained in Russia with her mother's family. She seldom wrote letters and no one really knew her, but it was said that she was a person of superior intellect, and an educated one.

The other children's mother had been Sarah, and all but one had red hair.

At the time of my Bilgoray visit, one of them, Sholem, had married, and lived in Tomaszow. Those at home were Avromele, Brocha, Taube, Samson and Esther.

Other members of the family said that if Uncle

Joseph had married one of his own kind his children
would have turned out brilliant like himself: but
Sarah had been a simple woman, and the children
took after their mother.

Twenty-two at the time, Avromele had red hair
and sidelocks, and an amiable, submissive attitude
toward his father. Uncle Joseph, who himself seldom
studied, would not compel his children to do so, and
Avromele would wander about from home to house of
prayer to Turisk study house, and back again. He
used to chop wood for his father, bring water from the
well, and perform other menial tasks.

Brocha, the next eldest, and already betrothed,
had an alabaster skin and yellow hair. With her own
sewing machine she made clothes for the people of
Bilgoray, and handed her earnings to her father. But
he was as rude and abusive to her as he was to the
other children and even to strangers.

Taube, sixteen, came after Brocha. Tall, stout,
fiery red, and sickly, she twitched and squinted. She
was a good-hearted girl who, when feeling well,
would work hard serving everyone, but then suddenly, as if possessed, she would cry out about all kinds of
aches and pains. There was a different ailment every
few weeks. Old Doctor Gruszcinsky diagnosed it as
"nerves" and prescribed bromides.

Samson—the only one to survive the Nazi
holocaust—was the same age as I, and his hair was
dark. A decent, quiet boy not especially interested in
books, he was mortally afraid of his father. Like
Avromele, he too chopped wood, carried water, ran
errands, and executed various insane notions of his
vile-tempered father, but when his father became too
unbearable, Samson began to mutter under his
breath.

Esther, the youngest, later played a role in my life.
Eight at that time, she had some of her father's
intelligence, but she was a much gentler person. Her
red hair was in braids, and she attended an Austrian
school in town. Hasidic Jews considered it sinful to

send their sons to secular school, but for daughters it
was all right—and there was a grain of enlightenment in Uncle Joseph. He loved his youngest
daughter, played with her often, and asked her all
kinds of ridiculous questions. Aware of this favori-
tism, she conducted herself accordingly.

Now for the family of Uncle Itche.

Uncle Joseph's junior by fourteen years, Uncle
Itche still had dark hair, a blond beard, and piercing
eyes beneath bushy brows. Though he was pious, he
was also, like his brother, sharp and somewhat
skeptical. He knew Russian and, like the official
Rabbi he was, had subscribed to a St. Petersburg
newspaper. For years, the two brothers had been at
odds because even though Joseph was the firstborn,
Itche had been his parents' favorite, particularly his
mother's. Itche and his wife Rochele, daughter of the
well-known Rabbi Isaiah Rachover, had had two
sons, but the younger and most able had died during
the epidemic, leaving his parents in a state of
turbulent melancholy. Uncle had begun to resent
God and the world in general. Following her son's
death, handsome Aunt Rochele had become even
more gloomy and full of complaints than ever before.
Like the rest of the family, she had a spirit rooted in
the Middle Ages; she believed in black magic,
amulets, and visions, and the dead were as present to
her as the living.

Constantly on guard against evil intentions, she
would complain about her dead in-laws, insisting
that Grandfather, who had listened to the evil gossip
of those who envied her, had put a curse on her.

Moshele, their remaining son, was handsome,
aristocratic, soft-eyed, naïve, timid, and unhealthy.
Even on a hot day, he was not permitted to leave the
house without a shawl. "God forbid, don't catch a
cold..." his mother was always saying. "Don't fall,
don't get overheated." She was always feeding him
milk and cookies. The other cousins mocked Aunt
Rochele, who pampered her son.

Besides the families of Uncle Joseph and Uncle

Itche, there were the married children of my Aunt
Sarah, who with her second husband lived nearby, in
Tarnogrod, and there were other relatives in Bilgoray. In Warsaw I had just been another boy walking
down a street, but here everyone knew me and those
who had come before me.

Though everyone tried to make our stay in
Bilgoray a happy one, there was a great deal of
bitterness behind it all. Basing their actions on
Mosaic law that states that only sons are entitled to
inheritance, my uncles had taken it all, including
Grandmother's jewelry. Aunt Sarah and Taube,
being settled in their husbands' towns, made no issue
of this, but it disturbed my mother, who had received
only some of Grandmother's old clothes.

Besides this, my uncles were afraid that Mother's
arrival portended competition. Uncle Joseph had
taken over Grandfather's position, with Uncle Itche
as assistant Rabbi, but they were afraid that Father
would come along with a following and set himself up
as a rival. As a result, they kept complaining to my
mother about the difficulties of their situation.
Actually, they weren't too well off, since the present
Ridnik Hasidim (formerly Sandz and Gorlitz Hasidim) had chosen their own Rabbi, thus dividing and
diminishing Grandfather's old following.

Here, as in Warsaw, even I could see, there were too
many Rabbis and ecclesiastics, nor were the Jews too
well off generally. Before the war, the town had
exported sieves to Russia and even China, but the
Russian market was closed, and many Bilgoray Jews
had to work on the railroad the Austrians were
building. But the construction couldn't go on indefinitely.

Meanwhile it was a warm, pleasant summer. The
Gentiles sold blackberries and mushrooms cheaply.
Austrian, Hungarian, Polish, Bosnian, and Czech
soldiers were quartered in Bilgoray, and were a
source of business to the Jews. Jewish women
smuggled tobacco from Galicia....

Nevertheless, the Jews of Bilgoray were as

insecure as ever, and the bitterness of the Diaspora
hovered over them.

Aunt Yentel

"MY DEAR WOMAN," Aunt Yentel said to my mother,
"Holy Rabbis have kept me alive. Where would I be
today without these saints? My first husband wanted
children, and when I was still barren after ten years,
people told him to divorce me. My mother-in-law said
to me, 'You are a tree without fruit. I want profits.
Children come with labor pains, but grandchildren
are pure profit.'

" 'What shall I do, Mother-in-law?' I asked. 'If I had
saved my tears, I would now have a barrelful of
them.' I cried all the time, my bed was wet with tears,
and I told my husband, 'According to law, you can
divorce me. It's all my fault.'

" 'How do I know that?' he asked. 'Maybe it's me.
Besides, you're more precious to me than seven
children, as the weekly section of the Pentateuch
says.'

"Nevertheless, I went to Turisk. You can't imagine
what it's like there, Bathsheba. The Rabbi had a
silver Hanukkah lamp the size of this wall, and his
face shone like the face of an angel. Women were
allowed in Turisk, but this isn't true of Rabbis
elsewhere. Nevertheless, it wasn't easy. I had to wait
for days before seeing him, and then when I entered I
couldn't say a word.

"Finally I cried out, 'Rabbi, you don't know how

miserable I am...' This saint knew immediately what I meant. 'Go home,' he said, 'You will be helped.'"

"Did you have a child, Yentel?"

"No. But at least he gave me hope. It wasn't my fate to have children. How I must have sinned! The saint wished me well and strengthened my spirit. I visited Wonder Rabbis everywhere. After my first husband died, I had no desire to remarry, I cried and cried. But how long can a person be alone? My first husband had been wonderful, not a mean bone in his body. I could have gone for days without feeding him, and he wouldn't complain. My second husband, with all due respect, was a madman. Never have I seen a man who could get so angry. I can't say I hadn't been warned. People had said, 'Yentel, you'll regret it. He's evil...' but what will be, will be. I married him. He was a widower and impossible to please. He found fault with everything I did, including my cooking. I thought I'd go crazy. My grandfather would say, 'You've got broad shoulders, bear it...' My second husband almost killed me, but I bore it humbly. I thought this was the way that had been chosen for me to repent my sins. He'd had a daughter by his first marriage, which was proof that I was barren. But one daughter was enough for him, he didn't want any more. He was always grumbling and screaming. For weeks on end he would stay in the woods, because he dealt in lumber. I was living in Turbin then. We had a large property, an estate almost, my pantry was always full... we had a cow, chickens, ducks, and geese... more than enough for one family. Visitors, Jews high and low, would come, and I sent no one away emptyhanded. They all blessed me, but it didn't change my fate. My husband would grow infuriated when he came home: 'What are all those *schnorrers* doing here? Get them out!'

"But I told him, 'We'll profit from this. What can you take to your grave except good deeds?' And for twenty years we lived this way...

"He was healthy, strong as iron, could break a

table with a blow of his fist, but suddenly he became so weak he couldn't stand. He saw doctors in Lublin, but it was hopeless, his time was up. For a few months he suffered, then he died. I didn't want to marry again. Twice was enough.

"Then it was wartime and everyone began advising me. What he left me was taken away by his daughter and son-in-law, who even drove me from the house. I went to live with my brother in Byszcz, a small village. But I didn't care for life among the peasants, without Sabbaths or holidays. I enjoy hearing a Jewish word or two at the synagogue and listening to a preacher. The matchmakers wouldn't leave me alone and they suggested your brother to me, Reb Joseph, the Bilgoray Rabbi. I heard all about him. But even though they told me he was an angry man, I thought: 'He can't be worse than the last one—'

"They arranged a meeting so I could look him over, but when I got here they said he was sleeping. I said I'd wait. Taubele told me, 'He isn't sleeping yet. Go in and talk to him.' The first thing I saw beside him as he lay in bed was a band, the kind used to hold up a rupture. 'A fine reception for a bride,' I thought. But at our age, who can choose? It's enough to be able to stay alive. That's the story of my third marriage. Woe is me! He should remain healthy..."

That was how my Aunt Yentel spoke. I could listen to her stories for hours. Sometimes she'd tangle one story with another and couldn't find her way out.

But my cousin Brocha the seamstress liked to embroider tragic tales, particularly those of the cholera epidemic in which two of our cousins had died.

Brocha would tell our mother, "It's impossible to explain how it all happened. Six hundred people! No one knew who would be next. One minute you felt well, and the next you had a cramp in your leg. The only remedy was to rub it with alcohol, but there was no one to do the rubbing because it required strong hands, and besides, alcohol was hard to get. Only during an epidemic can you find out who's really good and who's been pretending. People who had been considered worthless would sit up nights massaging the sick until they themselves became ill. Those who played the part of saints were hiding. But you can't hide from God.

"Those who became sick died. There couldn't have been more than ten people who recovered. In the beginning there were funerals, but afterwards there was no one to dig graves, and nobody dared cleanse the bodies. The Austrians ordered all corpses buried in lime. There weren't even any shrouds. You'd talk to a person one day, and the next he'd be underground. Auntie, how much is human life worth—any more than that of a fly or a worm? When Henia the magnate became sick, the paupers were gratified. 'The world isn't only for the powerful,' they said. But a plague doesn't differentiate between rich and poor. It was too much for Doctor Gruszcinsky, but people were afraid to call the military doctors, who would take the patient to the hospital. There they died of thirst. There wasn't anyone to give you a drop of water or even rub you with vodka. One patient dragged himself to the slop pail, drank, and died on the spot. But what can you do with a fire inside you? They didn't even notice if a corpse was Jew or Gentile, but just buried them all in lime, with their clothes on. Soldiers were posted along the roads to keep everyone from leaving town and spreading the epidemic. An old mendicant was told to go back but didn't have the strength. So they stripped him and washed him in a well. If we weren't so affected by tragedy, it would have been funny.

"Auntie, you can't avoid fate. Many people tried to behave as the doctors told them, didn't eat raw fruit, drank only boiled water with whisky, but it didn't save them. Others, who drank ordinary water and ate raw apples and pears, were spared. They say that the stronger you are, the less you get sick, but that's not true. The stronger ones died even faster...

"Women went to the cemetery to measure the

graves with strings that were later used as wicks for candles in the synagogue. They said it was good luck to marry an orphan at the cemetery. Yosele Hendele and...no, Auntie, you wouldn't know her. People were so demented that they celebrated the ceremony with dancing. Boys ran about wildly. Next to the wedding canopy, graves were being dug. Each morning I would wake up asking myself, 'Am I still alive?' I really didn't know. I thought it could happen to anyone but Ittele."

And Brocha would tell how her sister and cousin had become sick. I don't recall whether they died at the same time. One of them, I think, died of typhus.

Listening, Mother would sometimes ask about someone, and Brocha would answer, "In the other world..."

"Woe is me!"

"Grass grew in the market place, Auntie..."

Mother shook her head, deep sorrow in her eyes, which were sometimes gray and at other times bright blue. Her face was pale, drawn, and uncomprehending.

Suddenly Uncle Joseph appeared from his study. "Enough!" he growled at his daughter. "Sew!"

"I'm sewing!"

"Where's Samson?"

"What do you need him for?"

"I want to smoke a cigarette."

He was a heavy smoker but never carried matches. Avromele and Samson had to strike matches for him. He behaved like a squire, treating his children as slaves.

He asked me, "Well, what goes on in your Warsaw?" But, without waiting for an answer, he dashed back to his study.

Old Jewishness

ALTHOUGH MOST OF THE BOYS at Bilgoray used the big study house, I went to the Turisk study house, which had belonged to my grandfather's Hasidim. Isolated on a hill, it had in it everything that a study house needed—a large clay oven, tables, and bookshelves, and besides, it was nearly deserted during the day, since prayers were said there only in the mornings and evenings. With the two pupils assigned to me, I began studying the Talmud; one was my cousin Samson, the other, Benjamin Brezel. Both were my age, but I was more advanced than they. We talked more than we studied. I described the vastness of Warsaw, the trolleys running everywhere, the stores on Marszalkowska Boulevard and the New World, and they discussed Bilgoray with me. When I was alone, I paced back and forth and browsed through the books, longing for a taste of something more worldly, such as I had found in Warsaw. *The Guide for the Perplexed, The Kuzari,* and also Cabala books intrigued me for a while, but my thirst for knowledge was insatiable and I felt that I had been condemned to antiquity.

When I first arrived in that town, almost every Jew prayed thrice daily, and there was scarcely a woman who did not cut off her hair, covering her head with a bonnet or kerchief rather than a wig. The common people were even more devout than the scholars. On the day preceding the new moon, everyone recited the

prayers of the minor Day of Atonement. Some people
fasted every Monday and Thursday, rose early in the
morning, lamenting in the kind of penitential
prayers that other communities had forgotten.
Enlightened individuals could be found in Tomaszow
and Shebreshin, but in Bilgoray the few "enlightened" ones still wore long gabardines and never
missed a prayer. Yiddish newspapers were seldom
seen, and although Peretz had come from this region,
no one knew anything about him. My grandfather
had insulated Bilgoray against evil temptation, and
the town's distance from the railroad helped. Before
the advent of the Austrians, some townspeople had
never seen a train.

The Yiddish I heard there and the kind of Jewish
behavior and customs I witnessed were those
preserved from a much earlier time. In spite of this,
two Jewish sisters became whores, setting up, on the
Sands, near the cemetery, a brothel patronized by
Austrian, Magyar, Czech, Bosnian, and Herzegovi-
nian soldiers. A military doctor instructed the
soldiers in precautionary methods against infection,
and the girls had to wear special kerchiefs on their
heads. Occasionally they strolled past the synagogue. Their father was a simple man who suffered
deeply because of them. I was present when my uncle
issued a divorce against the elder sister, whose
husband had gone to America and had sent the
papers by mail.

The evil spirit, I discovered, had a small following
even in Bilogray.

Everything was conspiratory there. Years passed
before I learned of the existence among the town's
workingmen of members of the Bund that had
participated in strikes and demonstrations in 1905.
Either unaware of the legality of socialism in
Austria, or pretending to be so, they kept their brand
of socialism as if it had an air of the occult.

There were also in Bilgoray a few admirers of
Zionism who had not yet made the leap to politics.
Todros the watchmaker, though dressed as a

traditional Hasid, was the town's pillar of enlightenment. I had heard of him in Warsaw, because, as my grandfather's pupil and something of a prodigy, he had suddenly abandoned his studies, learned watchmaking, divorced his pious wife, and married a wigless modern girl. On the Sabbath, instead of praying at the synagogue or the study house, he joined the workingmen at the tailors' house of prayer and read the holy scroll there, with grammatical exactness, as official reader. Skilled as a watchmaker, he also played the violin, was friendly with the wedding musicians, and brought up his children in a modern way. I had seen him on the street—short, hunchbacked, with a small black beard and large intelligent black eyes somewhat like those of Mendelsohn and Spinoza (although neither of them resembled each other). There is a kind of Jewish face that one finds in all parts of the world. This is the face of Spinoza, Mendelsohn, Einstein, Herzl, and Todros the watchmaker. There was something about the expression of his eyes which stirred me. I longed to talk to him, but I had been warned that if I did so, my reputation would be tainted and the status of my parents diminished. Besides, I was too shy. I want to digress here and mention something that still seems incredible to me. Moshe, the son of my cousin Eli, who had visited us in Warsaw, would attend the Turisk study house on the Sabbath. A year went by without either of us, grandsons of the same grandfather, exchanging a word. This is more the way two Englishmen behave than two Jewish boys from Poland. But it's a fact.

One Friday, late in the summer, in the month of Ab or Elul, my aunt gave me a glass of tea and a cube of sugar. When I bit off a piece of sugar, I was amazed to find that it had no taste. I thought myself the butt of a practical joke. Was it chalk? When I told my cousin Samson about this, he teased, "Only Warsaw sugar is sweet..." I was inclined to praise Warsaw at the expense of Bilgoray.

I went outside to the shed in the yard, sitting there

and trying to read a Russian dictionary. It was the only secular book I could find; my uncle had used it while preparing for examinations during the Russian occupation. The print danced before my eyes.

I was feverish. It was soon apparent that I had typhus, and I spent several weeks in bed, dangerously ill. A Czech military doctor treated me, a gigantic man with hands larger than any I had ever seen on teamsters or porters. He spoke to Mother, Uncle, and myself in German.

I had all kinds of hallucinations, and I recollect one in particular because of its complete absurdity. Three peasant women were tied around my neck and weighed me down. I asked my mother why they were there.

"You only imagine it," my mother said. "Poor thing, you have a fever, you're dreaming..."

"But they hang around my neck..."

"Who would hang peasants there? Poor boy..."

Later, when I recovered, my legs were so weak that I could scarcely walk. Like a child, I had to learn to walk all over again, which was novel and entertaining for me. About this time a letter from Warsaw arrived stating that my brother Israel Joseph was also ill with typhus. My mother had much to be sorry about and pray for.

In Bilgoray I was able to witness holiday celebrations that had not changed for centuries. On Yom Kippur Eve, the whole town wept. Never before have I heard such wailing. But the town had reason to mourn; the cholera epidemic had left many widows and orphans, and young men had died on the battlefront. I was frightened by what I saw in the large synagogue, whose courtyard was filled with low benches on which there were platters, saucers, and plates for holiday offerings, and beside them numerous cripples and paupers. The aged, the paralyzed, and the freakish were on display. Inside the synagogue stood worshippers in white linen robes and prayer shawls. A young man near the threshold lamented bitterly, having recently lost his father. Others said to him, "May you have no more sorrow..."

"Oh Father, Father, why did you leave us?" he cried.

Hay covered the synagogue floor. It was an old synagogue, the Ark carved by an Italian master. On one of the walls hung the matzoth eaten at the end of the Passover seder, the Aphikoman. A metal vase filled with sand contained the prepuces of circumcised infants.

On the lectern lay an ancient holy book of a kind no longer printed, a collection of penitential prayers.

In this world of old Jewishness I found a spiritual treasure trove. I had a chance to see our past as it really was. Time seemed to flow backwards. I lived Jewish history.

Winter in Bilgoray

SUMMER GAVE WAY to a wet autumn and a cold winter. A new Russian revolution was rumored and we heard that the rich were sweeping floors and lighting stoves for the poor. But for a long time I did not see a newspaper. No matter what happened in other parts of the world, Bilgoray remained unaltered beneath mud and fog. On market day, Thursday, crowds of peasants in sheepskins and bast shoes arrived in town, selling grain, potatoes, and lumber. The Austrian major, Schranz, and my Uncle Joseph were the administrators of a new soup kitchen which fed, it seemed to me, half the town.

Uncle Joseph contrasted strangely with Major Schranz, who was so straight and tall that when he walked into my uncle's study his cap nearly brushed the ceiling. Ruddy-faced, with short-clipped blond hair, he wore his uniform like a Prussian. Madame Schranz, his aristocratic wife, usually dressed in black, wore a hat with a black feather, and sometimes visited my uncle as a member of the committee to assist Bilgoray's Jews.

Even though my uncle knew no German nor they Yiddish, they managed to communicate. My uncle could not understand this military-minded Jew and spoke of him as a "dumb-ox." The charitable major, on the other hand, treated my uncle as if he were chieftain of some primitive tribe.

Schranz, on entering my uncle's study, would immediately demand that the window be opened because it was so stuffy. "But Herr Schranz," my uncle would protest, "it's wintertime and bitter cold..." He never permitted a window to be opened in the winter; besides, it was plugged with clay and stuffed with cotton. Then Schranz would say a few words and run out to breathe fresh air. For this my uncle called him a "dumb-ox."

I would like to describe other antics of this uncle.

Late one night I was awakened by screams. I had become accustomed to my uncle's nocturnal bellowing, but the screams this time were louder than usual. His matches had disappeared and the whole household had to be roused to look for them. He wouldn't think of leaving cigarettes and matches on the table; they had to be fetched by Avromele and Samson. In the kitchen, where I slept, I could hear my uncle roaring in the bedroom while his sons padded around barefoot, poking vainly into shelves and corners.

My uncle began to scream more loudly, calling his sons "Lousy dumb-oxes! Blockheads! Idiots!" His terrifying screams roused his daughters, who leaped out of bed to assist in the search. I heard everyone stumbling into each other and into the furniture. The shutters were closed and the kitchen black. A pot fell, a plate shattered, and the shovel leaning on the stove crashed to the floor. Aunt Yentel, elderly and heavy, was not too anxious to leave her bed, but my uncle's fury was so wild that soon her unsteady footsteps were also heard in the dark.

"Brocha, Taube, where are you?" she called out. "Where am I?"

One of my girl cousins came tapping around my mattress, like a blind person. The din increased. My uncle's urge to smoke was so pressing that he too got up; I heard his voice approaching.

"Dumb-oxes! Asses! Dopes!" he screeched. Then he gave an inhuman shriek. He had stepped into a basin full of laundry.

In the midst of the tumult, someone found the matches and lit one, and I witnessed a scene out of the Habimah. My girl cousins shuffled about in night-gowns, with disheveled hair, and my Aunt Yentel, having lost her nightcap, stood there half barefoot and in underpants, pale and frightened. Uncle Joseph, his snowy beard twitching, skinny legs visible beneath his long nightgown, blazed amid the wet laundry, in a puddle of water. "Scabby villains! Dogs!"

Pretending to sleep, I watched furtively. The girls collected the dripping laundry and wiped up the floor, while my aunt searched for her nightcap. My uncle took the cigarette and match offered by Avromele and drew in the smoke deeply. His face matched his beard. "Where were they?" he screeched.

He kept up the harangue for a long time. I thought the episode would have taught my uncle a lesson, but the next night his screams again pierced the darkness.

Another experience resulted from my uncle's capriciousness.

My brother Moishe and I used to sleep on a mattress on the kitchen floor. One night I awoke feeling that someone was lying on top of me, and thinking that Moishe had rolled over me in sleep, I said, "Lie straight, Moishe. Get off me!"

As I said this, I touched another head lying on the pillow next to me. This one was Moishe! I was terrified. Sound asleep, neither of them woke when I touched them. But I knew which was Moishe by his smooth skin and silken sidelocks. Then who lay on top of me? The hair was thick and the skin rougher than my brother's. A demon, I thought, had prostrated himself upon me, one of the company of Satan. I had read of such things in *The Righteous Measure, The Book of the Pious,* and similar works.

What could I do?

The only solution for a Jew was to shout, "Hear, O Israel!" But I am not the shouting kind. Quietly, I recited, "Hear, O Israel," and other prayers of a protective nature. But the demon on top of me was afraid of none of this. He lay there and breathed.

My only alternative was to cause a commotion, but it isn't like me to rouse people in the middle of the night, and I was afraid that my brother might wake up and faint from terror. There were so many conflicts within me that I decided to act as if nothing had happened. I still cannot understand how I managed to control myself so well. Even though I lay there in trembling silence, I did not stir. Mentally I repeated verses such as, "Let there be contentment," but I was petrified. I kept reviewing the sins for which I thought I was being punished. At any moment, I imagined, demons would seize me and carry me off. I might even be mated with a female devil, or Lilith herself.

Meanwhile the head slept on.

The fear itself finally exhausted me, and I too fell asleep. I don't know how long I slept but I awoke with the depressing conviction that I only need stretch out my hand....

Nevertheless, it was merely Cousin Samson.

That night, like all other nights, Uncle Joseph had demanded cigarettes and matches, but Samson had been so tired that on the way back from his father's bedroom he simply stumbled upon my mattress and fell asleep.

Yet even stranger experiences were beginning to come to me. My mind filled with thoughts that were both sweet and painful. I had suddenly become aware of the female sex. My own cousins stirred in me a shameful curiosity. I recalled secrets I had heard in Warsaw, and my mind dwelt on passages in the Pentateuch and Talmud that the teacher had said I would understand when I grew older. I felt that I almost knew the answer to the riddle. My dreams became frightening and pleasurable. I thought I was going crazy, or was possessed by a dibbuk. Desires and fantasies became all-consuming. I resolved to fast. But fasting had no effect....

New Friends

WHEN THE GERMANS took Lithuania and the Ukraine, Polish Jews who had fled to Russia and settled there during the war began to drift back. A number of families were also allowed to cross the border from revolutionary Russia, thus bringing us news of the Bolsheviks.

Shlomo Rubinstein, a white-bearded man who dressed in a combination of the traditional and the modern, returned with his wife and attractive, educated daughters. He was wealthy and enlightened, had been a kind of hedge lawyer in Bilgoray, and owned a large house in the market place.

Another returning family, the Warshawiaks— three sons and two daughters—were influenced by modern ideas, even though their father had been a pious scholar. Both parents were dead.

Ansel Shur, a professional preacher who frequently expressed new concepts along with the old ones, came back from the Russian village of Rizhin. His children spoke modern Hebrew as well as Russian, and the eldest, Mottel, sounded as if he had just come from Palestine. Ansel later became an official propagandist for the Orthodox Party.

The three families caused a stir in Bilgoray, particularly in the Turisk study house and the big study house. I had never suspected that there could be so many worldly people in Bilgoray. There were even some assimilated boys and girls who attended a high school in Lublin or Zamoscz and conversed among themselves in Polish.

I met Mottel Shur when he came with his father, Ansel, to worship at the Turisk study house. Two or three years my senior, Mottel was short and broad, with a kind of Russian face, small nose, light eyes, heavy lips, and he usually wore a jacket and a cyclist's cap. Good-natured and talkative, he nevertheless caused resentment among others because of an addiction to boastfulness. He criticized the worshippers of the Turisk study house for their errors in grammar and pronunciation, their fanaticism, and their idle, parasitical ways. The Turisk Hasidim labeled him "Gentile" and tried to throw him out, but his father interceded.

I was present at the incident and sided with Mottel, scandalizing the Hasidim, who did not expect their Rabbi's grandson to become the ally of a heretic. This was the first obvious sign of my corruption.

When Mottel and I talked things over, I was thrilled to learn that he had all kinds of books, reading primers, grammar texts, prose and poetry. I borrowed a grammar and attacked it with incredible passion. Although I knew a good deal of Hebrew, I had no knowledge of verb conjugation, and for six weeks I spent several hours a day studying until I could write Hebrew. Then I wrote a poem. Its poetic value was nil, but the Hebrew was good.

All the same, the poem astonished Mottel, who

accused me of plagiarism. But soon, convinced of the originality of the piece, he evinced pride and a little jealousy.

Mottel, because of his nature, could not keep the matter secret, and began to tell everyone that it was the result of lessons he had given me for six weeks. This proved not only that I was an excellent student but that he was a remarkable teacher as well. There was some truth in this; he actually was a superb teacher, in love with Hebrew, fervently Zionist, a good person and noble-hearted. His was the passion of the old "lovers of Zion" and devotees of the Hebrew language. Years later he was killed by the Germans.

His praise got me in trouble. All Bilgoray claimed that the Rabbi's grandson was absorbed in heretical literature, I was reproved and scolded by several men, and my mother said I was humiliating her and harming our family. She had planned to bring my father there as unofficial Rabbi, but how could he find a following with such a son?

I repented by studying diligently morning and afternoon in the Turisk study house, studying alone, with pupils, or with partners. My uncles made no move to correct my ways; this would have gone against the grain for them, and besides they were not opposed to having my father's rabbinical opportunities negated in Bilgoray.

The Hasidim were enraged, but, on the other hand, there was a sudden display of interest in me by the more modern citizens of Bilgoray, whom my grandfather had persecuted for years. Enlightenment had come to Lithuania a hundred years before; Bilgoray was a century behind.

Winter ended, and the summer of 1918 came. My brother Israel Joshua had gone to German-occupied Kiev to work on a Yiddish publication of some kind. Kiev, Kharkov, and Minsk were lively with Soviet-Yiddish writers—Markish, Schwartzstein, Hoffmann, Kwitko, Fefer, Charik, and others. Selig Melamed founded the Cultural League. The Ukraine was on the verge of pogroms; the Bolsheviks were

waging internecine warfare; the Germans were
beginning to fall back on the Western front—but
none of this touched Bilgoray substantially. What
difference did a soldier's uniform make? Instead of
Cossacks, now Austrians, Magyars, Bosnians, and
Herzegovinians strolled through Bilgoray. Propo-
nents of enlightenment gravitated toward me in a
conspiratorial way. Todros the watchmaker and I
discussed God, nature, the First Cause, and other
topics. In Grandfather's yard there was a spot
shielded by a wall on one side, a Sukkoth booth on
another, and the dogcatcher's potato field on the
third. At a fence there, under an apple tree, I studied
an eighty-year-old physics textbook. Although concealed, I could see the synagogue, the house of prayer,
the bath, and the vast fields that extended toward the
forest. In the apple tree birds sang, and storks soared
over the synagogue. In the sun, the leaves of the apple
tree gleamed like tiny flames. Butterflies and bees
fluttered everywhere. And the sky was as blue as the
curtain before the Holy Ark on the days between
Rosh Hashanah and Yom Kippur. Warmed by the
golden sun, I felt like an ancient philosopher who has
turned from worldly vanities to the pursuit of wisdom
and the divine. From time to time Aunt Yentel would
come out to empty the slop pail.

The physics book was difficult to read, its
sentences long and complex and the language
strange. But scientific knowledge, I knew, had never
been easily attained. This book was the culmination
of hundreds of discoveries over as many years. The
nineteenth century was not represented in the book,
but I learned a great deal from Archimedes, Newton,
and Pascal. I had trouble with the mathematics,
however, not having had more than a smattering of
arithmetic. Sometimes, out of habit, I chanted a
Talmud melody as I studied.

One morning, as I was studying, two boys in
uniforms with brass buttons and decorated caps
appeared before me. They were the town's only
Jewish high-school students, Notte Shverdsharf and

Meir Hadas, both of whom were significant in my later life.

Notte came from a fine family. His grandfather, Reb Samuel Eli, had been a wealthy scholar and a great philanthropist, and he had an aunt, Genendele, who could correspond in Hebrew and was distantly related to me. But time had diminished the family fortune and increased its worldliness. Notte, blue-eyed, blond, and Gentile-looking, was very near-sighted and wore thick-lens glasses. Known as artistic and an idealist, he reminded one of the kind of Polish student who as a member of patriotic clubs would attempt to shoulder all the burdens of humanity. An organizer of dramatic and Zionist groups, he was extremely enthusiastic, but never saw anything through to the end. Even though he still wore a uniform, I think he was at that time out of high school. Too absorbed in fantasies to get through all eight grades, he knew only one thing well—the Polish language. He spoke like a Pole and kept reading Polish books. There was always some book under his arm.

The other boy, Meir Hadas, was of low origin. His grandmother, oddly named Kine, had been good-looking in her youth, and had been savagely slandered for fraternizing with Russian officers. But she was an old woman in a wig when I came to Bilgoray.

Meir Hadas also looked like a Gentile, but a different kind, being erect, frivolous, and full of a Polish vivacity. Unlike Notte, who spoke good Yiddish, Meir's Yiddish was a blend of Jewish and Gentile. Meir, who actually was a high-school student, had not been improved by Notte, who involved him in too many wild schemes and fantastic ventures.

Having heard from Mottel Shur about my versatility in Hebrew and poetry, they had come to discuss with me the world in general and Bilgoray in particular.

I received them like Socrates receiving Plato. They

sat on the grass under the tree and we discussed
everything all the way from God to the plan to
establish a theatrical group in town. I expressed my
opinions with the decisiveness of one who had
thought it all over and come to conclusions long
before.... I reduced everything to dust, proclaiming
that life was worthless and the noblest thing a man
could do was kill himself. I was fifteen, pale, with red
sidelocks I let grow again, a velvet hat, and a long
capote. The old German physics book lay on my
knees. Both Notte and I realized this was the
beginning of a long friendship....

The New Winds

UPHEAVAL marked Bilgoray, for so long successfully
obscured from the world by my grandfather. Now its
immutability was being penetrated from many
sources. A Zionist society was established by the
young people in town. Bund members renewed their
activities. Certain young men indicated Bolshevik
sympathies. Youthful worshippers at the house of
prayer separated into two factions: the Mizrachi and
the Traditionalists. Notte Shverdsharf formed a
pioneer division, the Hachalutz or Hashomer, and as
a group leader was trailed by hordes of children who
called themselves Zebim, wolves. Whether larger
cities showed the same tendencies as Bilgoray, I did
not know. In the streets, boys, passing each other,
would straighten up, click their heels in the Austrian
manner, and shout, "*Chazak!*—Be strong!"

All kinds of evening discussions and parties were now being held in this town which a year before had been a sleepy Jewish community. A Warsaw stock company performed *Shulamit* in the firehouse. The Austrians, who had started a school in Bilgoray, erected a theater in the market place. The Hasidim resented my uncles because they made no objection to this, did not drive out the heretics as their father would have done. But his sons lacked his personality and strength.

Jonah Ackerman, an old bachelor and hedge lawyer, opened a Yiddish library in his house. He was the son of an enlightened man, a sharp-tongued opponent of Hasidism. When the Gorlitz Rabbi came to town to be greeted with music and bells, old man Ackerman, standing in his doorway, had hissed, "Idol worshippers!"

The son of this kind of father should, logically, have turned out to be a dedicated heretic, but Jonah Ackerman was dedicated to nothing but compromise. A lawyer, he said, must not antagonize his clients. In three-quarter-length surtout, Hasidic hat, and with a pointed yellow beard, he spent his Sabbath in the same Gorlitz study house that his father had vilified. Raised on Russian literature, not on Tolstoy and Dostoevsky, but on those before them, like Lomonosov and writers of moralistic works, he had a principle to apply to everything, and enjoyed moral discussions. Although his Yiddish was fluent, he had a tendency to translate his thoughts literally from the Russian. A pedant with a calligraphic handwriting, he was especially attentive to grammar and syntax. When I arrived in Bilgoray he was an old bachelor who had had to pass up several wealthy matches in order to marry off his sisters, having assumed this responsibility when his father died. Jonah was an anachronism, but I have come upon this type occasionally in Russian literature.

His personality seemed to have evolved from print. He had an amazing memory, was said to know certain codexes by heart, and owned numerous

dictionaries and lexicons. Finally he decided to open
a library and ordered both Yiddish and Hebrew
volumes. Since he had a motive for everything, I
suspect that one of these was to attract the town's
girls. He was in general a pure-hearted old bachelor,
old-fashioned and a bit eccentric.

If anyone but Jonah Ackerman had opened a
library of worldly books, his windows would have
been smashed. But Jonah was a respected lawyer,
had influence with the authorities, and no one
wanted to anger him. Strangely enough, he was even
admired by the Bilgoray Gentiles, who thought there
should be more Jews like him, calm, honest, and
polite. They even approved of his wearing the
traditional Jewish habit.

By this time my knowledge of Yiddish writers
included Mendele Mocher-Sforim, Sholem Aleichem,
Peretz, Asch, and Bergelson, but I had not read them
thoroughly. Now with the Hebrew books and readers
given to me by Mottel Shur, I read enthusiastically
the poetry of Bialik, Czerniochowsky, Jacob Cohen,
and Schneyur, and had an insatiable desire for more.
I had never forgotten the two volumes of *Crime and
Punishment* that had so intrigued me even though I
scarcely understood what I was reading.

Now, under the apple tree in the garden, Notte
Shverdsharf would bring me a book one day and I
would finish it the next. Often, sitting on an
overturned bookcase in the attic, I would read among
old pots, broken barrels, and stacks of pages torn
from sacred books. Omnivorously, I read stories,
novels, plays, essays, original works in Yiddish, and
translations. As I read, I decided which was good,
which mediocre, and where truth and falsity lay. At
that time America was sending us sacks of white
flour and translations of European writers, and these
books entranced me. I read Reisen, Strindberg, Don
Kaplanovitch, Turgenev, Tolstoy, Maupassant, and
Chekhov. One day Notte brought me *The Problem of
Good and Evil,* by Hillel Zeitlin, and I devoured it. In

this book Zeitlin gave the history and summation of
world philosophy and the philosophy of the Jews.
Sometime later I discovered Stupnicki's book on
Spinoza.

I remembered how Father used to say that
Spinoza's name should be blotted out, and I knew
Spinoza contended that God was the world and the
world was God. My father, I recalled, had said that
Spinoza had contributed nothing. There was an
interpretation by the famous Baal Shem, who also
identified the world with the Godhead. True, the Baal
Shem had lived after Spinoza, but my father argued
that Spinoza had drawn from ancient sources, which
no Spinoza disciple would deny.

The Spinoza book created a turmoil in my brain.
His concept that God is a substance with infinite
attributes, that divinity itself must be true to its laws,
that there is no free will, no absolute morality and
purpose—fascinated and bewildered me. As I read
this book, I felt intoxicated, inspired as I never had
been before. It seemed to me that the truths I had been
seeking since childhood had at last become apparent.
Everything was God—Warsaw, Bilgoray, the spider
in the attic, the water in the well, the clouds in the
sky, and the book on my knees. Everything was
divine, everything was thought and extension. A
stone had its stony thoughts. The material being of a
star and its thoughts were two aspects of the same
thing. Besides physical and mental attributes, there
were innumerable other characteristics through
which divinity could be determined. God was eternal,
transcending time. Time, or duration, controlled only
the modi, the bubbles in the divine cauldron, that
were forever forming and bursting. I too was a
modus, which explained my indecision, my restless-
ness, my passionate nature, my doubts and fears. But
the modi too were created from God's body, God's
thought, and could be explained only through
Him...

As I write these lines today, I am critical of them,

being familiar with all the defects and hiatuses of
Spinozaism. But at that time I was under a spell
which lasted many years.

I was exalted; everything seemed good. There was
no difference between heaven and earth, the most
distant star, and my red hair. My tangled thoughts
were divine. The fly alighting on my page had to be
there, just as an ocean wave or a planet had to be
where it was at a specific time. The most foolish
fantasy in my mind had been thought for me by
God...Heaven and earth became the same thing.
The laws of nature were divine; the true sciences of
God were mathematics, physics, and chemistry. My
desire to learn intensified.

Other boys, Notte Shverdsharf and Meir Hadas,
were not, to my astonishment, at all interested in my
discoveries. My absorption amazed them, just as
their indifference shocked me.

One day Notte approached me and asked if I would
be willing to teach Hebrew.

"To whom?"

"Beginners. Boys and girls."

"But what about Mottel Shur?" I asked.

"They don't want him."

I still don't know why they didn't want Mottel
Shur, unless it was because he quarreled with the
founders of the night school that now sought my
employment. Mottel had a weakness for telling
people what he thought of them, also he boasted too
much—and perhaps he asked too high a fee. I hardly
dared accept the position, knowing it would embar-
rass my mother and cause consternation in town. But
something made me accept.

In the private home where the first lesson was
held, I discovered that my pupils were not, as I had
assumed, children, but young men and women, and
somewhat more of the latter. The girls, my age and
even older, came dressed in their best clothes. I faced
them in a long gabardine, velvet hat, and with
dangling sidelocks. How, when I am naturally shy, I

had the nerve to accept this assignment, I do not know, but it has been my experience that shy persons are sometimes unusually bold. I told them everything I knew about Hebrew. The lesson created a furor in town—to think that the Rabbi's grandson had lectured worldly boys and girls on the Hebrew language!

After the lesson, the girls surrounded me, asking questions, smiling. Suddenly I was dazzled by a particular narrow face, a dark girl with coal-black eyes and an indescribable smile. I became confused, and when she asked me a question I did not know what she was saying. Many novels and a lot of poetry had filled my mind by then; I was prepared for the turmoil that writers call "love"...

Isaac Bashevis Singer

Winner of the 1978 Nobel Prize for Literature

SHOSHA	23997-7	$2.50
SHORT FRIDAY	24068-1	$2.50
PASSIONS	24067-3	$2.50
A CROWN OF FEATHERS	23465-7	$2.50
ENEMIES: A LOVE STORY	24065-7	$2.50
THE FAMILY MOSKAT	24066-5	$2.95
IN MY FATHER'S COURT	24074-6	$2.50